GLAMOUR NUDE PHOTOGRAPHY

Robert and Sheila Hurth

Amherst Media, Inc. ■ Buffalo, New York

Published by:
Amherst Media, Inc.
P.O. Box 586
Buffalo, NY 14226
Fax: 716-874-4508

Publisher: Craig Alesse
Editor/Designer: Richard Lynch
Associate Editor: Frances J. Hagen
Editorial Consultant: Dan Schwartz, J.D., Ph.D.
Proofreader: Ellen Bumbar
All photos and diagrams by: Robert and Sheila Hurth

ISBN: 0-936262-47-8
Library of Congress Catalog Card Number: 96-84431

Printed in the United States of America
10 9 8 7 6 5 4 3 2 1

Notice of disclaimer: The information contained in this book is based on the authors' experience and opinions. The authors and publisher will not be held liable for the use or misuse of the information in this book.

Table of Contents

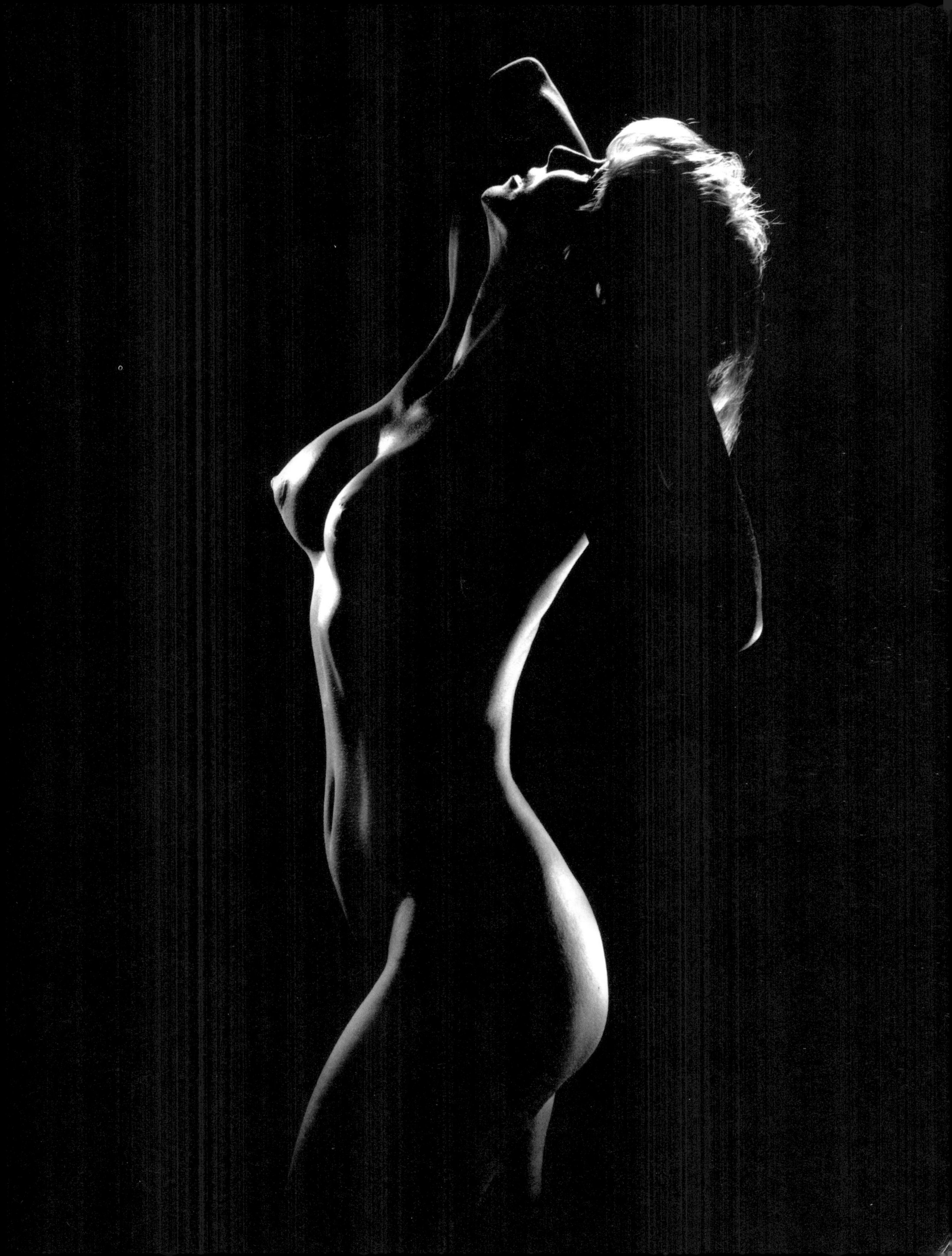

Introduction

"...produce stunning and tastefully executed images of the human form."

The human form has captivated the imagination since the beginning of recorded art history. Recording the human figure — especially the female figure — has been one of the most popular aspects of the creative visual arts. And, photography has played a prominent part for the past century and a half. But, the real question is why? Why has there been such fascination with the nude human form? There have been a lot of reasons.

While there are many books on nude photography on the market, most are nothing more than a compilation of photos. Most of these books contain no clear-cut information or instruction as to how the photographs were conceived or made.

They are intended mainly for those who enjoy viewing this art form, rather than those who want to practice it themselves. We wanted to satisfy the needs of the aspiring photographer of the human form.

If you have read our book, *Secrets Of Boudoir Photography*, then you should note a number of parallels between that book and this one. Some of these parallels are subtle; others are more obvious.

Whether the similarities are great or small, this book has the same basic goal: to help you produce stunning and tastefully executed images of the human form.

Boudoir imagery has been very much a commercial endeavor for us. We shoot to please the client and the intended recipient of the boudoir images. By contrast, when we initially started doing nude photography, we did so for the sake of the art form alone; for our own creative pleasure, and fulfillment; to sharpen our skills and talent. However, within relatively short order, these reasons melted into the background; our nude photography began to take on a great commercial appeal as well.

Today we not only book and shoot nude photo sessions for customers on a routine basis, but we are doing more and more nude photography in conjunction with our boudoir photo sessions.

In about forty percent of the cases when we do boudoir photography, the customer will want us to create at least one photo scenario where we photograph her in some state of nudity. Figure photography — which is a natural and logical extension of our boudoir work — has extended our experience, fulfillment, and reputation as creative photographers.

It has also enabled us to offer a greater pictorial variety for some of our boudoir subjects. And all of this has meant a tremendous addition to our overall business success. However, all of this did not come about overnight

To get to the point that we are at today meant that we had to become involved with and knowledgeable in both traditional and contemporary styles of nude imagery. We had to know and understand the traditional nude, from old master paintings, as well as the contemporary nude existing in present day art work. This took a great deal of time and effort.

Accordingly, and to make your transition into this field easier, this book presents nude studies in both of those styles.

Many of the images reproduced in this book follow in the tradition of the great artists of the past. However, we have also attempted to blaze new trails and to deviate somewhat from the accepted norm and seek a more modern approach.

Consequently, we would like you to treat this book as a guide through a learning adventure. Its purpose is to teach you — the amateur and the pro alike — how to execute this sensitive form of photography and to spare you some growing pains (time, effort, money and aggravation) while you learn.

Although we presently use all three camera formats when we engage in nude photography — 35mm SLRs, medium-format (of the Hasselblad type), or view cameras — for the purpose of learning how to execute the photos depicted herein, it really doesn't matter what camera format is used.

We assume that most readers will own and use 35mm SLR camera equipment; however, the information provided in this book applies regardless of which camera format is chosen.

Whether you are a typical 35mm enthusiast, prefer the larger, 4x5 or even 8x10, formats, or some format in between, we invite you to read on and follow us through the adventure.

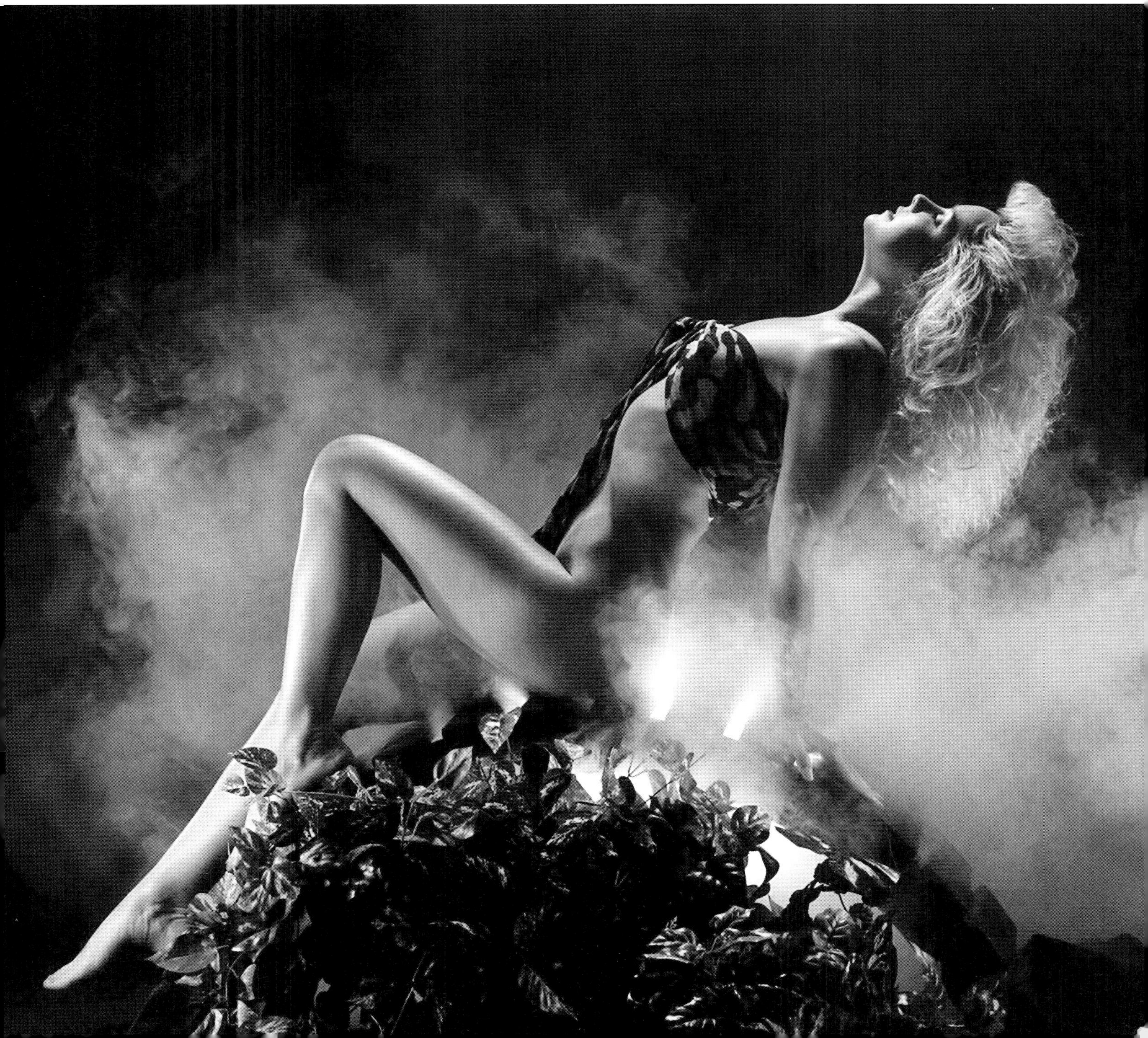

CHAPTER ONE

Types of Figure Photography

"...have a good foundation of information to draw upon."

Although photography is not as time-honored as some of its older brothers (the history of paintings and sculptures date back to ancient times), nonetheless, some forms of photography have come to be considered legitimate art forms.

This does not mean that all great photographs are automatically art, but neither are all paintings nor sculpture. Not all photos will rise to the dignity of seriously executed artistic nude photos simply because the photos depict men or women without clothing. It takes much more than this.

For example, before a photographer can produce seriously executed nude or figure photos, he or she should have a good foundation of information to draw upon. This involves, among other things, having knowledge and understanding of three major factors or areas:

1. Terms and concepts
2. Types, styles or categories
3. Ingredients

Terms and Concepts

For our purposes, definitions of most "artistic" words and concepts are too academic. They are often debatable and not required knowledge for the study of figure photography. However, there are terms and concepts that need explaining.

Naked Versus Nude

To us, there is an important difference between a photo of a naked person and a photographic nude study. The distinction is more than semantic and both types usually yield a very different reaction when people hear the words.

Unfortunately, a look at our dictionary doesn't help us understand this problem. It defines naked as being "...without clothing or covering on the body; nude." At the same time, it defines nude as being "...without clothing; naked."

These definitions would have one believe that the words naked and nude are interchangeable; that they are synonymous. In fact, and especially in the context of the visual arts, the words are not synonymous and have very different connotations.

For example, the word naked has a clinical, analytical overtone, while the word nude suggests an artistic interpretation or treatment of the bare body.

As photographers of the artful nude, it becomes imperative that we thoroughly understand the difference between these two terms.

Without such an understanding of the terms, it would be difficult, if not impossible, to engage in serious nude photography. Since we wouldn't be able to formulate a clear idea of how we wanted to photograph a subject, we couldn't possibly capture a good photo no matter how hard we tried.

For our purposes, it will help if you think of a naked body becoming a nude, in the artistic sense, only when that body is well posed, lit, styled, and depicted, not for documentary, clinical, or informative purposes, but for an aesthetic, interpretive end. The photographer of the artistic nude should seek to extol a subject's physical form and not exploit it.

More than the Bare Essence of a Subject

An unimaginative documentary photo of the naked form, no matter how beautiful the subject may be, will generally not rise to the dignity of being a work of art. It may be a starting point but something more than this will be needed to make his or her photographic image artful.

The subject's body should usually be idealized and made more appealing through the skill and talent of the photographic-artist. The body should not be merely documented but explored by his or her camera.

The subject's body, the form, should be photographed in such a manner as to symbolize woman- or manhood. Then and only then could the unclad figure rise from a mere naked form — with all the imperfections that all human beings have — to the attractive art-object that is sought: the artistic nude.

Summary

This book and its photos are addressed to the nude photo-study of the female and male form. The pure photographic nude study seeks to approach the level of art, whereas photos of naked men and women are often thought of as mere documentary photos, photos without life or substance, and sometimes as trash.

Understanding this essential difference is important in the context of understanding what this book is all about. It is not about the human body in a direct manner. It is about the art of interpreting the beauty and meaning of the human form.

If you approach your photographic sessions and your undressed subjects with this noted difference in mind — seeking to produce art and to idealize the subject and his or her figure — your subjects will frequently think of themselves as being dressed and perfectly at ease with you and your camera.

When is A Body Nude?

Must a subject for nude figure photography always be totally nude in a photo composition in order to have the image be the legitimate subject matter for a nude photo study? No. Sometimes partial draping or covering of a subject is desirable, either for aesthetic or contextual reasons, or simply to cover a less-than-perfect body part. The selective revelation or concealment of body parts can even be achieved by means other than drapes or articles of clothing.

For example, a body part can be "clothed" in deep shadow, so that no detail is shown in that area. Or, a body part can be hidden either behind another part of the body or a separate object.

The point is that not only can a partially clad figure constitute a legitimate nude study, but the photo composition for such a study need not necessarily show the subject's entire body. A close-up image of a body part — of an exposed leg, of one exposed breast or of the small of the back with the buttocks being displayed — can legitimately constitute the proper subject matter for what is normally understood as nude or figure photography. However, there is a word of caution.

If the materials covering a subject are articles of clothing rather than just a drape of material, and if there is no total nudity involved, although legs, arms, midriff and even much of the bust may be amply revealed, you'll often find yourself photographing in the sphere of boudoir photography rather than nude photography. The crossover point from one photographic expertise to the other is often very subtle.

By removing or even adjusting some of the clothing worn by a subject during a boudoir photo session, an image — otherwise classed as a boudoir image — can easily be transformed into a partial nude photo study.

A lot will depend on the intent of the photographer, the manner in which the photo was styled, the way the subject was posed and lit, as well as the purpose of the photo. A boudoir image is almost always a personal statement or the revelation of one specific woman or man for one specific viewer.

On the other hand, artistic figure photography typically has as its purpose the revelation of woman- or manhood in general, for a larger-based viewing audience.

Pornography

Our dictionary defines pornography as "...the depiction of erotic behavior meant chiefly to cause sexual excitement; written,

"The subject's body should usually be idealized..."

graphic or other forms of communication intended to incite lascivious feelings... ." The words "dirty" or "immoral" are conspicuous by their absence but even so, this definition really doesn't help. It is subject to too much interpretation and error.

Ultimately, a photographer and the viewers of his or her images must determine whether a particular image is art or sexually explicit. The borderline between the two is almost impossible to define, either aesthetically or legally.

Indeed, even Supreme Court Justice Potter Stewart has stated, "I don't know exactly what pornography is, nor exactly how to describe it, but I know it when I see it."

We believe an image is pornographic when it offends a viewer not merely because eroticism is present but because we sense or think that the image is demeaning to womanhood in general, and the woman depicted, in specific. We further think that an image is pornographic if it exploits, rather than glorifies, the erotic human qualities of a person.

Although pornography is often associated with visual imagery of the human form, we can assure you that nude photography that is done with honesty, sensitivity, and integrity is not only one of the most challenging and difficult art forms to create, but it is nearly the extreme opposite of anything that might be regarded as obscene.

The artful nude can be one of the highest tributes paid to a subject, a fact which pornography can neither match nor subscribe to.

Types of Figure Photography

- **The two major art categories are classical art and contemporary art.**

What definitively makes a painting, sculpture, or a photographic image a work of art is almost always open to debate. What we do know is that the subject matter itself is generally not the controlling factor.

In other words, just because you have selected a legitimate subject matter — a meadow, a nude study, a sunrise, a lovely flower and so on — does not, in and of itself, guarantee that the finished product will be classed as a work of art.

There is much more to something becoming a work of art than this. However, once the work in question does rise to the point of being considered a work of art, then it becomes capable of being classed in accordance with certain recognized and accepted artistic standards.

And, the reason that it is important to classify any work of art is so that we, the viewers of an artistic image or artifact, can have a better understanding of the work of art itself, its message and perhaps, even what its creator intended.

When photography does fall within the spectrum of being photographic art, it will fall and be classed in only one of two major categories; it will be either classical or contemporary in style.

However, in addition to a major category, it will also fall within one or more minor categories. Since within each of the two major categories there are numerous minor forms and styles of figure photography, it is not unusual to have a given piece of art classed in one of the major categories and, at the same time, two, three, or even more of the minor categories.

For example, a piece of art could be classical in style (the major category) as well as erotic, graphic, and impressionistic, all at the same time.

The Two Major Categories

Art has only two major categories for us to concern ourselves with: classical and contemporary. To have you better understand the distinction between the two major art categories, we must define some terms. The definitions will help you learn some guidelines; guidelines that you can follow and that will help you when you attempt to photographically create either one or both of these styles.

Classical Art — Strictly speaking, Classical art refers to art of the ancient Greek and Roman eras. However, for our purposes, the definition can be a bit more flexible. Classical art need not be exclusively of ancient Greek and Roman times but can also include European art that was created up to the late 19th century. It is usually art that has survived the test of time and is thought of as setting a standard from which other pieces, more modern in nature, derive much or at least some measure of their origins.

Although the medium of photography itself is relatively new, photographs that mirror the classic or traditional styles of the old master painters are considered and said to be classical photographs. For

Right and Below: *Even though these images are both figure studies, they demonstrate how images fit into different categories — both major and minor categories. In the photo on the right, the model is looking right at the camera. This image would most likely be classified as a personal nude. The photo below, however, has the model's backside facing the camera. This image would be classified as an impersonal nude.*

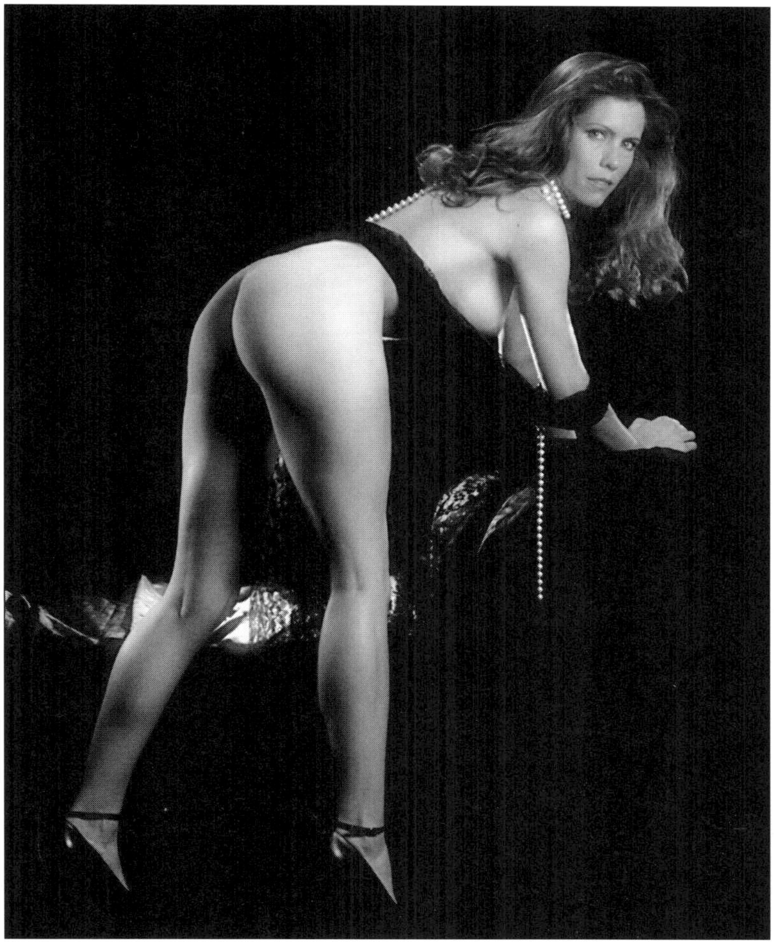

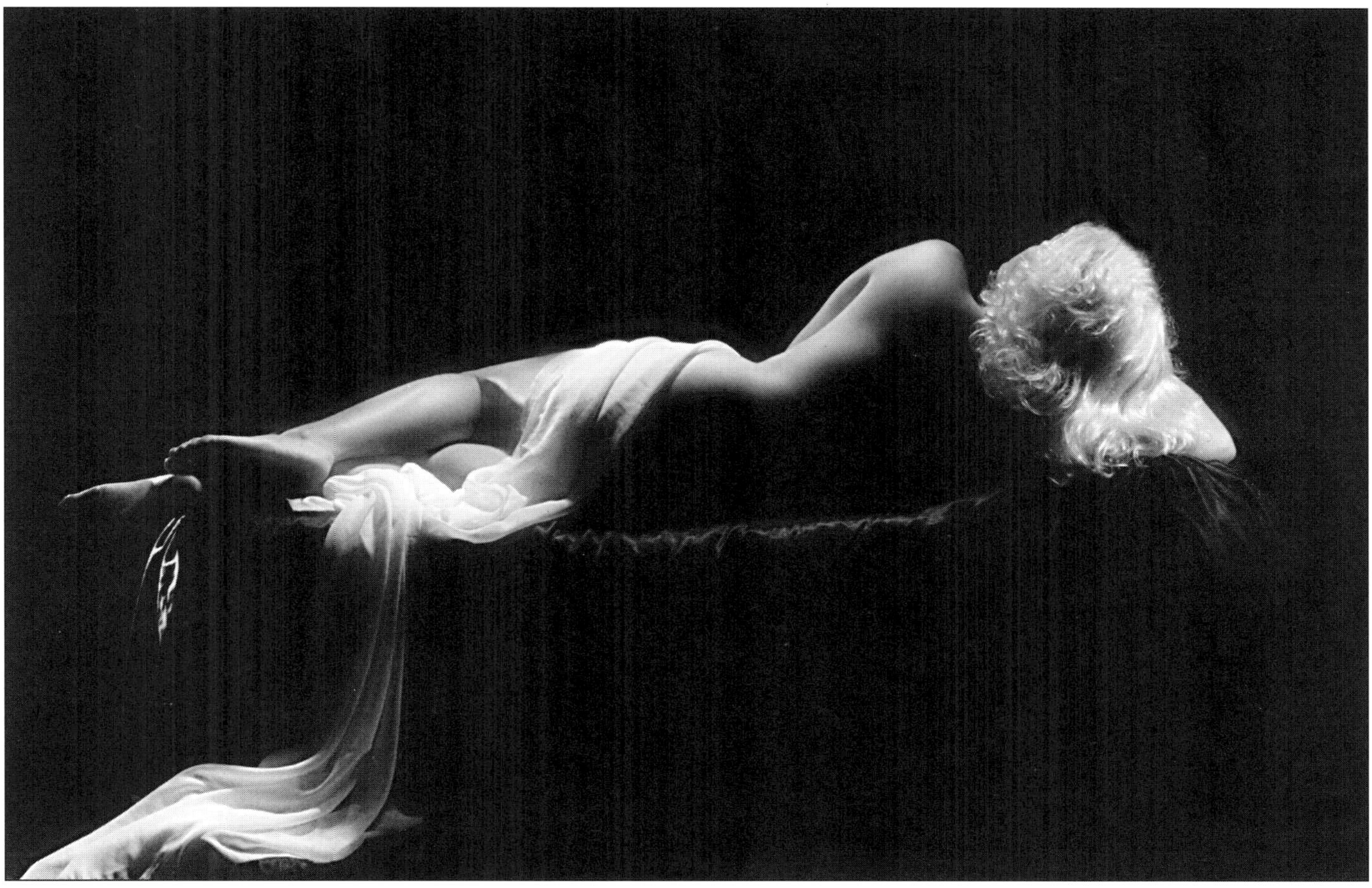

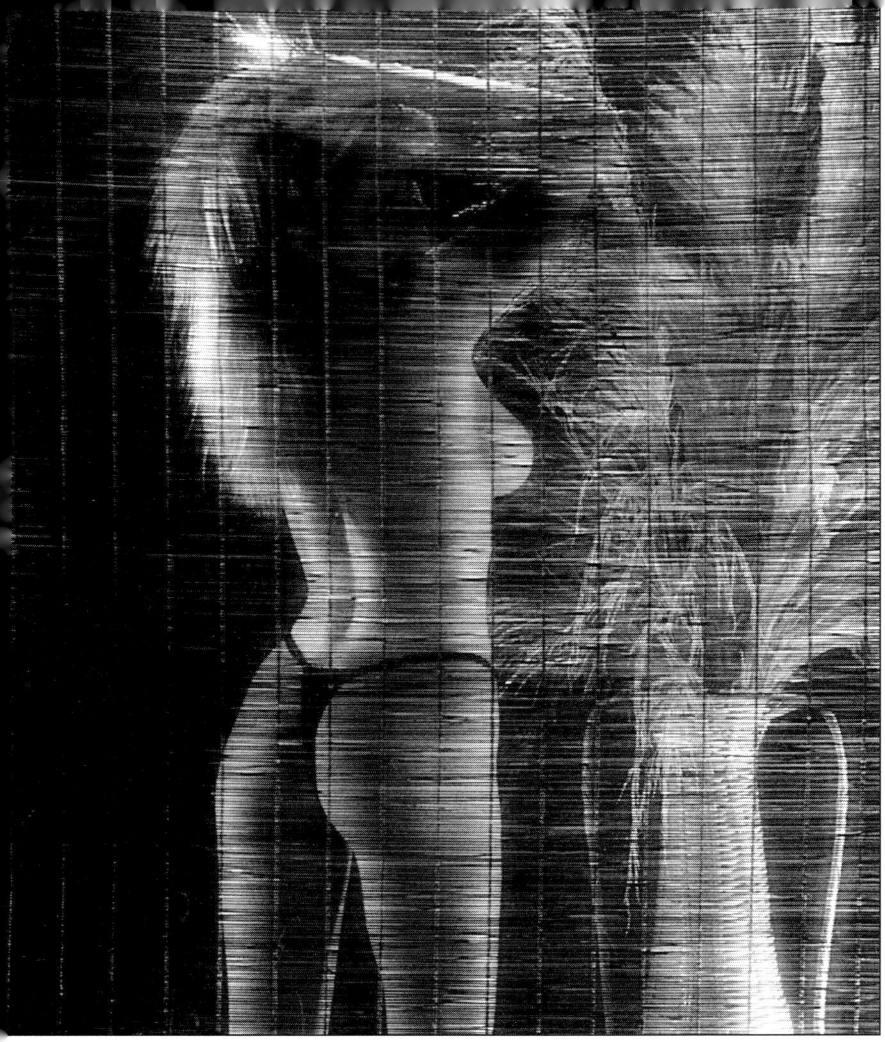

Above and Right: *These images exemplify the different categories of figure photography. The photo above is an impersonal nude while the photo to the right would most likely be called a personal nude. Both images are stunning, but in very different and dramatic ways — they demonstrate the pictorial variety found in this art form.*

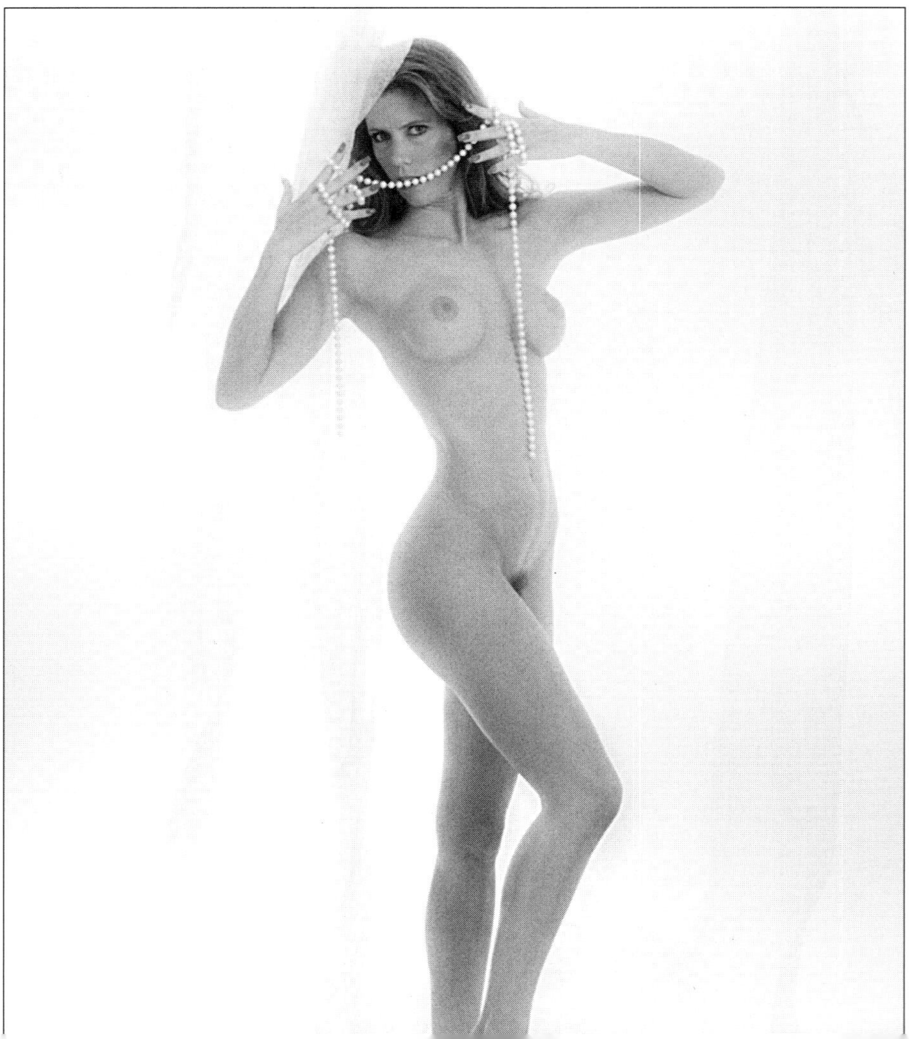

example, Renoir was and is considered to be a great 19th century painter.

If a photographer created an image of a full-bodied woman, posed nude in a setting of trees and flowers in the woods, in style, lighting, posing, and setting of a Renoir painting, it could be said that the photographer had created a photographic nude study which was in the classical style.

Contemporary Art — Contemporary art does not draw upon traditional aesthetic standards of posing, color selection and balance, composition, and lighting to be appreciated and recognized. It is original art and not merely a mirror image of an old master's work, style, or technique. In the same vein, contemporary photography, especially in recent years, has been bold and experimental.

Even a brief and superficial study of photographs made during the latter part of the 19th century and early years of the 20th century will reveal that not only nude photography, but also what we today call boudoir photography, was popular in those times.

Nude photography then, as now, was done mainly for the sake of art, for personal satisfaction and in both the classical and contemporary styles. However, a few "profiteers" exploited females and their naked forms and photographed solely for profit. Many of those early photos were often referred to as "French postcards;" 19th century pornography.

The Minor Categories

If a photographic nude study does find itself being classed as a work of art, then, as we have noted, it will not only fall within one of the two major art categories, but within one or more of the minor categories as well.

There is a definite value to categorizing any work of art. At least in theory, categorizing helps a viewer better understand the artful image or artifact. A minor art category can be thought of like chapters within a given book. Chapters in a book help to more specifically explain or define a book's essence.

Thus, a photographic nude study, which is either classical or contemporary in style, will also fall within at least one, but often two or more, minor categories.

For a better understanding of the minor categories and the effect they can have on an image, here is a list and explanation of a few categories:

Impersonal Nude — This minor category of figure study is one in which there is no suggested contact or communication between the subject and the viewer of the photo; there is no eye contact by the model with the camera. The subject's face is often hidden by some material, is placed into shadow, or even turned away from the camera. When a subject is so posed, the resulting photo is sometimes referred to as a concept shot.

The purpose of the impersonal or concept nude is to primarily reveal an aspect of the subject which is hard to obtain with other methods. This method also deemphasizes the subject as a person because the subject's face is hidden or obscured.

The impersonal or conceptual nude photo studies can yield some of the most striking images. Since the subject's face is obscured or hidden, a viewer's attention of the image is directed elsewhere, usually to a portion or all of a subject's body, depending on how the subject was styled, illuminated, and posed.

Personal Nude — This kind of image is designed to make personal, intimate contact between the subject and an intended viewer of the image. There is generally eye contact by the subject with the camera and therefore the viewer of the photo. A personal nude photograph is usually made with one specific viewer in mind: a boyfriend, a husband, or significant other. In this sense, almost all boudoir images fall into the minor, personal category.

Erotic Nude — This kind of image has deliberate sensual and sexual overtones. A pose is usually structured to dramatize the more erotic body parts; the breasts or buttocks, and even the eyes, mouth, or legs of a subject. With this type of image, there is usually direct subject eye contact with the camera.

For this kind of image to work, in a tasteful and artistic manner, it is important for the photographer to work with restraint. Sensuality is a powerful thing and it should be revealed with great subtlety.

There is often a very fine line between an extremely erotic image and a pornographic one. From our standpoint, pornographic images just don't sell. Admittedly they might sell extremely well in men's

- **Figure photography has six minor categories.**

"A pose is usually structured to dramatize the more erotic body parts..."

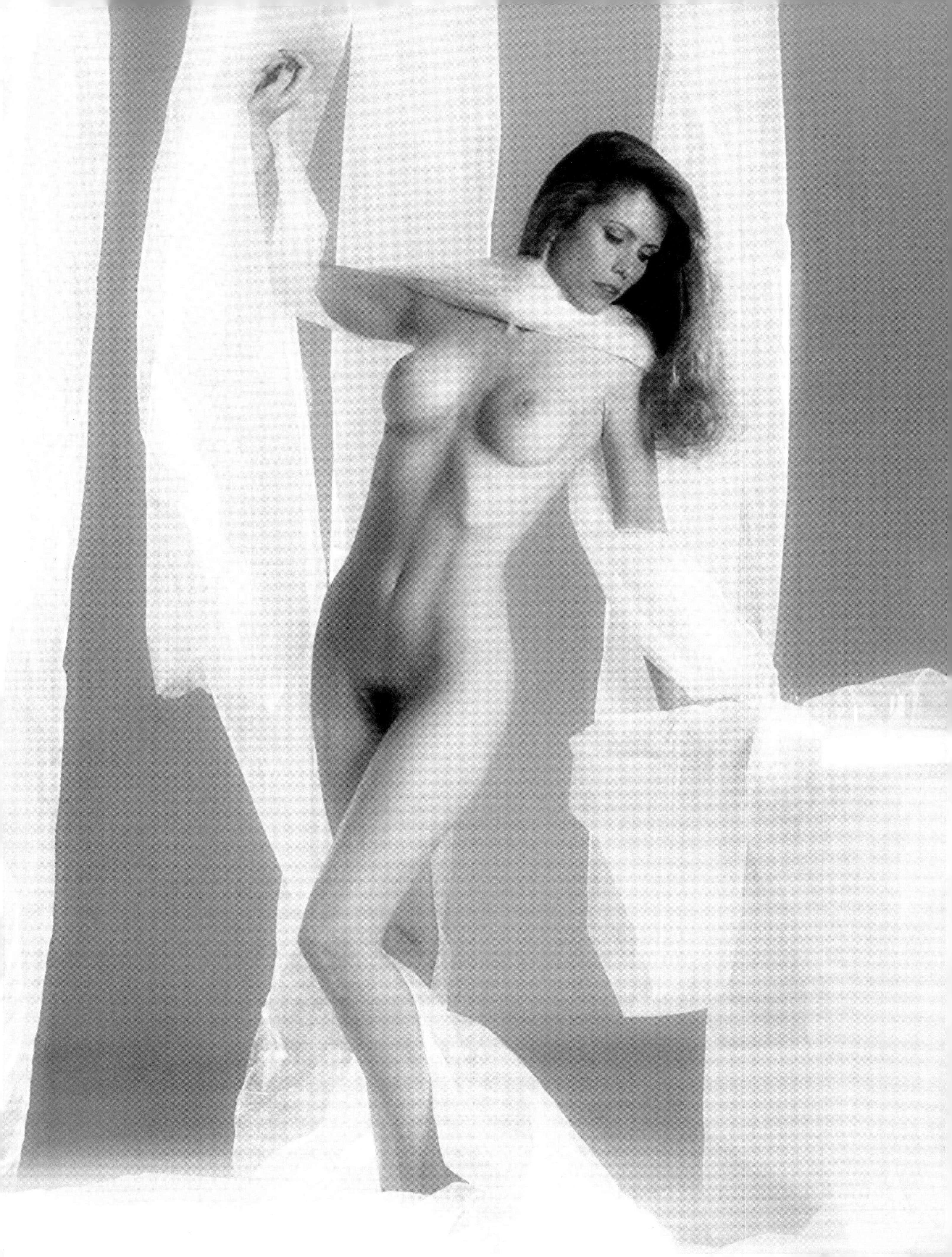

magazines or from an X-rated book store. But from an established photo studio — one which is attempting to build a solid business — pornographic images are financial losers. Therefore, a prudent photographer must exercise great care not to cross the fine line which separates one from the other.

Graphic Nude — The graphic nude exploits and explores the graphic possibilities of a human form. By appropriate posing and lighting, visual poetry is created by the curves and lines of the body. Background selection becomes extremely critical for a graphic nude study. It must complement and augment rather than compete.

For example, a black silhouette of the subject's figure against a stark white background makes a startling graphic image. Although full-length, graphic figure studies are common, one should not forget that graphic nude studies of selected body parts can be very effective.

Abstract Nude — Abstract paintings emerged in this country around 1940 and attained prominence in the 1950s. Photographically, abstract art — especially of nude figure studies — did not gain a measure of popularity until two decades later.

Today, it still has some popularity in figure photography, but on a very limited basis. Abstract art does not emphasize the subject matter (the human figure). It tends to accentuate the manner in which the subject matter or nude was photographed and at the same time distort, obscure, exaggerate, or inaccurately represent a subject's nude figure or portion thereof.

For example, instead of a subject's nude figure being literally captured and made photographically prominent in a photo composition, it's made a secondary element. Blurs of colors, some form of motion (such as moving the camera during exposure), or a billowing mass of materials partially or totally obscuring the nude subject, are a few methods in abstract photos to obscure the artful nude.

Impressionistic Nude — This artform came into existence in the late 19th century by such notable artists as Monet, Renoir, and Cezanne. This style is considered a classical style. Photographers who mimic the style of these impressionistic artists usually make the subject's nude figure primary in a photo composition, but alter (at least to some extent) the literal qualities of the subject matter.

In other words, they interpret the subject's nude figure rather than just record or document it. Photographically, this interpretation can be brought about in a number of ways.

During the printing process, an otherwise literal or straight-forward image could be altered by projecting it through distorted glass in an enlarger, or by tilting one end of the printing easel while the image is being projected onto photographic paper. During the actual photographic process, images could also be altered by shooting through distorted optical glass (such a shower-type glass), or by using certain spurious filtrations. (A glass filter smeared unevenly and erratically with Vaseline would be one technique for accomplishing the result.) Another favorite shooting technique to accomplish an impressionistic photo is to improperly use a given focal length lens.

For example, if you posed a subject so that her legs were closer to the camera than the rest of her torso and face, and then used a wide angle lens up close, you would photographically misrepresent the subject's figure. You would distort and exaggerate the subject's legs (the foreground objects) and, at the same time, would cause the subject's torso and face (the mid and background subject matter) to greatly recede and appear much smaller in the photo.

If you want to practice photographing impressionistic photos, try taking a photograph of a landscape from inside your house. Wait until a very rainy day then,

"...graphic nude studies of selected body parts can be very effective."

Opposite page: *Here is an example of a traditional, impersonal pose. Shots like this one are easy to create. We used a three light set-up: an accent light, housed in a 4-inch snooted reflector with an amber gel; a Balcar Opalite with a 20-degree grid spot and plastic diffuser cap (main light); and a 3x4 foot softbox (fill light). The fill light had its power set to two f-stops lower than that of the main light. The main light was set about 45-degrees to the right of camera axis and the accent light, which had its power set to one f-stop lower than the main light, was affixed at about 100 degrees to the right of camera axis.*

while the rain is heavily striking a window pane, shoot an outdoor scene, from inside your home, through the rain drenched or splattered window.

The photo results will yield wavy compositional lines, somewhat blurred colors and tones, and your subject matter (trees, grass, or flowers) will appear less than sharp. The effect can be very nice — for a landscape. However, we usually don't care for this particular style or technique when it comes to our nude photography. In our opinion, it most often is not as flattering to the human form as we and most of our customers would like it to be.

Ingredients of Figure Photography

Whether you engage in classical or contemporary nude photography, and irrespective of which minor category a nude study might fall within, there will always

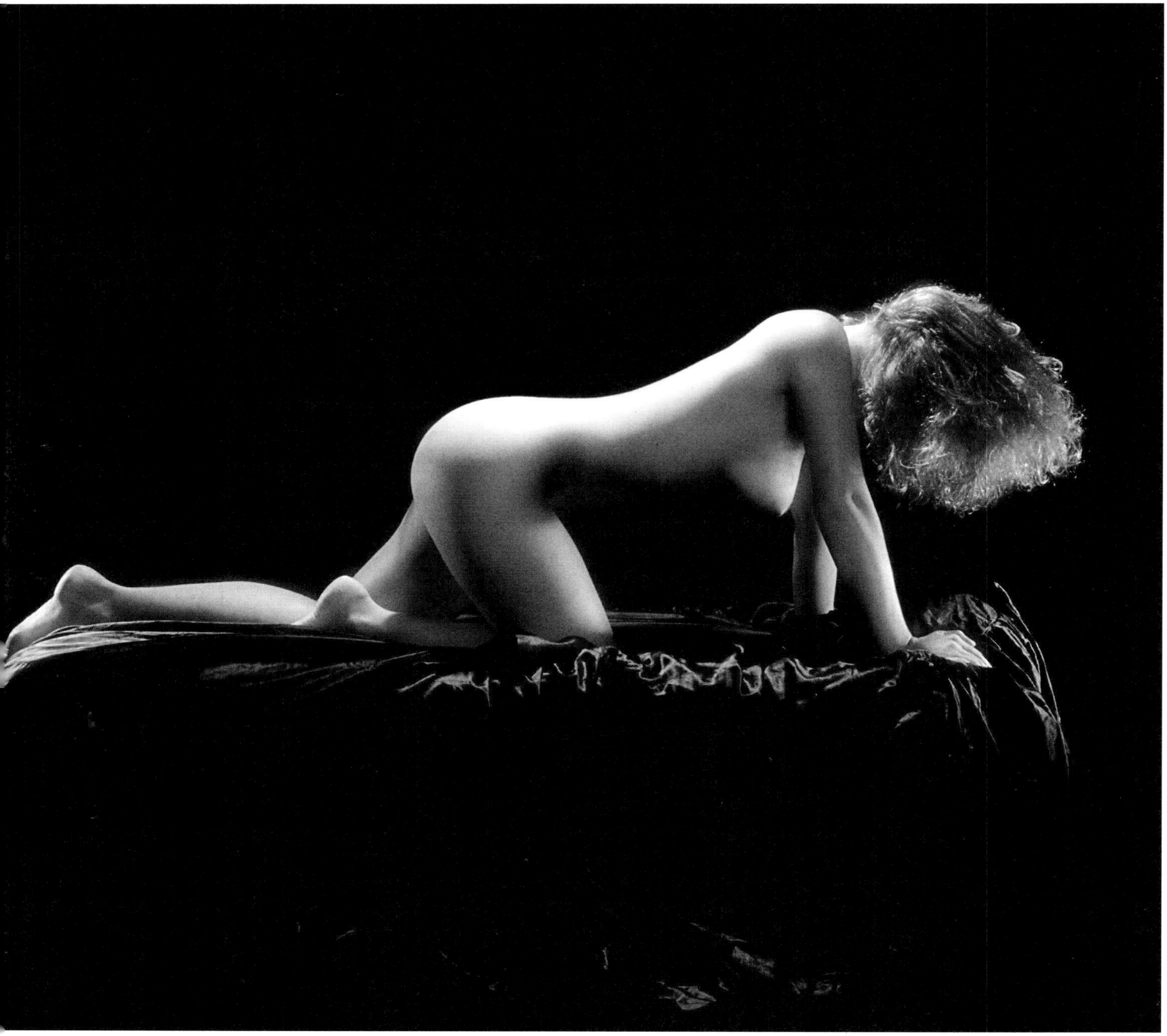

***Above:** We call this a "cat" pose, in a simple, low-key setting. Because the subject's face is not discernible, the image becomes "impersonal." The face was intentionally concealed so that a viewer's eye would go to other areas of the body. Notice how light (a single Norman 4-inch snoot) was used to flatter important areas such as the breasts and hair. The line of her back, buttocks and upper legs were illuminated by another Norman light in a 6-inch bowl reflector, suspended on a boom stand and directed down onto the subject's back.*

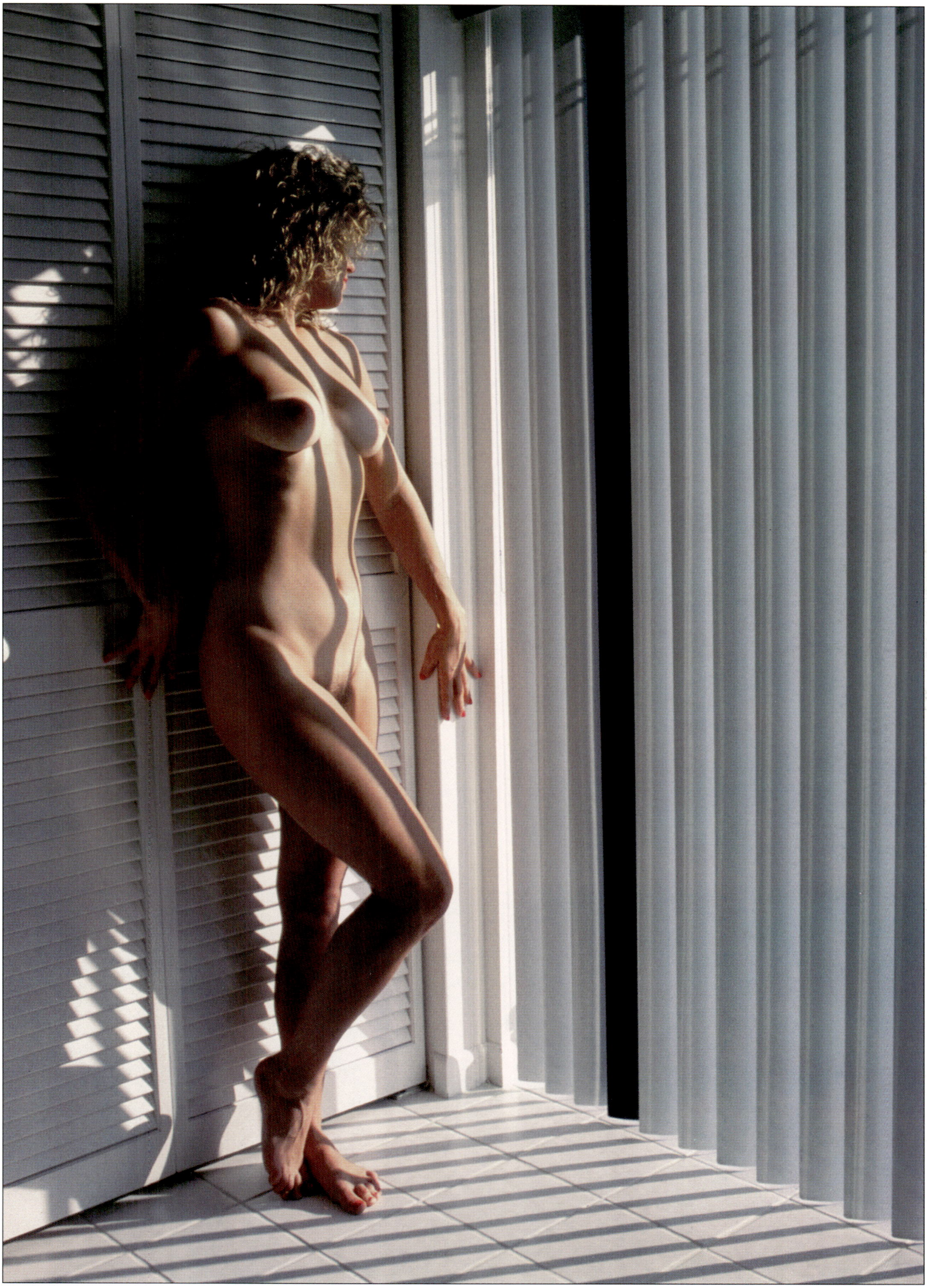

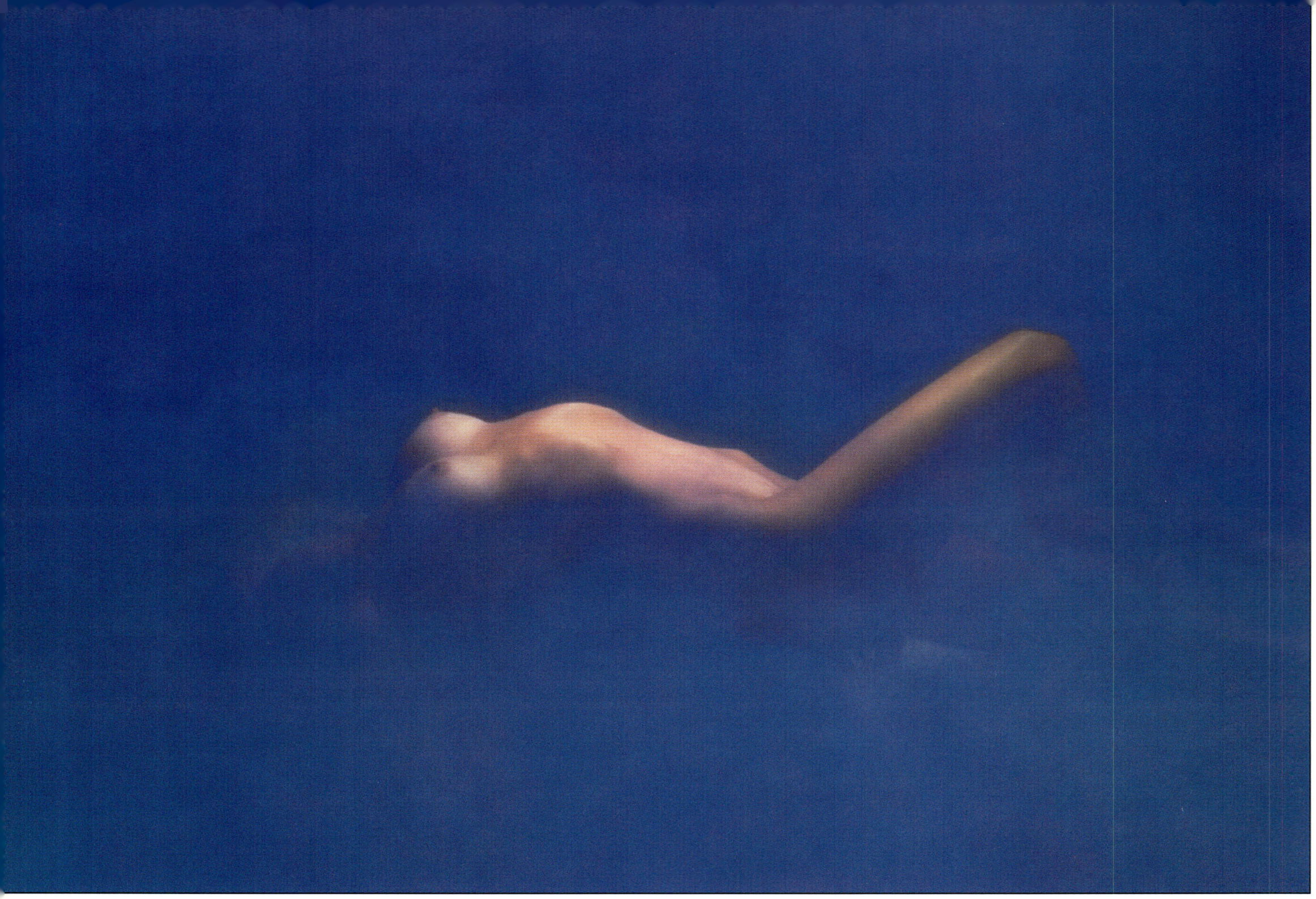

Previous page: *In this photo, a single, fixed light source was used — daylight. The subject's torso, from her shoulders to her legs, is the feature of main interest. Her stature is enhanced by the shadow line that continues to run down the length of her leg, making her look taller than she actually is.*
Above: *This image is not only timeless and dramatic, it will also support different interpretations. An image of this type is often well received by viewers. It can be admired just for what it is or it can cause a viewer to become an active participant, providing his or her own story or meaning.*
Right: *Artificial fog always makes for interesting photography because it is unpredictable and non-repeating. Because of this, we suggest that when you use fog, make a number of exposures of each setup before moving on to other poses or lighting situations. In addition, and because fog has a tendency to soften any image, we rarely use a soft-focus filter when we employ fog. It would degrade an image too much for our taste.*

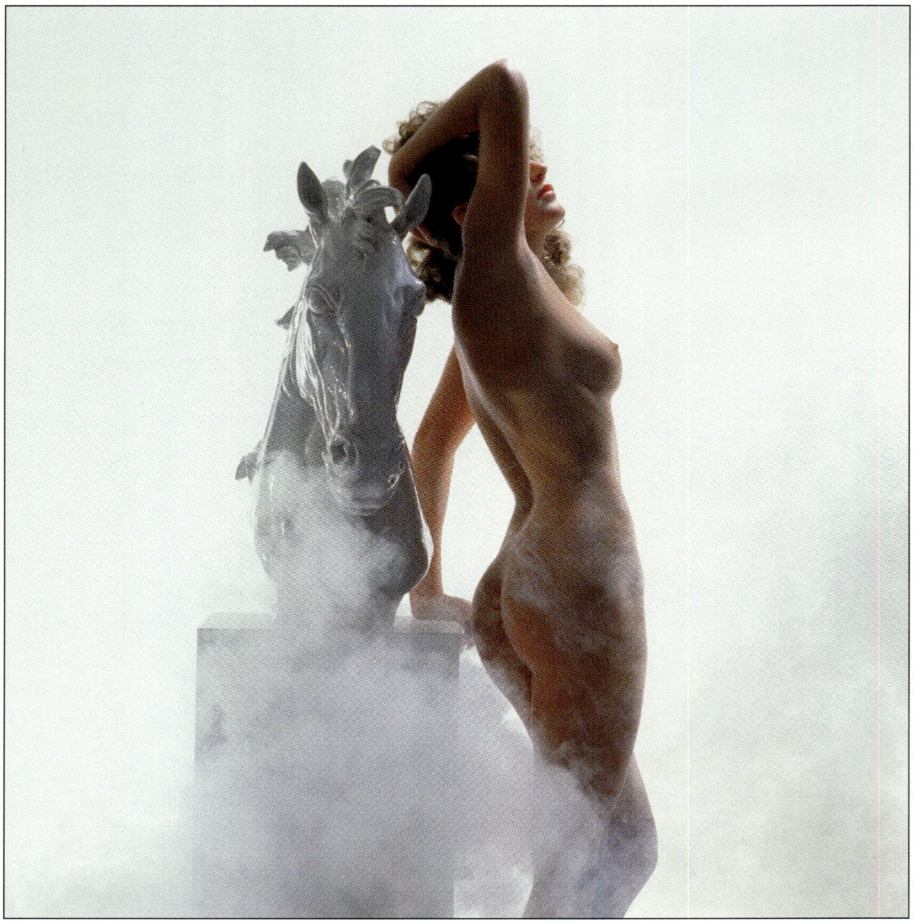

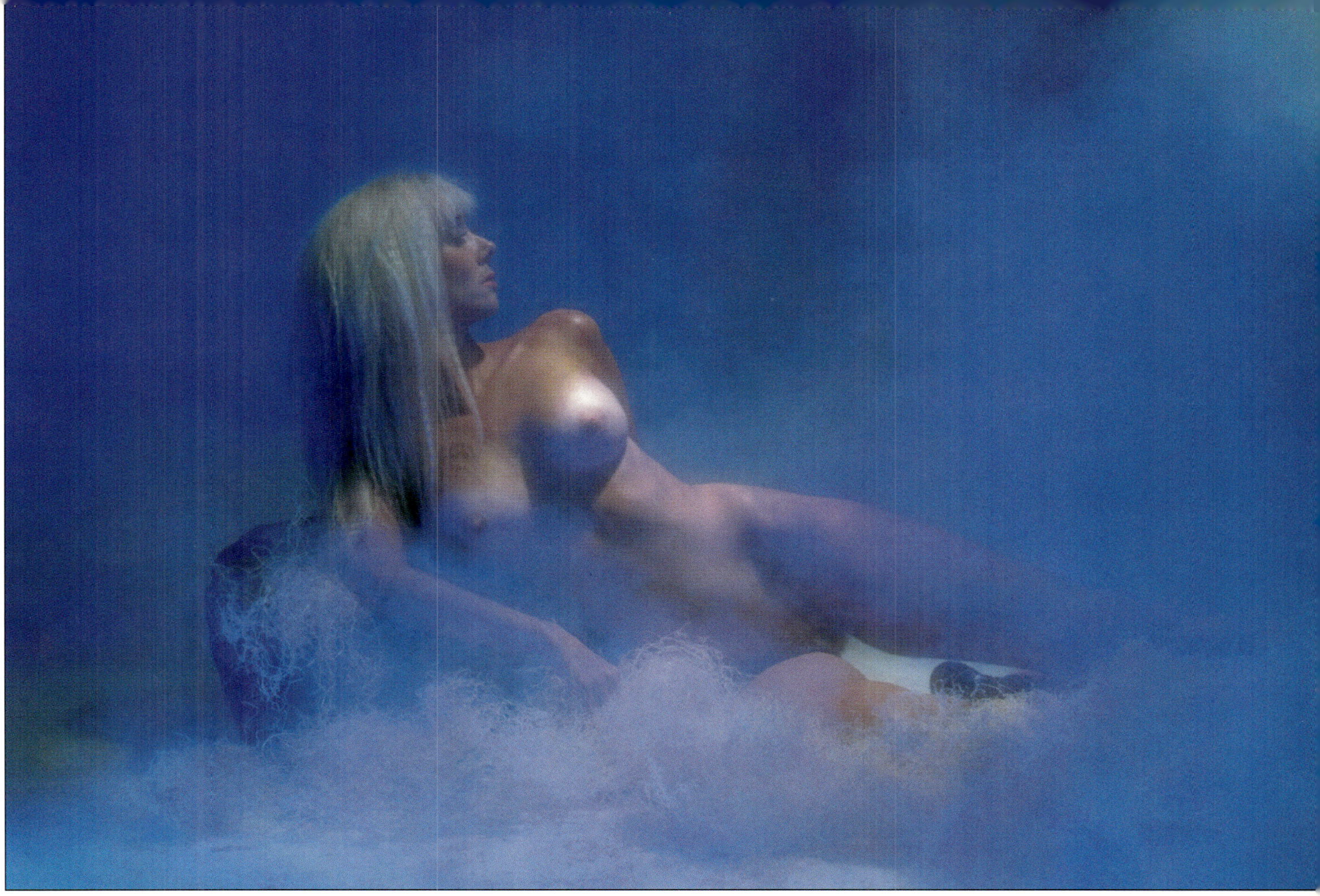

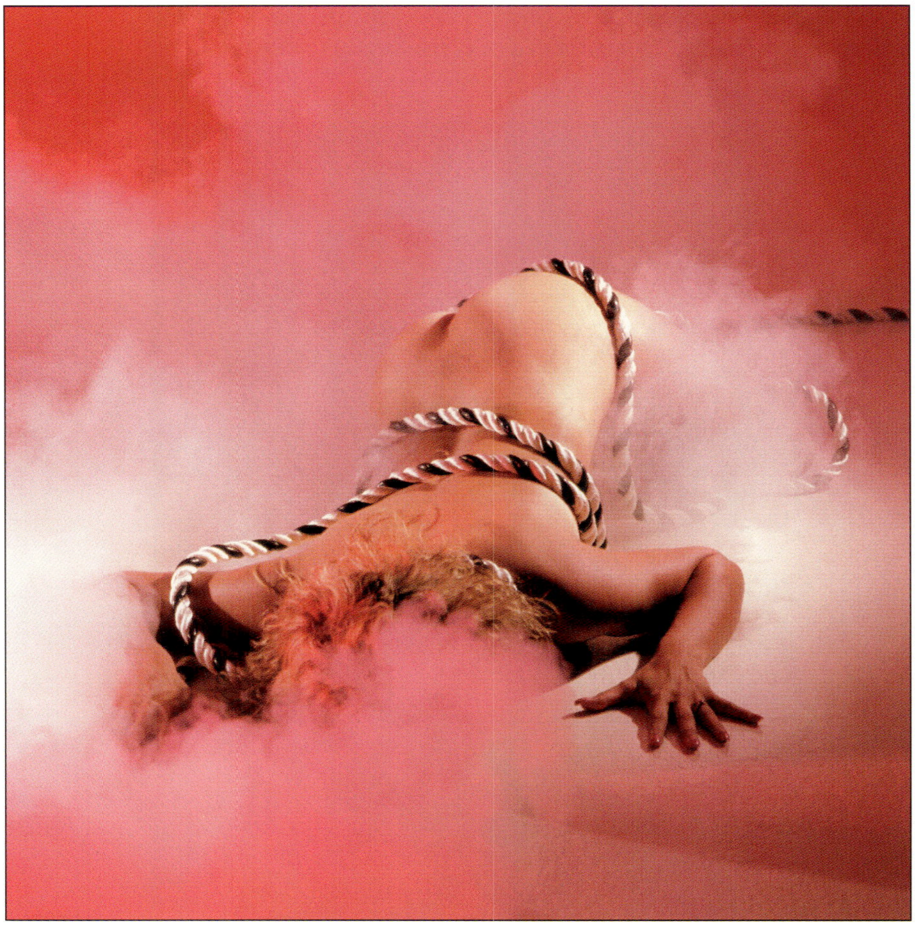

Above: *This type of photo, like the one on the opposite page, is one that demands enlargement. The larger these type of images are portrayed, the more impact the image has. Also note how the change in poses has given these photos a very different appearance and concept. It is important to know how to manipulate and vary any setting, the lighting, poses, props, camera angles, and so on. By doing so, you'll get the greatest visual variety and be able to achieve variety in mood, effect, and meaning from one image to the next.*

Left: *This is one of our favorite photographs, largely because it offers a viewer a wide range of possible interpretations. The interpretation any given viewer might give to this image might say as much about the viewer as it would the image itself or even about us, as its creator. Many of our subjects truly enjoy being involved in this kind of photographic story telling. We enjoy it too — it exercises our imagination.*

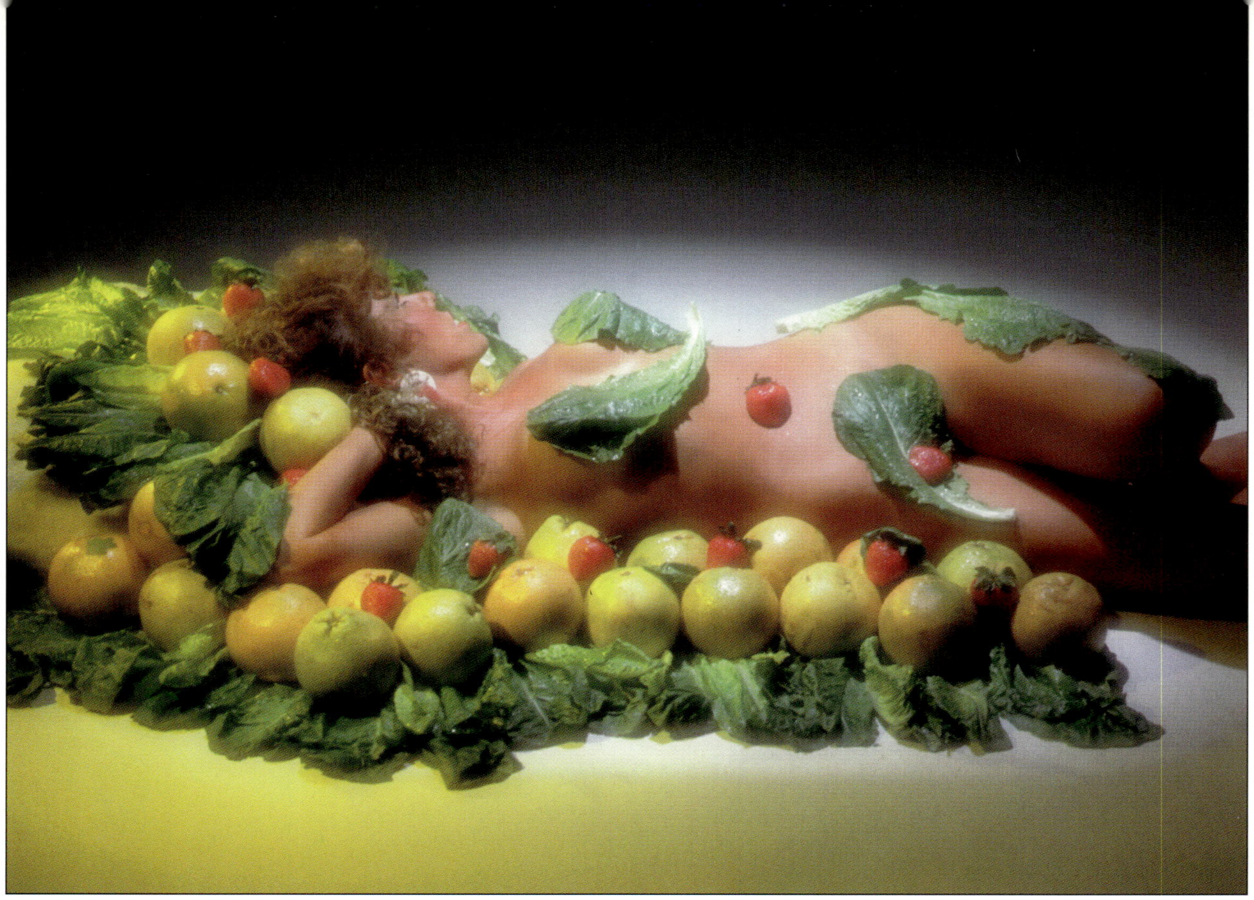

Above: *One way to come up with ideas for nude studies is to ask a subject what he or she does for a living and any hobbies she or he may have. In this case, the subject told us that she and her husband were in the produce business. The result: a stunning and fun-type shot.*

Below: *For this image, we used our "autumn leaves" scenario. As you can see, it is very simple and easy to set up, and yet very effective. Two lights were used: one, housed in a five-inch bowl reflector with an amber gel, was placed on the floor to the far side of the subject, just beyond the left edge of the image. The main light, also housed in a five-inch bowl reflector, was suspended from a boom stand and placed almost directly above the subject. Notice the modeling this provided on the buttocks and back. The background light was put at a power setting of one full f-stop less than the main light.*

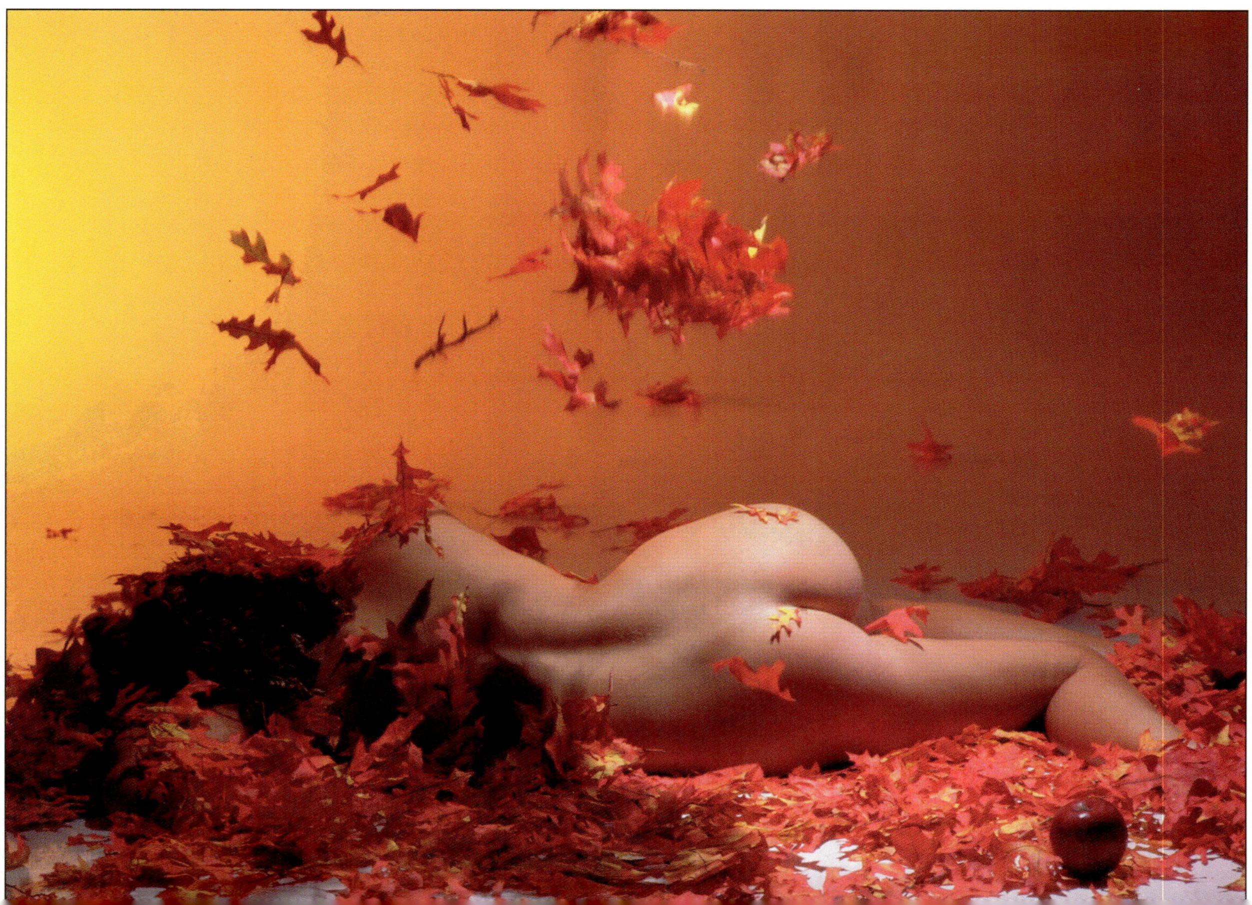

be a certain number of ingredients which comprise any artful photographic nude study. Some of these ingredients will be primary and some will be secondary; however, all will be important and should exist in order to insure a successful and desired photographic result. Seriously executed nude photography will involve at least four primary ingredients:

1. A well-conceived concept or idea.
2. A well-chosen subject.
3. An appropriate pose.
4. Appropriate lighting.

Not one of these ingredients is more important than another. All should exist and should interact with each other during any given photo session to attain satisfying images and an artful result. For example, if a photographer has an excellent subject, with a wonderful pose, but has inappropriate lighting, the shoot will be less than a total success. The results will be mere

• **Figure photography involves four primary ingredients.**

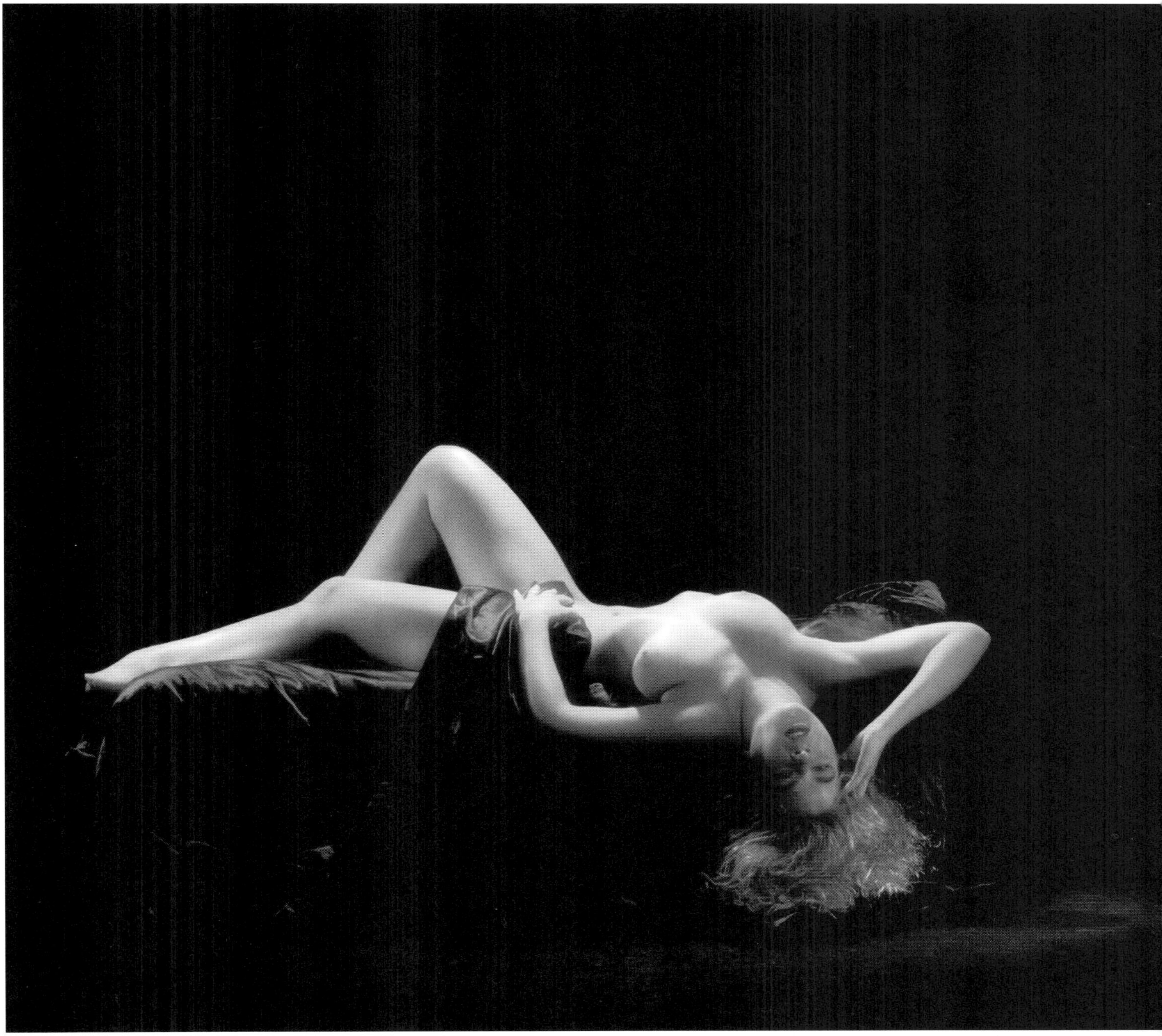

Above: *This pose is quite dramatic and very sensuous. The unusual view of an upside-down face adds drama, as does the loosely hanging hair. Although you can discern some of the face, the image is still "impersonal." This is because the face has not been prominently lit but has been allowed to go rather dark (one f-stop darker than the body). Accordingly, and like the image on the opposite page, the image becomes representative of womanhood in general rather than of the specific woman posing.*

"The goal, of course, will be to realize on film, the concept you had pre-visualized..."

photos of a naked subject and not an artful nude study. Although these ingredients will be discussed in detail throughout the book, for now, it's important that you to generally understand the importance of working with these ingredients.

During any practice session with a subject, we suggest that you concentrate on a limited number of poses. Work on just five or six, over and over again. Initially, don't concern yourself with lighting, but only with the poses. Learn how the various facets of a subject's body can be affected through minor posing changes; how the arch of the back, the turn of a leg, the placement of an arm and hands can affect an entire pose, the subject's look, and the photographic end result.

Then, while staying with one specific pose, practice using three or four different lighting arrangements. Learn what each arrangement can do for a subject and how each can affect an overall mood and final image. Finally, practice combining some of the poses you liked with the lighting combinations you favored.

The goal, of course, will be to realize on film, the concept you had pre-visualized in the first instance. This will be achieved much easier if you take things in steps. You should not work with too many ingredients at one time; it could become confusing.

Subject Selection

Subject selection requires a great deal of thought on the part of the photographer. To help you with subject selection, consider the following:

Choose stereo-typical subjects: Our thinking is constantly being bombarded by stereotypes and symbolism. Words such as motherhood, doctor, and wedding ring provide us with mental pictures from which we — in varying degrees and based upon life's experiences — conjure up pre-conceived ideas. Doctors are supposed to look like doctors, judges like judges, models and ballet dancers like models and ballet dancers, and so on.

As a result, and to make any photographic image easily and readily comprehensible to a viewer, we are well-advised to follow the accepted stereotypes.

Not all subjects, no matter how attractive they may be, are going to be suitable candidates for a nude figure study. Not all women will have the talent or inclination to convey on film the symbolic pictorial representation of the beauty and glory of womanhood; or, they simply will "not look the part" in keeping with your preconceived ideas. Such subjects will be the wrong choice for an artful nude figure study.

As you view the results of your first attempts at figure photography, you might not understand why you're not getting the startling images you were hoping for. However, with time and experience, you'll see that the problem might have been in choosing the wrong subject for your photographic interpretation.

To generate the greatest impact and clearest meaning for your intended viewers, choose a subject who has physical qualities and features that are consistent with your preconceived ideas for the final image.

For example, if the intended concept is one of gentleness and vulnerability, you would not want a powerful, muscular model to be your subject, no matter how attractive she may be.

Choosing an appropriate subject for your concept might also involve selecting a subject who is more mature rather than youthful in appearance, one who is more full-figured than slim, one who is an African-American or Asian rather than Caucasian, or a male instead of a female. All of these factors should be taken into account.

Once you have chosen your subject, the main concept you had pre-visualized must be structured around him or her. If the chosen person is not the main subject matter, the end photo result may be a lot of things (e.g., a product or scenic shot with a naked subject shown secondarily in the photo composition), but it will not be a nude photo study of an individual.

Mixed or combined nude studies: Most figure photography is of a single subject and usually female. However, it is not rare for two or more female subjects to be photographed together, for male subjects to be depicted either alone, in pairs, or groups, or for there to be some combination of male and female subjects.

When you photograph more than one subject, you should determine whether each should be given equal prominence in the image or if one should be the "lead" character while the other, or others, play a secondary part. The poses, composition, and lighting will have to be

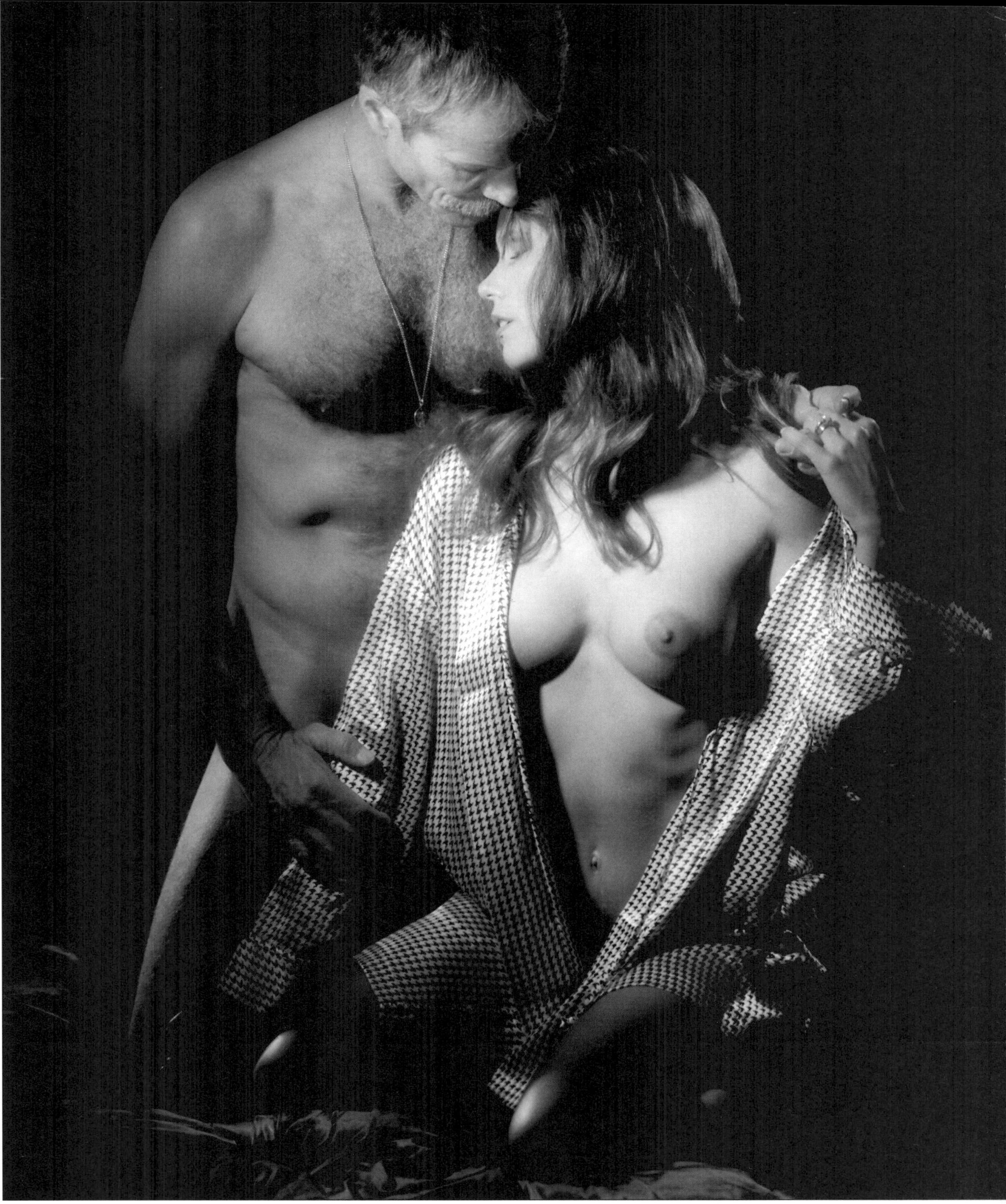

Above: *We love to create "couple" images like this one. We used black and white film (T-Max 100 by Kodak) and very selective lighting: a Broncolor 20-degree grid spot acted as the main light (placed 90 degrees left of camera axis and in line with the female subject's nose); two accent lights and another light with a grid as a fill light. Each accent light was in a 4-inch snoot-type housing. One accent light was behind her and directed toward the back of her head. The other was placed low and positioned about 110 degrees left of camera axis. It served to rim the male's leg as well as both knees of the female. A fourth light, mounted onto a boom stand and positioned just above and in front of them, acted as a fill light source. This light was housed in a 5-inch bowl reflector with a 10-degree grid spot covering it.*

"mixed nude studies can be profound."

• **Figure photography also involves one or more secondary ingredients.**

structured based on the way you choose to shoot the combination of the figures.

In many of our photographs of couples, the secondary subject may be: farther in the background, lit less brightly, slightly out of focus, or looking away from the camera.

In today's enlightened world, it is perfectly acceptable to make photographic nude studies of woman and man together, in equal prominence, or where one is primary and the other secondary.

For the best sales results, the images should most often clearly demonstrate that one sex is not taking an unfair advantage nor demonstrating cruelty.

The photography of mixed couples puts the greatest artistic demands on both the photographer and the models. The achievement of images that are natural, believable, and appealing confronts all the participants with a special challenge. Self-consciousness, triteness, and awkwardness must be avoided at all costs. The subjects must be comfortable with each other and not feel intimidated by the presence of the camera or photographer.

However, if the photographer is successful in working with two or more subjects at the same time, mixed nude studies can be profound. This fact has been proven over and over again, in other art media, most notably in some of the sculptures by Auguste Rodin. His sculpture, *The Kiss*, is a clear example of two subjects having equal prominence with no suggestion of chauvinism, inequality, or cruelty.

Whether you are photographing in the classical or contemporary style, mixed nude studies can offer tremendous potential for creativity.

However, some value judgments must be made and some pitfalls should be avoided before engaging in this type of work. For example:

1. When two or more subjects are used, you need to decide whether one or more subjects are to dominate the scene with the remaining subjects acting as supporting elements, or whether all are going to be equally involved in representing the main concept.

2. A value judgment must be made as to the degree of nudity for each of the subjects you intend to use in each photo. It sometimes helps to emphasize the separation of main and supporting subjects by having the main subject totally nude while the supporting "players" are partially draped, or the other way around.

There are no hard and fast rules governing this point and you must decide which avenue to take, based upon your preconceived idea of the end result. Don't wait until the last minute to make the decision. Let your subjects know, well in advance, what it is you expect of them.

3. Prepare to spend some time coaching your subjects before and during a photo session. We have found that relatively inexperienced, amateur female models are generally more cooperative and less self-conscious than their male counterparts. Fledgling male models frequently concentrate on assuming a macho look. This can be an asset only if this is the type of look you're after.

If you want a variety of other looks from your male subjects, which do not strongly suggest the symbolism of power, strength and virility, you will often have to spend time coaching them. You'll often need to talk them into a proper pose and mental attitude in order to achieve your desired result.

4. Be cautious about too much frivolity during the photo session. When working with two or more non-professional subjects, posing nude, you may encounter a situation in which one or more of the subjects may openly become too frivolous. While this may seem like fun and a good idea, if it is allowed to go unchecked, it could adversely affect the outcome of the shoot.

This doesn't mean that you and your subjects shouldn't have fun during the session. You should shoot in a light-hearted atmosphere. However, you, the photographer, must retain sufficient control and influence over your subjects during the session to achieve the end results you want.

Secondary Ingredients

An artful nude photo session will also involve one or more secondary ingredients. These include the following:

1. A suitable setting.
2. Proper makeup for the subjects.
3. Proper hair styling.
4. Appropriate props.

5 Appropriate accessories for the setting and subject.

Although the primary ingredients must always exist for an artful nude study, the secondary ingredients are not mandatory. In subsequent chapters, we will be discussing these secondary ingredients in more detail.

For now, it's important for you to note that any one of these ingredients could be used during a nude photo study session, in any combination, all at once, in varying degrees, or none at all.

Note: Just because we have labeled these ingredients as secondary, you should not ignore them.

Once you have decided to use one or more of the secondary ingredients, you must be as critical of them — in terms of selection, lighting, and placement — as you would be of the primary ingredients. If you are not, the secondary ingredients are likely to prove more of a hindrance than an aesthetic asset.

Summary

Figure photography promotes an escape from the commonplace and forces one to strive for a level of creativity that is hard to achieve in almost any other photographic area. Indeed, it is a very special and powerful art form.

If we had to choose one single thing about nude figure photography that is more special than any other, we would probably tell you that it is the aesthetic and technical challenge of doing justice to one of the most beautiful creations on earth — the human form.

Even just one model offers the creative, inventive photographer an infinite number of variations and possibilities to capture on film.

For example, one could photograph a subject's full figure or just a body part. One could prominently show a subject's face or conceal it; the model could make eye contact with the camera or avoid it. The photographer can even emphasize or de-emphasize parts of a subject's figure by carefully selecting an appropriate camera viewpoint and lens choice.

One could vary the way in which a subject was lit as well as the pose. All of this is done to suit the photographer's previsualized concept of the image. In addition, one could create a realistic image or a graphic, abstract one. The list is almost endless.

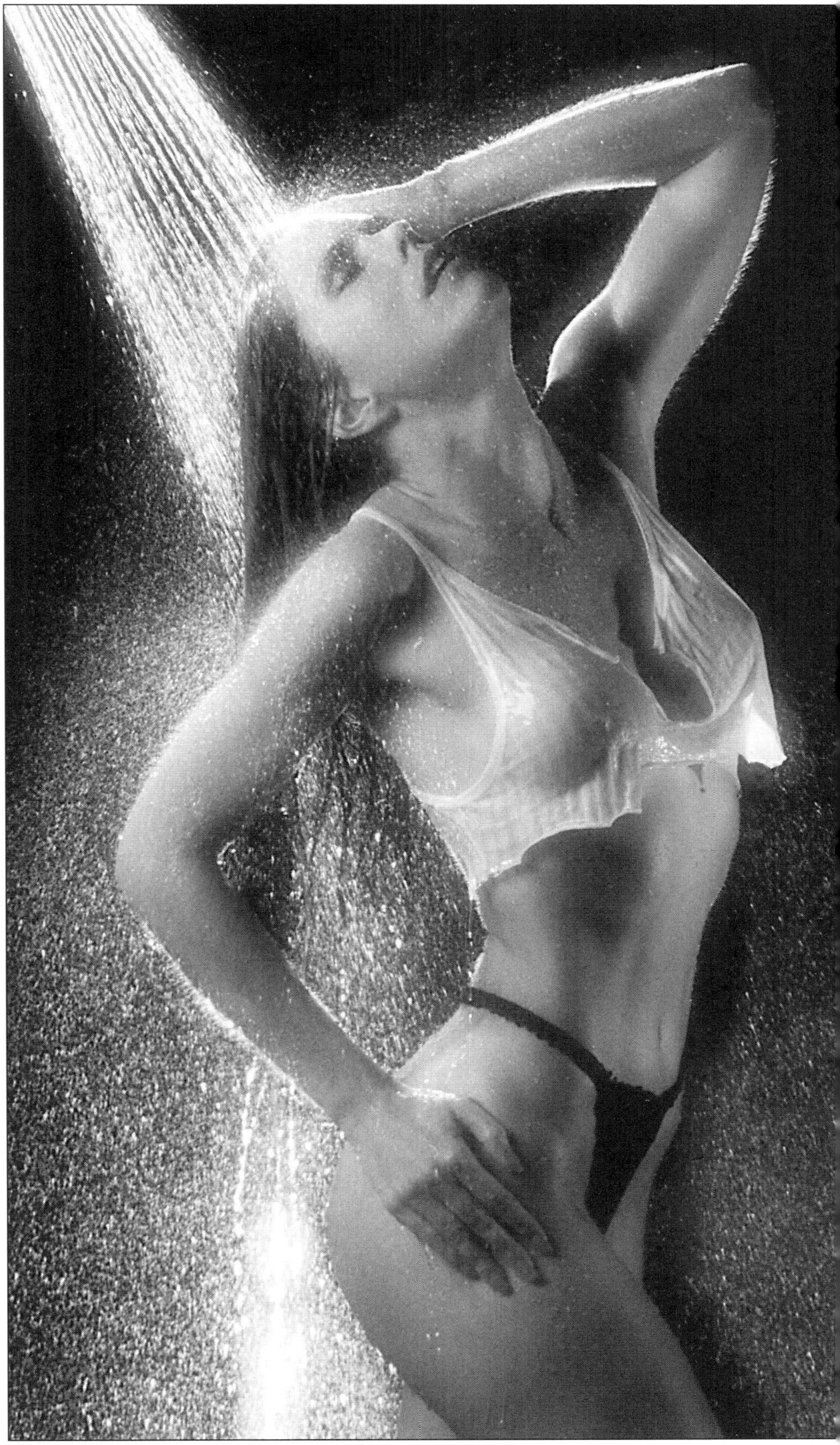

***Above:** How can this photo be a nude study when the subject is clad? To us, it serves to demonstrate that the human form need not be sans clothing and barren to be "nude." The fact that you are able to discern the subject's breasts and nipples through the water soaked, torn shirt causes the images to rise to the dignity of a nude study.*

Chapter Two

Finding and Preparing Models

Finding and preparing a model for a nude photo session is often no easy task. Among other factors, it requires an understanding of subject selection.

Subject selection involves an understanding of three separate, distinct, but interrelated problems: a photographer's credibility, knowing where to look for subjects, and knowing what to look for in a subject. As if this were not enough, there are other factors involved in getting a subject for nude photography.

For example, once a willing and proper subject has been found and selected, a subject must be properly instructed so that he or she can adequately prepare for a photo session.

And, once both the selection and preparation facets have been dealt with, a photographer is then frequently and typically confronted with a fifth problem: legal considerations.

Credibility

"...credibility is what you'll rely upon..."

In the beginning of your photographic career, before you have had an opportunity to gain a reputation, your credibility is what you'll rely upon to persuade a subject to pose for figure photography. Credibility can be established in a number of different ways.

Be Honest and Sincere

One of the worst things you could do is to lie to a subject or misrepresent yourself. There really is no need to. Every photographer had to get his or her start at some point; people are not born knowing how to do figure photography.

Therefore, if you have never photographed a subject nude before and even if you're not a professional photographer, don't lie to a prospective subject about your accomplishments or expertise. Not only will most subjects appreciate your honesty but many will find it charming that they might be helping you launch your career.

Never misrepresent your intentions during any photo session. If you do, your conduct will come back to haunt you. At the very least, a subject will bad-mouth you to friends and family and a poor reputation could ruin your career.

A Professional Manner

Figure photography is an extremely delicate and sensitive area of photography; consequently, you simply cannot afford to treat it with a cavalier attitude. A poor, non-professional manner can go far in putting you out of business before you ever get started. By contrast, if your approach to a prospective subject is pleasing, sensitive, non-threatening, straight-forward, and business like, you'll find your subjects reacting in a more favorable and positive manner.

Professional Shooting Locales

Unless you are an established photographer, with years of experience behind you and have an excellent and untarnished reputation in your community, you simply can not afford to be haphazard in your selection of shooting locales. This does not mean that you must have a 10,000 square feet photo studio, in the busiest part of town, with a half a million dollars worth of equipment, in order to attract prospective figure-photography subjects. To the contrary, some of you might not have a real photography studio to work out of and still be able to attract good subjects. So long as the area you've selected to photograph in looks and suggests legitimacy, this will usually suffice to calm the anxieties of the most cautious of subjects. But, there is another word of caution.

If you are not photographing in a real photo studio, from a legitimate business location, then you should make absolutely certain that the location which you have chosen is not one which might bring some sort of nefarious activity to the prospective model's mind.

For example, advising a prospective subject that you intend to conduct a photo session in your bedroom, in the confines of your private office (either late at night or during a time of day when no one else will be around), or in some dimly-lit, back-alley warehouse area, is not how to attract subjects. It's also a good way to get yourself into trouble.

Business Stationery

To many subjects, a professional-looking business card, stationery, and the like will go far in bespeaking the fact that you have a measure of credibility. This will be true even if you don't have a real studio to work in or out of. The more costly and elaborate your stationery and business cards are, the more initial credibility your subjects will ascribe to you.

Many of these people will think that if you have gone to the time, trouble, and expense to produce costly cards, and other printed business material, then you must be legitimate.

Obviously, this type of thinking is not totally accurate (since many con men work on this premise too); however, it, along with one or more of the other credible factors we've listed here, will usually suffice in allowing you to gain a subject's initial attention and confidence.

Be Careful of What You Say

If you're in this business long enough, you're bound to come across at least one or two people who will have vocabularies worse than five angry truck drivers; every other word will be a colorful, four-lettered metaphor.

Notwithstanding the fact that some subjects may take such liberties with the English language, you should never follow their lead; watch what you say very carefully. It could cost you a lot of professional credibility if you don't.

"...watch what you say very carefully."

For example, whether he or she is a paying client or not, never, under any circumstances, use any profanity in the presence of a subject. In addition, never use any words which might have a sexual connotation associated with them. Never use any crude language to describe any portion of their anatomy.

A subject may feel perfectly at ease referring to their own posterior by some crude or colorful term; however, you should not follow suit. You should be careful to use more appropriate language; use socially accepted words such as buttocks, derriere, or posterior when referring to that specific body part.

An Assistant

Under no circumstances would we ever engage in boudoir or nude figure-photography without the presence of three people in the shoot-room area at all times: my wife, myself and the subject; my wife, the subject, and an assistant, or myself, the subject and an assistant. When an assistant is used, we always use one who is of the same sex as the subject. This helps make a subject feel more at ease, less guarded, and far less intimidated.

A Portfolio

If a photographer can show a prospective subject a good portfolio of his or her previous figure photography work, it can be a great factor in quickly building credibility. However, if the photographer hasn't done nude photography before, then some examples of glamour photography should be shown. If this type of photography is not available either, then some other type of photographic work must be shown.

- **Have a portfolio of your work to show a prospective subject.**

No matter what the subject matter might be — family portraits, scenic, still-lifes, and so on — some photos should be shown, provided they are the photographer's best work. Without some evidence of a photographer's work being shown,

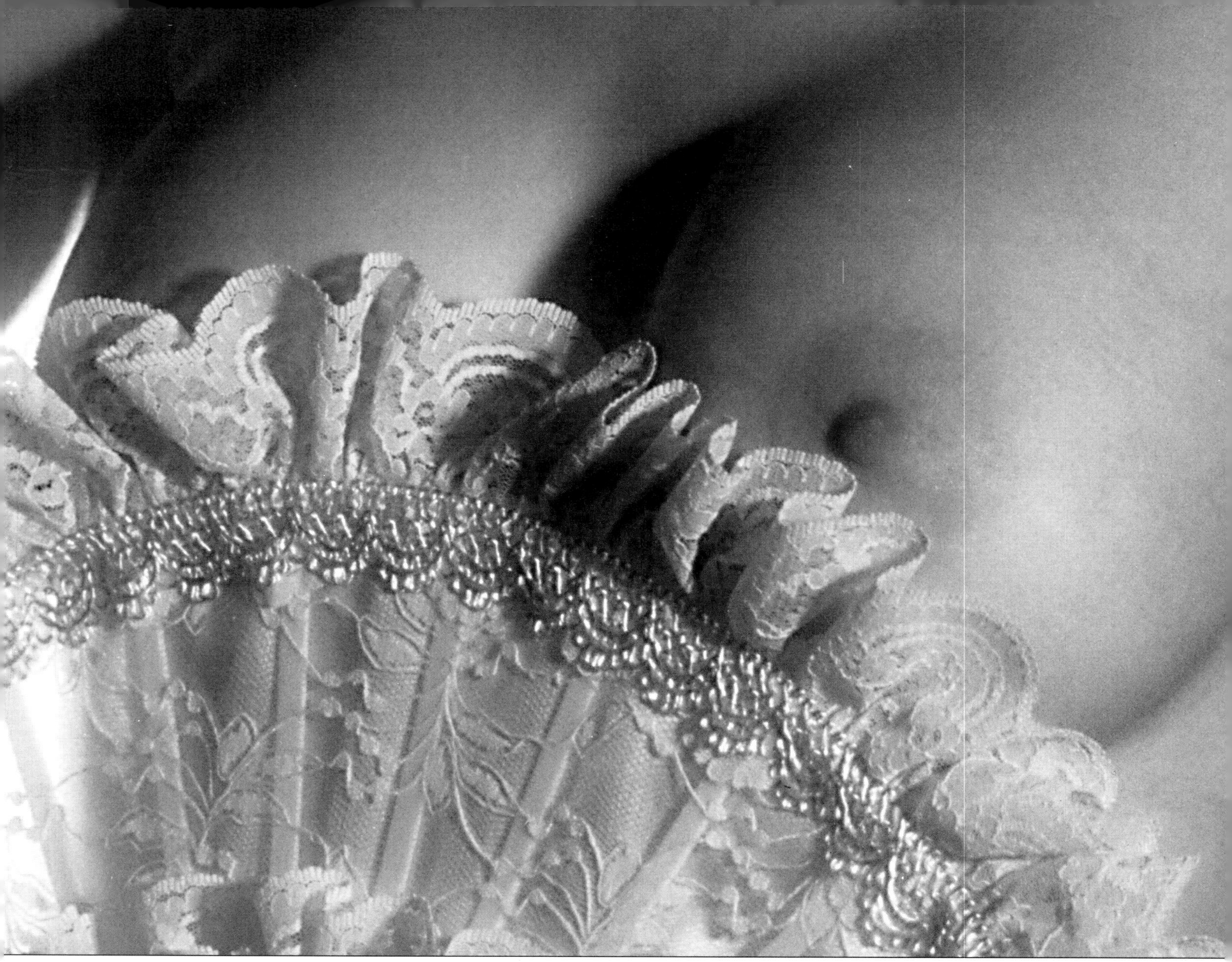

Above: *This particular subject had a bust augmentation performed just a few months before this photo was taken. On the day of the photo session, she told us that she not only wanted a photo which would remind her of the event but also wanted a photo which she could give to her plastic surgeon; a memento of the occasion. In addition, she was concerned that her identity remain unknown. This body-part shot filled the bill.*

most otherwise willing prospective subjects will usually turn off and tune out. Some might even question a photographer's motives and intentions and want to report the photographer to the authorities.

Where to Look for Models

Obviously the following is not an exhaustive list of where to look for models; however, it will give you a good starting point.

Former and New Customers

If you have photographed a subject in the past — at a portrait session, a wedding, some candids of a friend — you should not hesitate to ask this person to pose for you. This, of course, is provided you think that the person would otherwise be a suitable subject.

If you operate or work in a professional studio, the group of women who will go through your doors during any given week, month, and year will often be your best source for models. They're already familiar with you and your work and are most likely to trust you. For us, this has certainly been our biggest and best source for model candidates.

To give you an example of how lucrative this source can be, when the photography for this book was initially planned, we were absolutely convinced that we would need to hire professional models to pose (nude photography being the sensitive area that it is, plus the fact that the photos were to be used in a national publication). To our amazement, we didn't have to; many of our clients actually volunteered to pose for us.

In fact, we had more of our clients ask to pose for this book than we had ask us with respect to our boudoir book: *Secrets Of Boudoir Photography*. As a result, all of the subjects shown in this book, with the exception of one, are non-professional models.

In addition, and with the exception of the one pro, all of the subjects in this book were strangers to professionally created figure work. This, of course, gave us an ideal situation.

First, it allowed us to write and demonstrate how one can take inexperienced women — often with less than perfect features; who were otherwise unaccustomed to being in front of a camera without clothing — and still produce stunning (and salable) figure photographs.

Secondly, we were able to draw upon a large number of different posing candidates, all for a very reasonable cost: no money actually changed hands; it cost us one photographic print for each photo.

However, you may not be as fortunate as we, since we have a large number of people passing through our doors during the course of any given year: customers as well as people browsing, asking for a price list or information regarding an individual portrait, family photo session, and so on. This gives us a very large audience to draw upon whenever we are in need of photographic subjects.

Family, Friends and Acquaintances

If you approached some of your acquaintances, friends and family members and informed them that you needed a volunteer to pose for some practice portrait photos, most would probably agree to sit without thinking twice.

Unfortunately, if you were to approach these same candidates and ask them to pose for nude photographs, you'll most likely find a negative response. Some may even get angry or openly question your motives and intentions.

You'll often need to spend time convincing and assuring your prospective subjects that your motives and objectives are totally professional and that your end results will be in the best of taste. This can be hard to do, especially with friends and relatives.

However, don't give up if you are initially turned down. Try to educate those around you on the history and meaning of nude art in general and figure photography in particular. Those in your immediate circle of friends and family can be an excellent source for models, especially when you are first starting out.

If absolutely necessary, allow a friend or relative of the prospective model to sit in on the photo session.

This will go far in convincing an otherwise hesitant subject that your intentions are legitimate. Normally, however, we do not favor having people sitting in on shoots. Spectators tend to be a distraction to both the photographer and the model.

"Spectators tend to be a distraction..."

Art Schools

If you are fortunate enough to live in an area that has an art school or a college with an art department, you'll find that such schools and departments can be an excellent source for subjects.

The fine-art division of such schools will often have excellent figure models. Not only will the schools have a number of models to work with but, as important, the models will most often be accustomed to posing in the nude, having done so many times for the school's art students. Many will also possess the requisite bodily agility that is so important in figure-photography work.

- **Art Schools are a good source for subjects.**

Even the cost is not prohibitive with these models. Most will usually charge a very modest modeling fee, such as $5 to $10 per hour.

Other models may even agree upon a smaller and flat fee (such as $20-$25 for the entire day's (4-6 hours) photo session) provided you also agree to give each woman one or two photographic prints from any photo session in which they were involved.

Model Agencies

A reputable model agency can be an excellent source for experienced subjects. It's not, however, a source we would favor. Professional models for nude photography can be very expensive — $50 to $200 per hour, or even more, is not uncommon — and this can make their use prohibitive for the average amateur photographer.

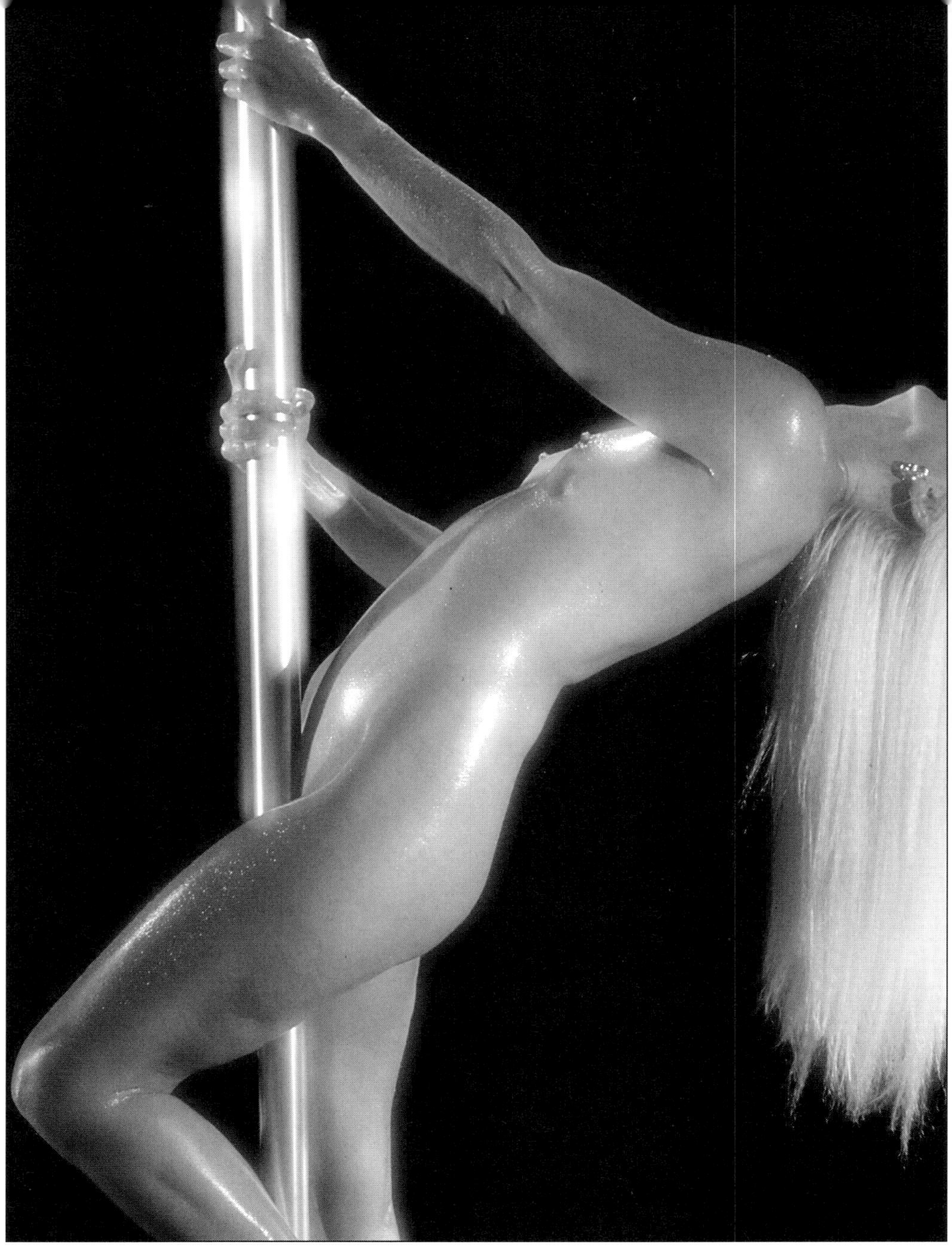

***Above:** Baby oil was applied to the subject's body to complement the glistening pole. Not only did this help to beautifully highlight the skin, it also gave the subject a very convincing "athletic" appearance. For contrast, we used a black background. For nude studies, direct eye contact by the subject with the camera is not always suitable. By having the subject's eye directed elsewhere, more emphasis is given to the subject's body. The subject is thereby seen more as a symbol or man or womanhood than as one specific subject.*

Also, well trained and experienced models in fashion and advertising work sometimes lack the freshness and spontaneity of a less experienced, but enthusiastic, amateur model.

On the other hand, many agencies will be happy to offer you a large selection of fledgling models who are in need of experience working before a camera and who also need to build a photo portfolio. For their posing services — at least in our area in Florida — it is customary to pay such inexperienced models no money but to give them one or more 8x10 enlargements from each of their photo sessions. However, this relatively "free" service usually applies only if you are seeking models for regular portraiture, fashion or glamour photography.

For boudoir or nude photography, not only will the agencies have fewer people to send you, but, as we noted, the charge becomes quite substantial: from $50 to $200 per hour even for inexperienced models. Such charges are generally out of the question for mere practice sessions.

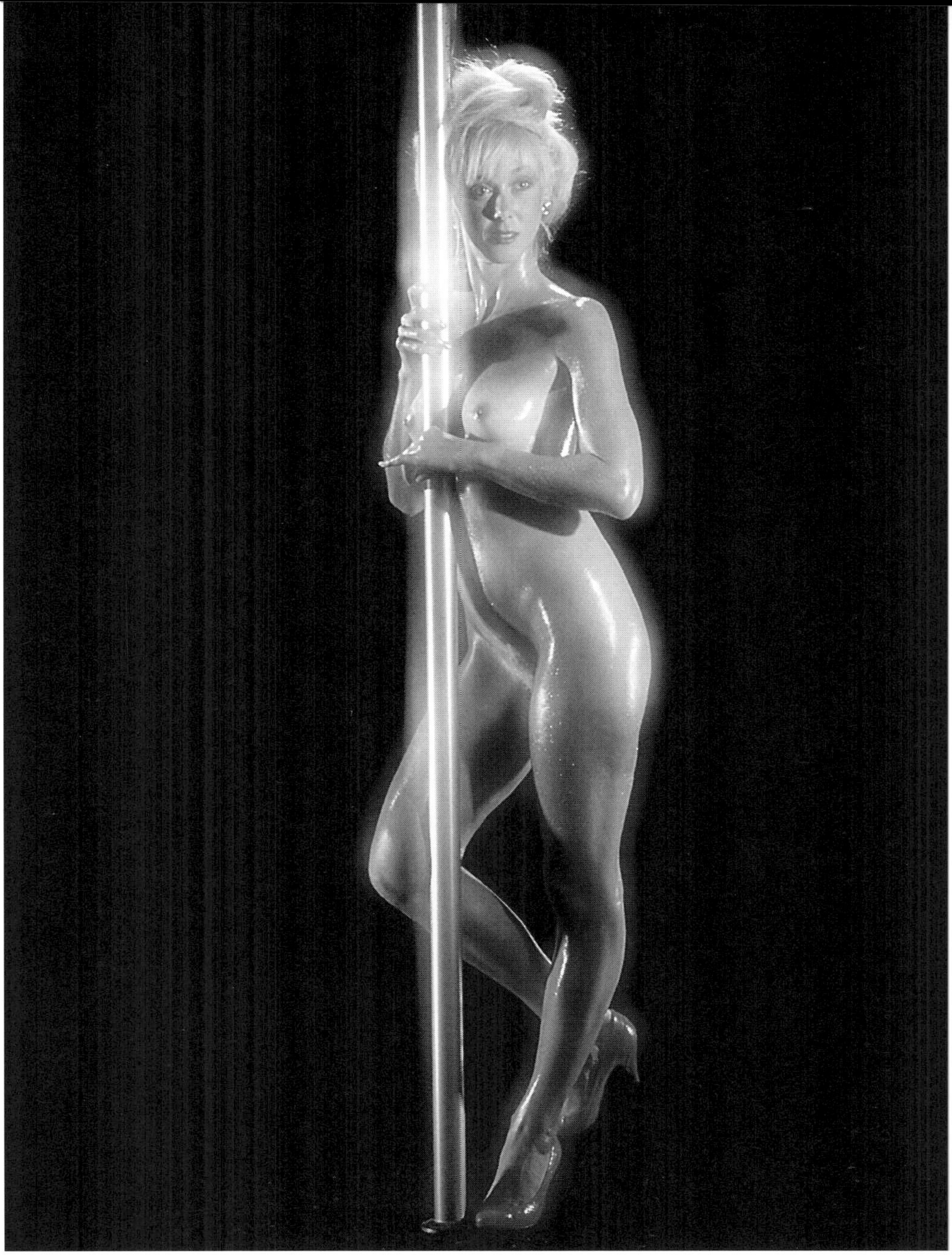

Above: *When using any pole as a posing probe, be quite sure that it is secured firmly enough to taken any weight and stress a subject may place on it. A subject's safety and well-being must be paramount during any photo session. In this photo, where the subject is just standing, apparently resting between exercises, the eye contact with the camera seems quite appropriate although a downward or upward glance would have been just as effective. Each would have evoked a different response from the viewer.*

Why are the charges for nude modeling so high? First, most of the modeling agencies we know think that high charges help ensure the legitimacy of a photographer's motives. It also represents added compensation for the "hazard" of engaging in a form of photography which, even though totally legitimate, is still regarded by many as taboo. (It's thought of much like combat pay.)

In addition to high charges by a modeling agency, most will always insist that the women be protected by exchanging very comprehensively and carefully worded "General Releases."

They'll want to ensure that your photos do not end up in some national magazine, with you being paid thousands of dollars for the photos while the girl who posed for you only got a couple of hundred. (We'll be discussing model releases later in this chapter.)

Dance Schools

Like art schools, dance schools can be a good source for prospective models.

Dance instructors as well as their students can be excellent figure-photography candidates, even though they may not have had any prior training in modeling.

Dancers usually have a certain physical agility, expressiveness, grace, and vitality which will more than compensate for their lack of modeling skills or training.

It's also been our experience that most dancers will generally be happy to pose in exchange for photos; most will expect little or no financial remuneration.

However, there is one caveat. We have found that most dancers who have never posed before hesitate to start a photo session totally nude. Most need to start out slowly, such as with glamour head shots or even full-length shots in a dance leotard until confidence is built.

Once they realize that nothing more than great photography is going to happen to them, most will contrive; and be relatively uninhibited about their bodies. In addition, and once they get into the

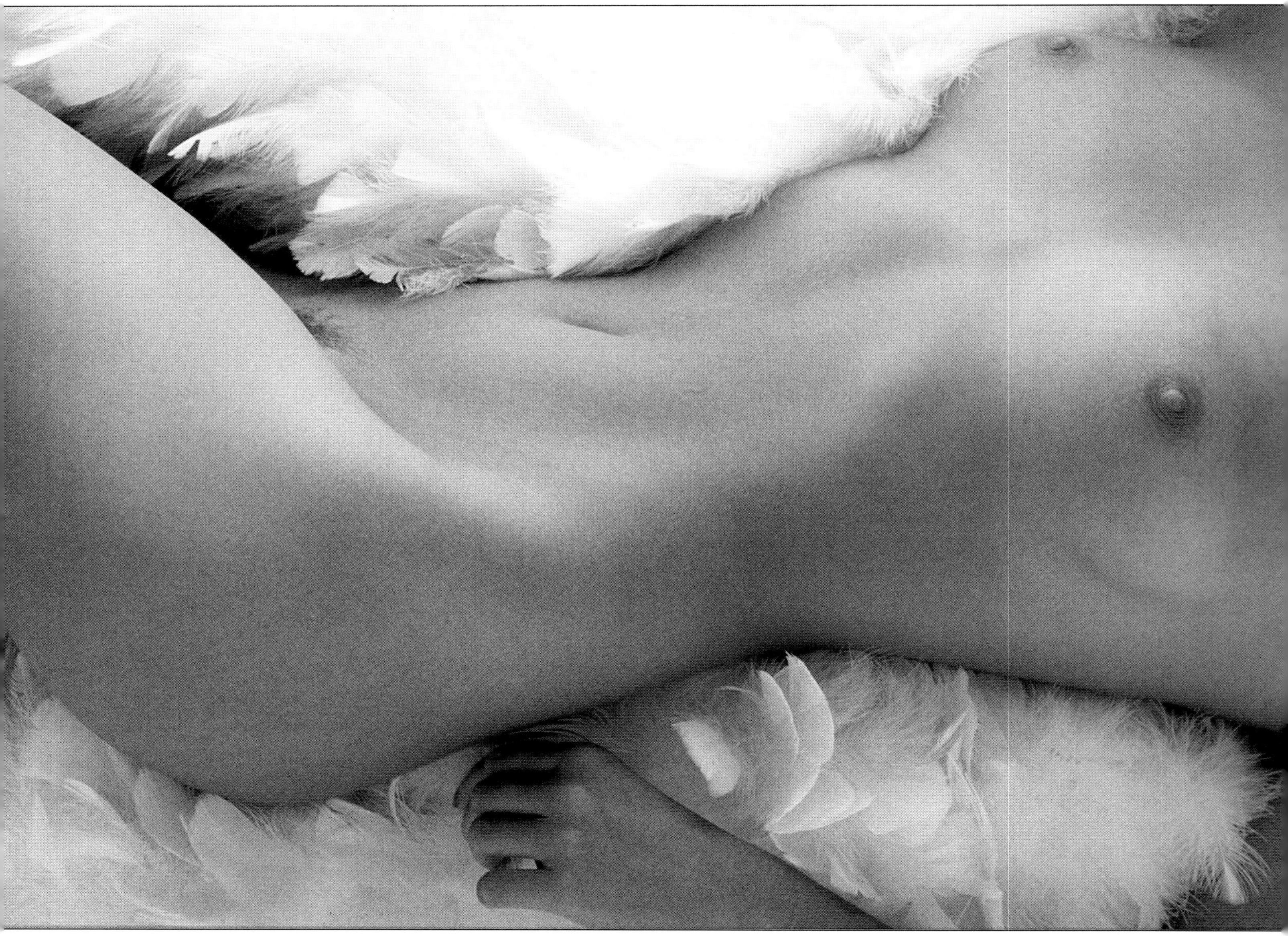

Above: *Achieving a pose that appears natural to the camera demands some very special skills on the part of both a model and her photographer. A good and experienced model will have a pretty good idea of what the camera is "seeing" and will pose accordingly. However, the ultimate control rests with the photographer. To get a full view of the reclining figure and to keep all parts of the body in the same plane, we shot down vertically from a six-foot ladder. The main light source consisted of two electronic flash heads in a 4x7-foot light panel. The subject was facing the full length of the panel. The fill source was a white 4x8-foot foamcore reflector, laid horizontally on the side of the body opposite the main light. Because of its size and close position, it filled in the shadows for the entire length of the body. To retain the overall soft effect, the shadow side was only on f-stop less bright than the highlighted side.*

spirit of a figure photography session, dancers tend to make the very best of models. They work hard trying to please and they like being creative with the movements of their bodies.

Nightclubs

High-caliber nightclubs that feature exotic dancers can also prove to be an excellent source for subjects. If you intend to visit them, be sure to take some samples of your best and most appropriate work; you'll need to show prospective subjects the level of your work and prove your legitimacy.

If you seek only models that have a high level of agility, grace and beauty and you intend to rely on exotic dancers as a source for posing candidates, we urge you to seek out dancers who only work for the better clubs. Some of the lower-class clubs we have encountered only seem to have two requirements when it comes to hiring exotic dancers—they must be female and they must be willing to appear nude. (Not an exhaustive criteria.) Such clubs often don't concern themselves with true talent, experience, or beauty. Some don't even care if a person can really dance.

In our experience, most exotic dancers will pose in exchange for just photos without expectation of other payment. Others will ask for a flat fee of between $50 and $100 for a three to four-hour posing session.

With an experienced dancer, one who knows how to move gracefully and has no inhibitions about her nude body, payment of such a sum can be worthwhile.

What to Look for

Women of varying sizes and shapes, from diverse walks of life and from all age groups, are all possible subjects for most forms of people-photography, including boudoir photography.

But, because nude photography is much more demanding and restrictive, and, because fewer women are likely to agree to pose nude, the number of good subjects available to the average photographer will usually be limited.

As a result, your inclination might be to photograph just any willing subject who happens your way. Don't. You must be more discerning.

For example, you must be aware of a subject's ability to conceal certain portions of her physical and emotional self. In addition, you must learn to select the right type of subject, one of desired weight, with good skin (both in quality and tone) and hair. You should also seek out a subject that has a certain measure of physical agility as well as a proper attitude.

If you don't follow some sort of guidelines or rules such as these (whether they be ours or ones you've self-imposed), and if you settle for just anyone you'll usually find that you have done a disservice to both yourself and the subject; the photographic results will most often be poor, or at the very least, inappropriate.

Concealment

Even though you may have found and approved an otherwise willing candidate for posing, you might find yourself being disappointed once the photo session actually gets underway.

Once the subject is sans clothing, waiting to be photographed, you might be shocked to find that the candidate does not really possess the physical, emotional, psychological, or artistic qualities you were either looking for, or initially thought she had.

Often this will be due to a two-fold condition which we call concealment—physical and emotional concealment. It's a problem which typically confronts figure photographers, and one not commonly associated with other types of people-photography.

Physical concealment: The nude figure photographer doesn't usually get to see everything that he or she is going to photograph when first meeting an intended posing candidate or model.

Typically this is because the subject is dressed during the initial meeting and interview. Therefore, the subject's clothing, being restrictive and concealing, makes a photographer's first encounter and assessment of the subject somewhat superficial.

You won't be able to see, with any degree of precision, a subject's figure lines, her body's total skin tone, her skin markings, her body blemishes and so on. This often puts a photographer in an awkward position; he or she must speculate about how a subject will look when she is totally nude.

"...you must learn to select the right type of subject..."

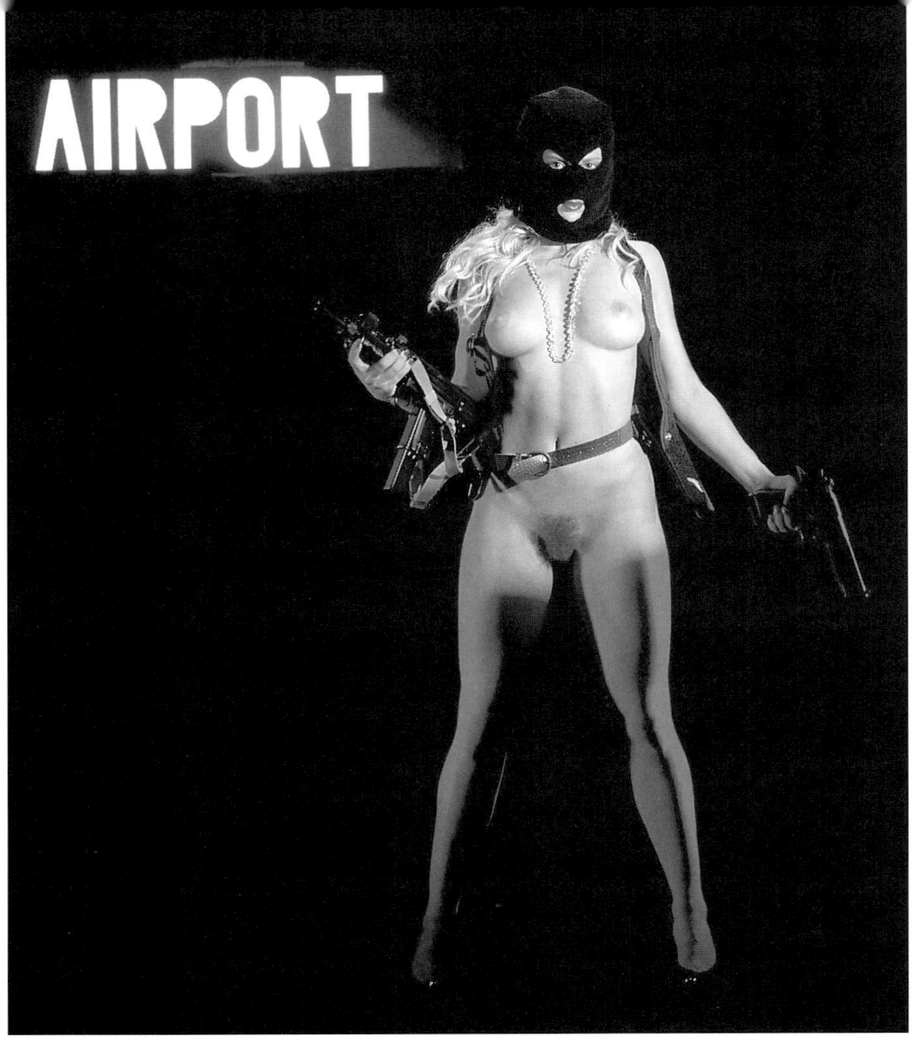

Above and Right: *In today's fast-paced, troubled world, we thought that we would provide a light-hearted change of pace by photographically creating a spoof on the very poignant topic of terrorism. That was the basis for these images and we have entitled them "Airport." In the image above, the body language — the subject's open and unguarded stance — suggests strength, tension, toughness, preparedness and readiness for a confrontation. There is a pictorial incongruity: the soft lines and curves of the subject's body. It seems totally inconsistent to have such softness and grace present such a threat. But therein lies the spoof. We consider this a fine figure study rather than an exploitative one.*

While the subject seems to be threatening a confrontation in the above image, the one to the right seems to indicate an "after-the-fact" situation. The subject has apparently already engaged in confrontation and is now contemplating what has occurred. Many different photographic interpretations can be derived from the same subject simply by making a pose change. It is a very powerful photographic tool.

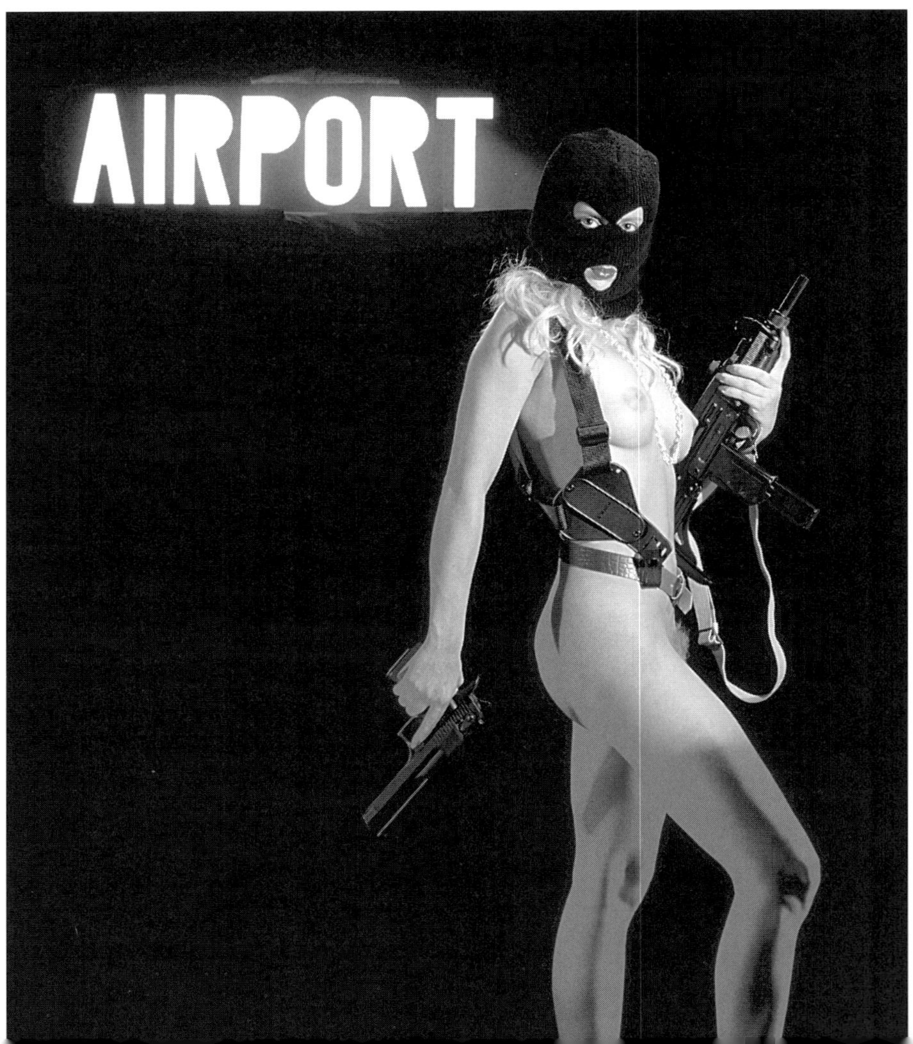

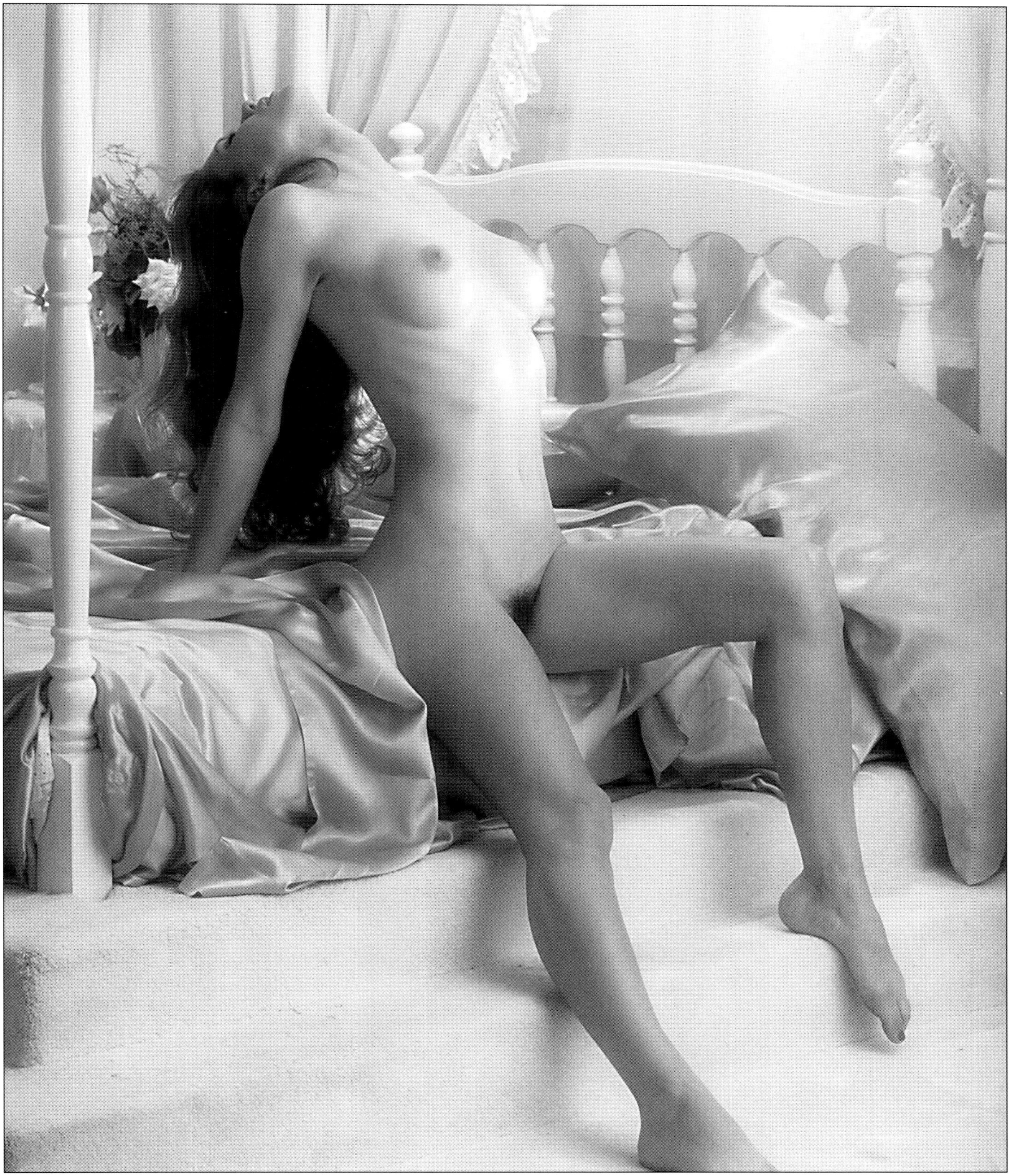

Above: *Since you often will not know who the viewer of the intended images will be, it behooves you to offer as much pictorial variety as possible; you want your images to have great appeal. In this case, we took several photos using this setup — some with a bit of clothing draped around the subject and some like the image above where the subject was without clothing. The image displays frontal nudity yet the subject was able to project a quiet elegance. This fact, along with poses, lighting and setting lead to some beautiful images.*

"Nudity makes some people free spirits."

This state of affairs might well provoke a couple of questions. For example, why worry about such things? Why not just ask the subjects in the first place if there are any problems with their figures that you can't see, and that you should be aware of?

Unfortunately, and even though we typically ask a prospective subject this type and a lot of other questions prior to engaging in nude photography, the solution is not always this simple.

It's not that subjects will intentionally lie or give misleading information, its that it's hard for most subjects to be very objective about their figures in the first place and harder, if not impossible, to have them judge how you, the photographer, are going to perceive their particular figure.

We recently were hired to do some nude photos of a woman who was in her late 30s. Days before the photo session (a typical procedure at our studio), Sheila had a pre-photographic consultation with the subject.

During this meeting, and among other items discussed, the subject was specifically asked if she had any body markings, blemishes, scars, or other skin conditions that we should be aware of.

The subject replied that other than a "small," one-half inch tattoo on her left thigh, there were no skin conditions to worry about. Sheila accepted the subject's self-assessment without further query; Sheila didn't ask to see the tattoo so that she could make her own evaluation of the body marking.

On the day of the photo sitting, we were shocked when we saw the "small tattoo." Although it was true that her tattoo was only about one-half inch in size, the subject neglected to tell us that this measurement was its width; that it was one-half inch wide and 16 inches long: a tattoo of a lightening bolt which ran all the way from the top of her left knee, all the way up the side of her left thigh.

To avoid being confronted with such a situation as this, you might well ask yourself, why not just ask the subject to disrobe during the pre-photographic interview or conference and then evaluate her nude body for yourself? It just isn't done; it's not professional.

In our opinion, it would be out of context. It would be like laughing during a very dramatic moment in a classical play. It's one thing to see a nude subject before you during a photo session, since the photo session adds an air of professionalism and legitimacy to the entire event.

However, having the subject disrobe just to look at her might be offensive. At the very least, the subject would feel very uncomfortable and surely question your motives.

Emotional concealment: Far worse than physical concealment is emotional concealment. Many subjects act completely different once they are on a set, nude, waiting or being photographed, than they were when they were initially interviewed.

Nudity makes some people free spirits. It makes them open-up, become demonstrative, aggressive, gregarious, and so on. At the other extreme, others become withdrawn, shy and retiring when the armor of clothing has been removed. Still others will act silly and giggly. All of these manifestations are nothing more than defense mechanisms.

From time to time, you're going to come across a subject that will react in a completely different way from how you thought she would. Unfortunately there is no sure way for a photographer to guard against, or prepare for, a subject's emotional shift.

However, it's not a catastrophe. With time and experience, you will learn how to shoot from the hip you'll learn how to quickly deal and cope with such emotional shifts of a subject on the spot, without batting an eye, and without it affecting your photo shoot.

The Right Type of Subject

We have previously touched upon this point; therefore, we shall not belabor the issue. Suffice to say, you should select a subject who has a figure that is appropriate for the effect or pictorial representation that you want to create.

In other words, don't look for a woman whose figure is perfect, there is no such person; however do look for a subject whose figure will best represent your preconceived ideas.

For example, if you want to create a delicate, ethereal image, don't choose a model with a clearly powerful-looking, muscular build. Or maybe you want to symbolize a stalking tigress in your image. Don't select a delicate, slight-of-

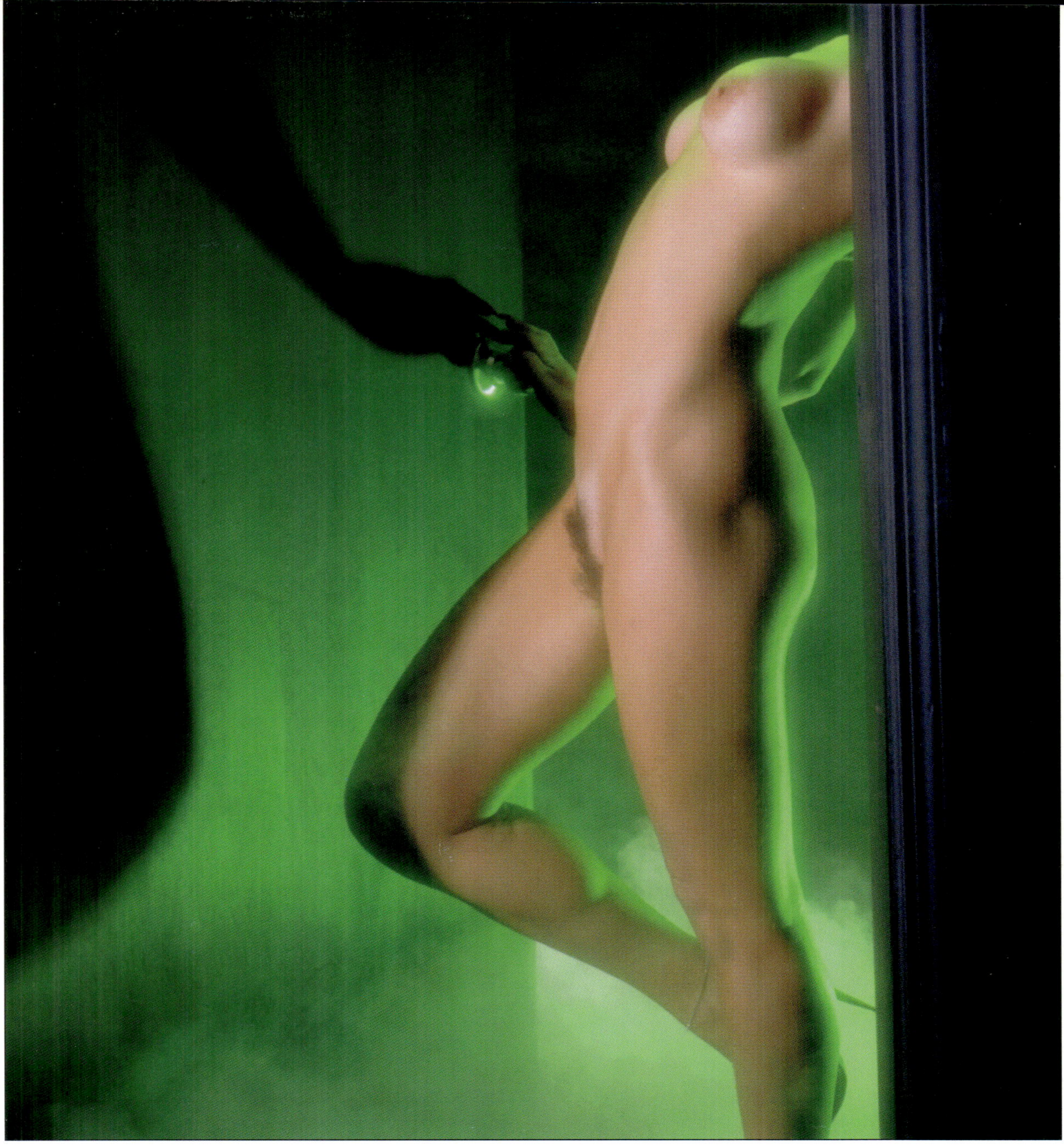

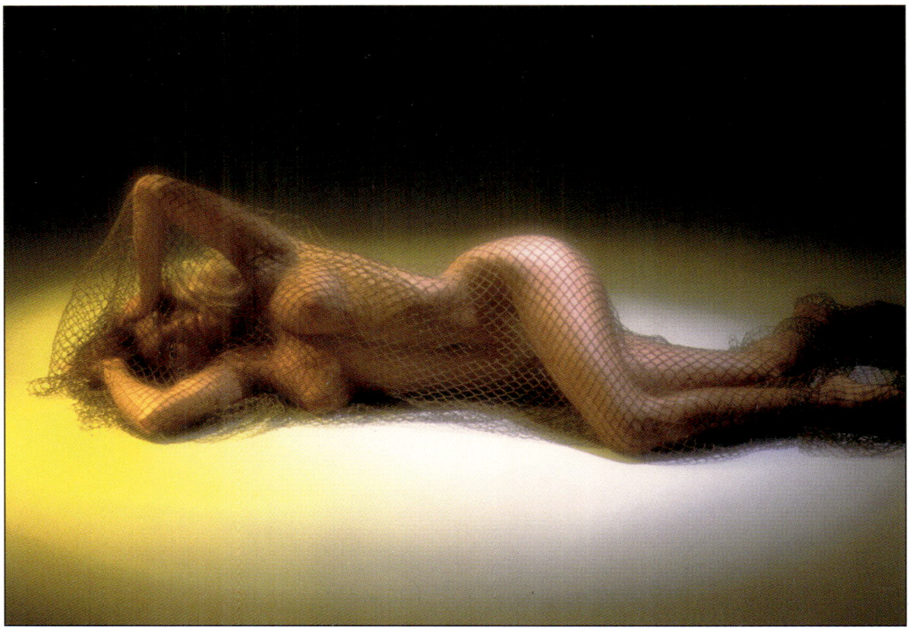

Above: *Several factors make this an almost surrealistic image: the head being completely hidden from view, the low-key setting, the distorted shadow on the door, the eerie color produced by the green-gelled light, and the subtle use of fog. The main light, without gel, was a Balcar Opalite with a 20 degree gridspot and plastic diffuser cap, placed about 90 degrees to the left of camera axis and feathered. Gelled green illumination was used about 90 degrees to the right of camera axis.*

Left: *In this photo, we worked with one major prop — a fish net. There always seems to be something especially exciting about a subject whose body is covered by something, yet is clearly nude.*

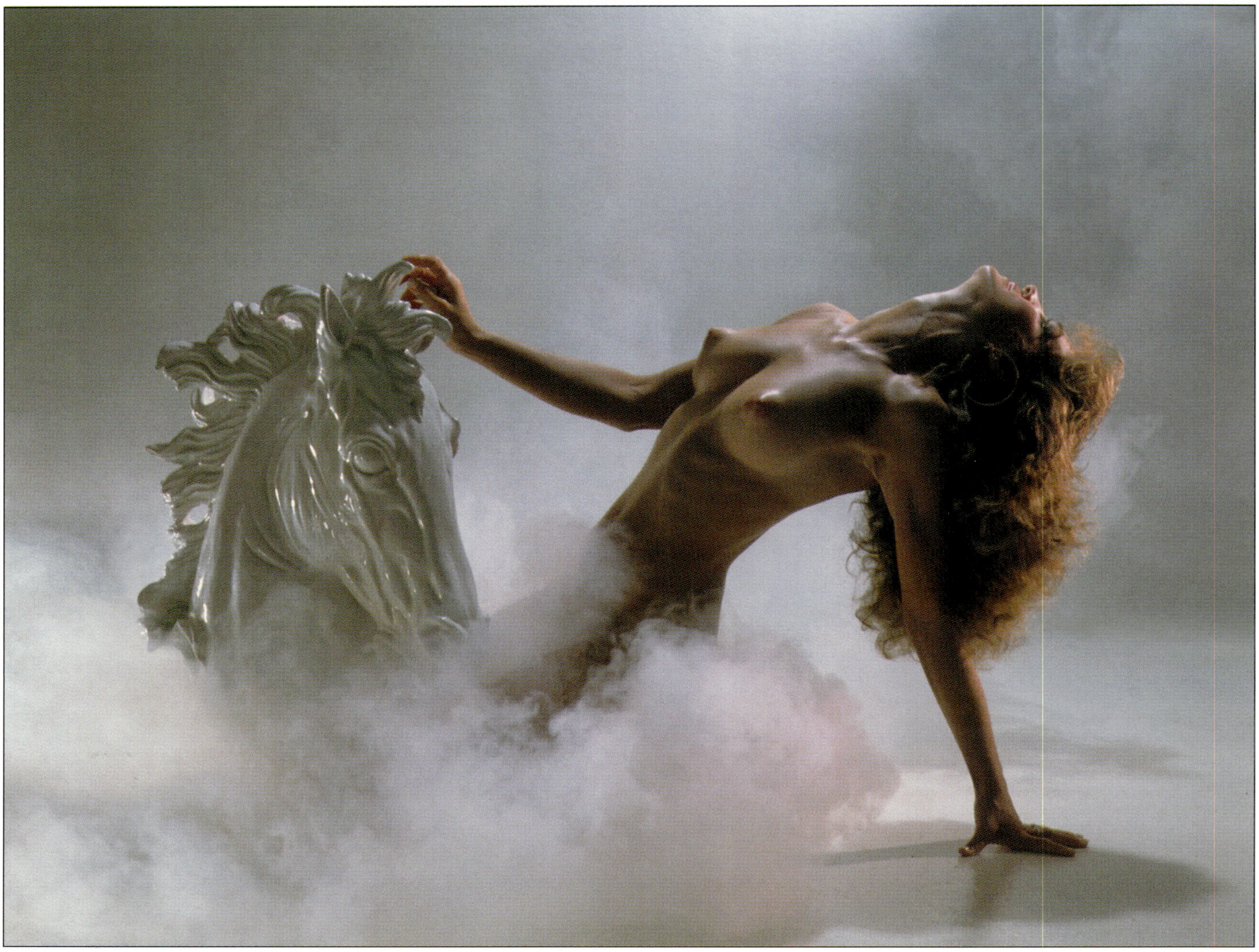

Above: *Artificial fog was used as well as one major prop — the horse's head. In this photo, we placed the subject close to the horse and had her touch its ear by extending her arm. This provided enough contact to unify the image into one concept. The most convenient way to generate fog is with a machine specially designed for the purpose. These machines can be rented from theatrical supply houses. We only use fog fluid that is guaranteed safe and we advise you to do the same. There are other ways of creating fog, too. For example, you can use dry ice or smoke pellets. Whatever is used, make sure you understand how it works and take all the safety precautions to protect you, your assistant, and your subject.*

Right: *Daylight was used as the single fixed light source for this image. The shadow lines cause emphasis to be placed on the subject's bust and upper portions of the legs.*

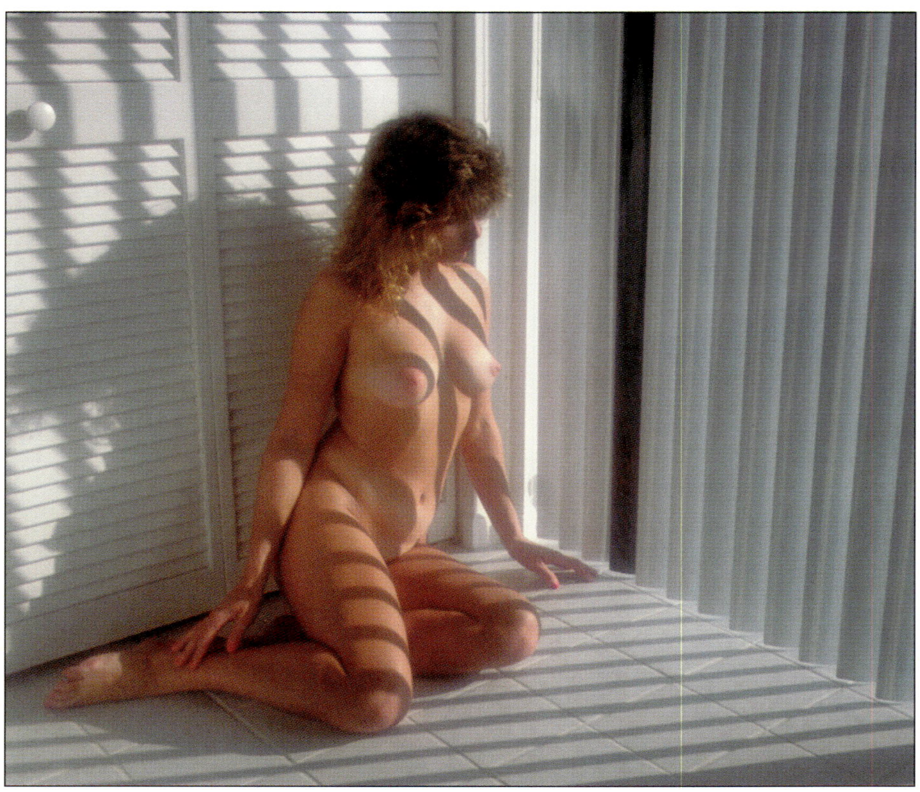

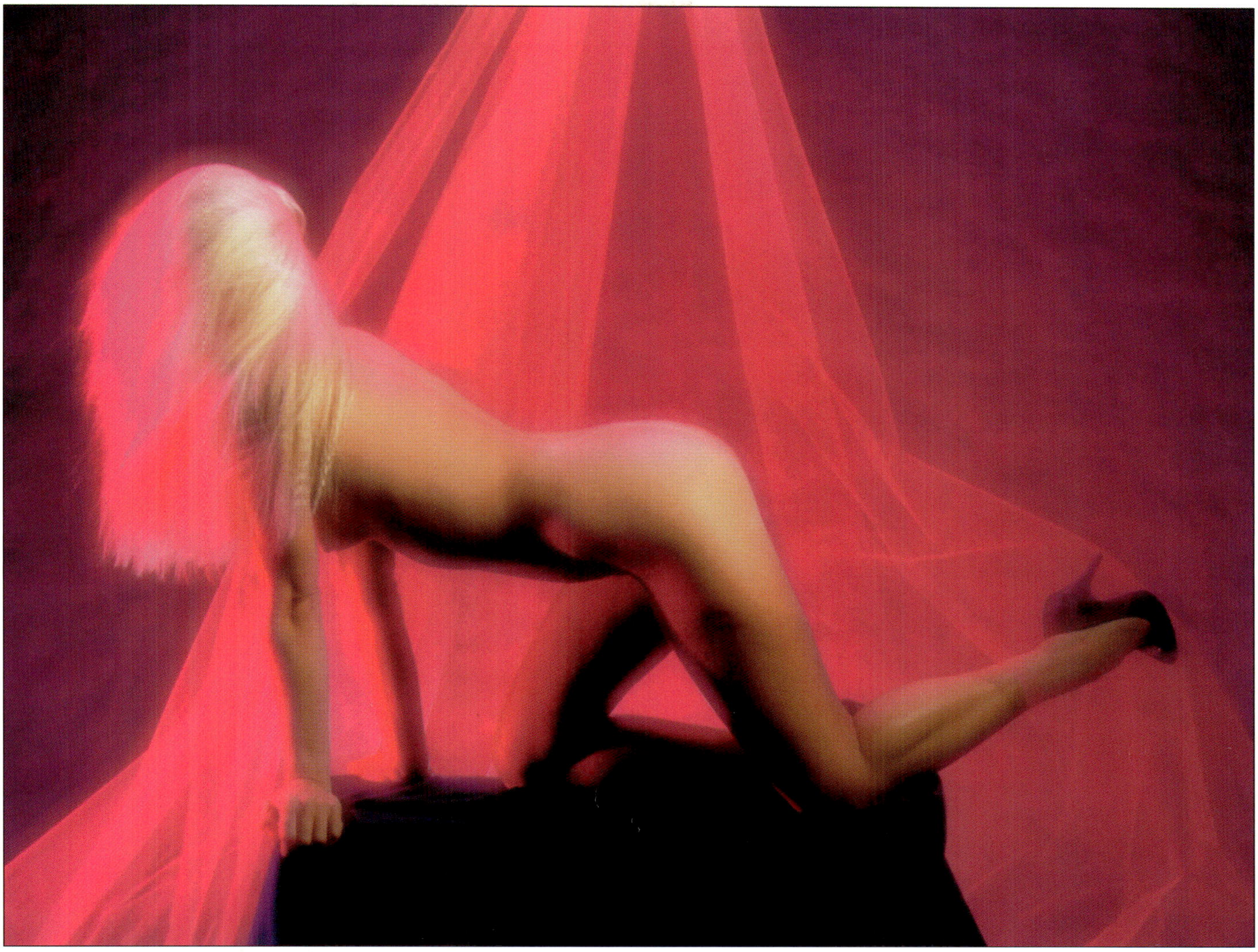

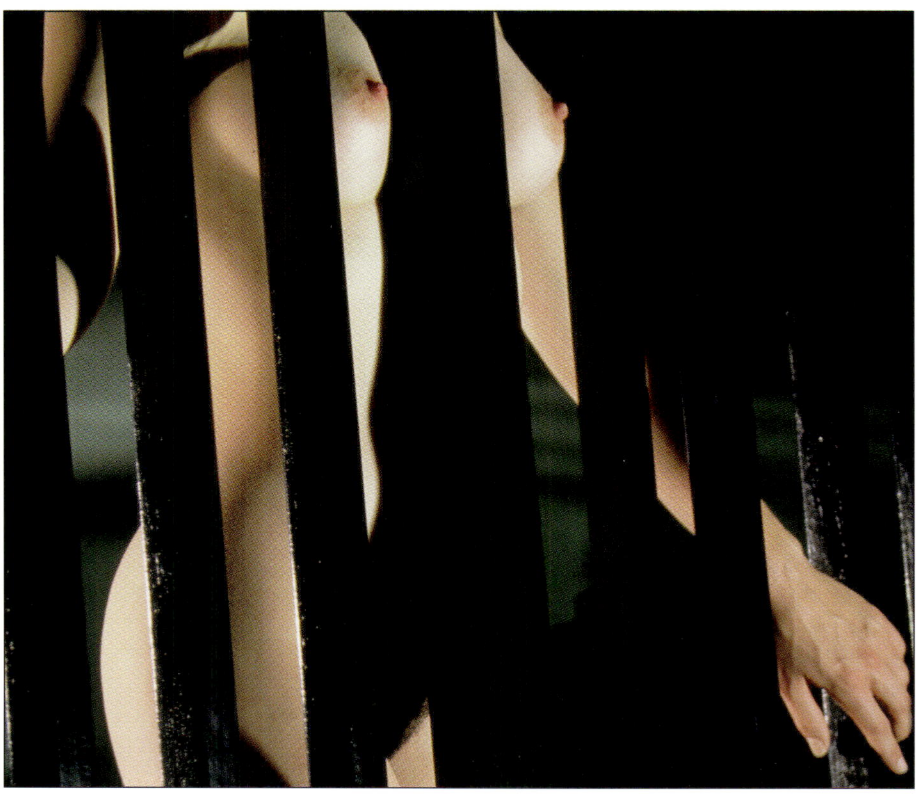

Above: *There can be a number of reasons why you might wish to photograph a figure study and keep the subject's face hidden from clear view. For example, you may want the viewer to concentrate on the subject's body. This effect creates an "impersonal" nude study.*

Left: *When shooting in a subject's home, always be aware of potential settings for an image. Even though you may have already visited and scouted the subject's home for ideas of where to shoot, other photographic opportunities may arise during the actual session due to natural lighting changes, etc. Do not overlook these opportunities, but use and work the setting to its fullest potential. We hadn't considered this shot prior to the day of the session, but when we saw how the subject, light, and staircase all interacted together for an interesting image, we set up and took the photo.*

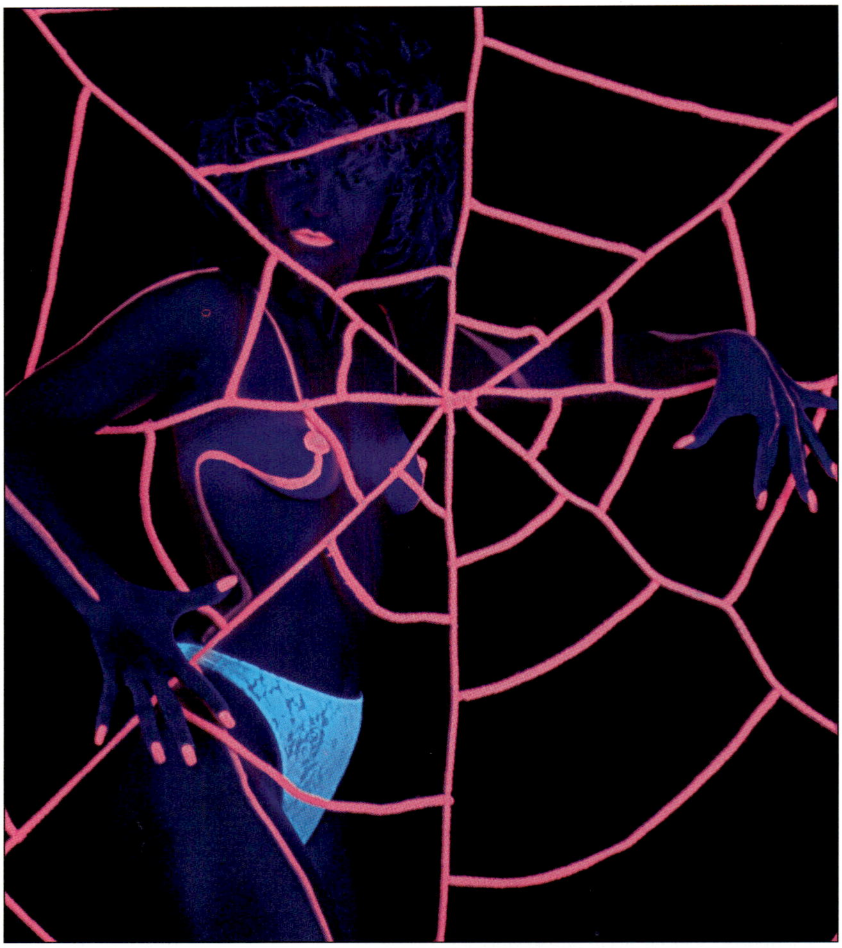

Above: *The web is made from 1/8th inch rope which was cut into pieces and hot glued together to get a "web-like" look. It was then attached to a pole just above the subject, then drawn taut and secured on the left and right side. The web and subject were painted with a special Rosco paint. We used a large, round, 10 inch, self-contained black light as a main light. Be prepared for some rather long exposures. This was shot a f-5.6 at 30 seconds.*

Right: *When we use colored gels on lights, we will have at least one light (usually the main light) be color-free. A four-light setup was used. Three of these lights were covered by a magenta gel. One light was placed on the floor and directed onto a dark background. The second light was placed 90 degrees to the left of the camera-subject axis. The third light was placed about 110 degrees to the right of this axis. These lights had power adjusted to emit one f-stop less than that of the white main light. This white main light, from a Bowens Monospot, was limited to a very specific area of the subject's body to achieve graphic effect and impact.*

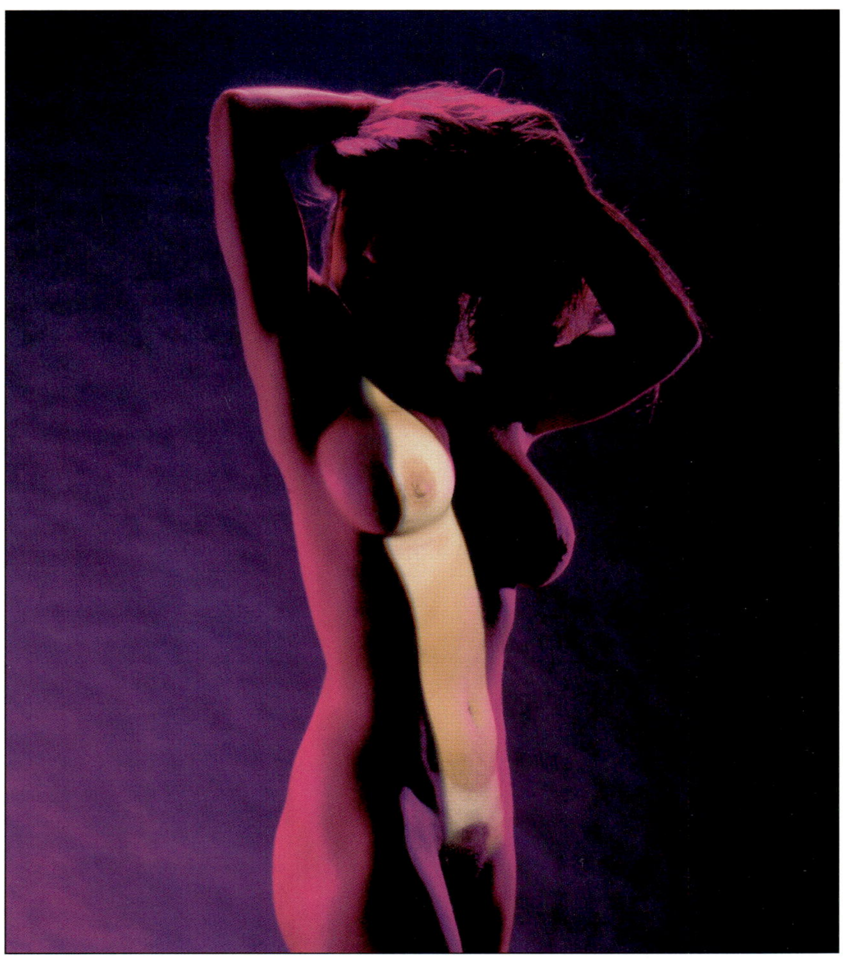

build model. And, don't choose a subject simply because she is pretty.

A Subject's Weight

Beauty tends to be largely a matter of fashion of the time. Thus the typical nude female figure in paintings, exemplifying womanhood, used to be a plump figure, with a full face and heavy thighs, arms, legs, and waist.

This type of woman is often referred to as the Rubenesque-type; she's the type that typically would wear a dress size between 14 and 40.

Up to the beginning of the 20th century, this robust type of woman was the type which was extolled, idealized, and admired. Thin women were often made fun of; they were thought of as being too delicate, having little stamina, and being incapable of dealing with the rigors of daily life.

Today, quite obviously, the opposite is true. Thin is "in." Today it is not stylish to be heavy. In fact, in today's face-paced world, we have become a society of health-conscious, figure-conscious, weight watchers, seemingly on perpetual diets. Tomorrow? Who knows?

We don't mean to suggest that we don't photograph women with slightly heavy figures. We have and we do. However, a very heavy subject is not usually a preferred subject for us for one major reason: self-consciousness.

Our experience has shown that most very heavy subjects — even the very willing, attractive, and paying clients — are usually poor candidates for figure studies. They tend to be so busy worrying about their weight, that they often fail to devote the needed concentration on the photography at hand.

As you can see from the photos in this book, most of the subjects chosen were thin. Most all of our subjects were health and fitness conscious and worked hard to get and keep their bodies in good condition and shape. This is most typical. Figure models (the pros and nonprofessional models) are most often very proud of their physical appearance, and are not ashamed to be seen in some state of nudity.

Read that last sentence again; it's a very important aspect for successful nude photography. No matter whom you choose to model for you and no matter how you pictorially intend to depict her, your model must always think of herself as looking good, and looking good to others. If she does, there's a good chance that you will be able to record that special look or beauty successfully on film. If not, your photos will be poor at best.

Skin Quality and Tone

When you photograph a nude figure, it's axiomatic that you'll usually be depicting a major portion of a subject's skin. Therefore, her skin must be of good quality, tone, and texture, and as free as possible from flaws.

Skin quality — Very few bodies are totally free from markings of one kind or another, so you should be prepared to deal with at least minor body flaws. For example, minor flaws, such as small cuts, scars, bruises, and blemishes can easily be covered by makeup, hidden in shadow, or even covered by a subject's long hair, if she has it. On the other end of the spectrum, you should avoid using prospective models if they have major body marks: prominent scars, large bruises, large tattoos, or other large markings. Nude photography is difficult enough without having to cope and deal with these problems.

Notwithstanding this warning, sometimes you may find a model who is so good in every other respect that you'll be more than willing to accept some skin imperfections, even if they are fairly prominent. However, be prepared for the consequences. If makeup and concealment through shadows, long hair, or an appropriate pose don't work, you may have to resort to retouching on the final image and this can be very expensive.

Skin tone — Tone involves and refers to not only a skin's color, but also a skin's condition. Skin of a slightly dark tone is often advantageous, not only because it has a good, healthy appearance, but because it often tends to keep overall image contrast down. This can be especially important in color photography. In other instances, such as high-key images where almost everything in the image is of light tonality, a very fair skin is often best.

If your subject insists upon sunbathing, she should do so only in the nude, and she should be very careful to get as uniform a tan as possible. Tan marks from a swimsuit are a definite no-no for a figure

"Beauty tends to be largely a matter of fashion."

- **The subject should only sunbathe in the nude to avoid uneven tanning.**

"...we must often request unusual and difficult body positions..."

model. However, we always advise our subjects not to get a sun tan prior to a photo session. The chances of their bodies getting uneven illumination from the sun are too great and we don't want their skin looking red or blotchy on the day of the photo shoot.

The other type of skin tone really pertains to the firmness of a subject's skin and not to a subject's overall weight. For example, a subject may be thin, but have poor skin tone; she may have upper arms and breasts which sag.

Such a body condition can cause a photographer some consternation during the course of photography. Ideally, you should seek out a subject who has some degree of firmness to their upper arms, legs, stomach, and bust.

Hair: Length, Color and Quality

Generally speaking, and all other considerations aside for the moment, it has been our experience that if a woman's hair looks and feels nice to her, she will think of herself as being more beautiful. However, if she thinks her hair is dull looking, messy, too long or too short, and so on, she will think that her entire appearance is poor.

You might not agree. You might think that she and her hairdo look just great. However, most of the time your opinion will be of little consolation to the subject and her negative thoughts about her appearance will be just enough to ruin most of the posing for the photos you had in mind.

It's important to remember to seek out a subject who has the hair length, color, and quality that would be more in keeping with the type of image you wanted to create. For example, if you intend to do a nude study which has a "turn-of-the-century" theme, it would be appropriate to seek out a dark-haired subject, with long hair (perhaps styled in a bun) and not a woman with blond hair and a short hairdo.

Long hair, without a doubt, provides the most versatility in figure photography. It not only enables a subject's face, or even other body parts, to be selectively concealed but also provides an excellent prop for draping parts of the subject's upper body.

This does not mean to suggest that you should rule out models who have short hair. As we have already pointed out, most of the time the length of a subject's hair will largely depend upon the type of images you want to create. Along these same lines, the color of a subject's hair is not generally very important unless, again, you want to create a special effect or atmosphere.

For example, often, you would not want to select a model with black hair if your aim was to produce a high-key image, nor would you usually select a blonde for a somber, low-key image.

In any event, long or short, dark or blond, the quality of a model's hair should always be immaculate — unless you're deliberately trying to create a special effect.

Physical Agility

For simple portraiture and even most boudoir imagery, a subject generally needs very little physical agility and flexibility. Most of the poses that subjects are required to assume in those photographic areas are quite simple.

In figure photography, by contrast, we must often request unusual and difficult body positions, angles and poses to bring out certain lines and shapes. This requirement puts much more demand on a subject's physical agility.

To avoid finding out at the last moment that the subject you've chosen cannot execute any but the simplest of poses, you should, well in advance of any photo session, ask some questions of your prospective model.

For example, find out if your subject has ever taken ballet lessons, or if she has any abilities in dance, gymnastics, swimming, or other sports and activities. Sports and activities such as these demand some measure of agility as well as bodily coordination.

If a subject is, or was poor at all of these things, or hates the thought of doing or being involved with any of these things, chances are better than 50-50 that they will not be a good posing candidate for figure photography.

In addition, inquire if she has ever modeled for a photographer or at an art school. If the answer to these questions is also negative, you might save both you and the intended model a lot of time by passing her by and using someone else to pose.

A subject may have none of the above experiences and still be a natural, creative, and agile model. Therefore, before you reject, be absolutely sure you're not losing someone who is actually or potentially very worthwhile.

Psychological State

A subject for nude photography should be psychologically prepared to be uninhibited and comfortable without clothing from the beginning of the photo session.

From the inception of a sitting, the subject should be able to project that she is perfectly at ease in the state of undress and be prepared to be directed into artistic as well as sensuous and provocative poses. However, not many subjects (unless they're professional models) are able to attain this state of mind quickly. A subject may often be shy, somewhat embarrassed, and a little guarded. However, as a sitting progresses, this anxiety usually fades.

Toward session's end, most subjects become very willing and even enthusiastic, showing an ability to display their figures freely and assuming quite sensuous

"A subject may often be shy..."

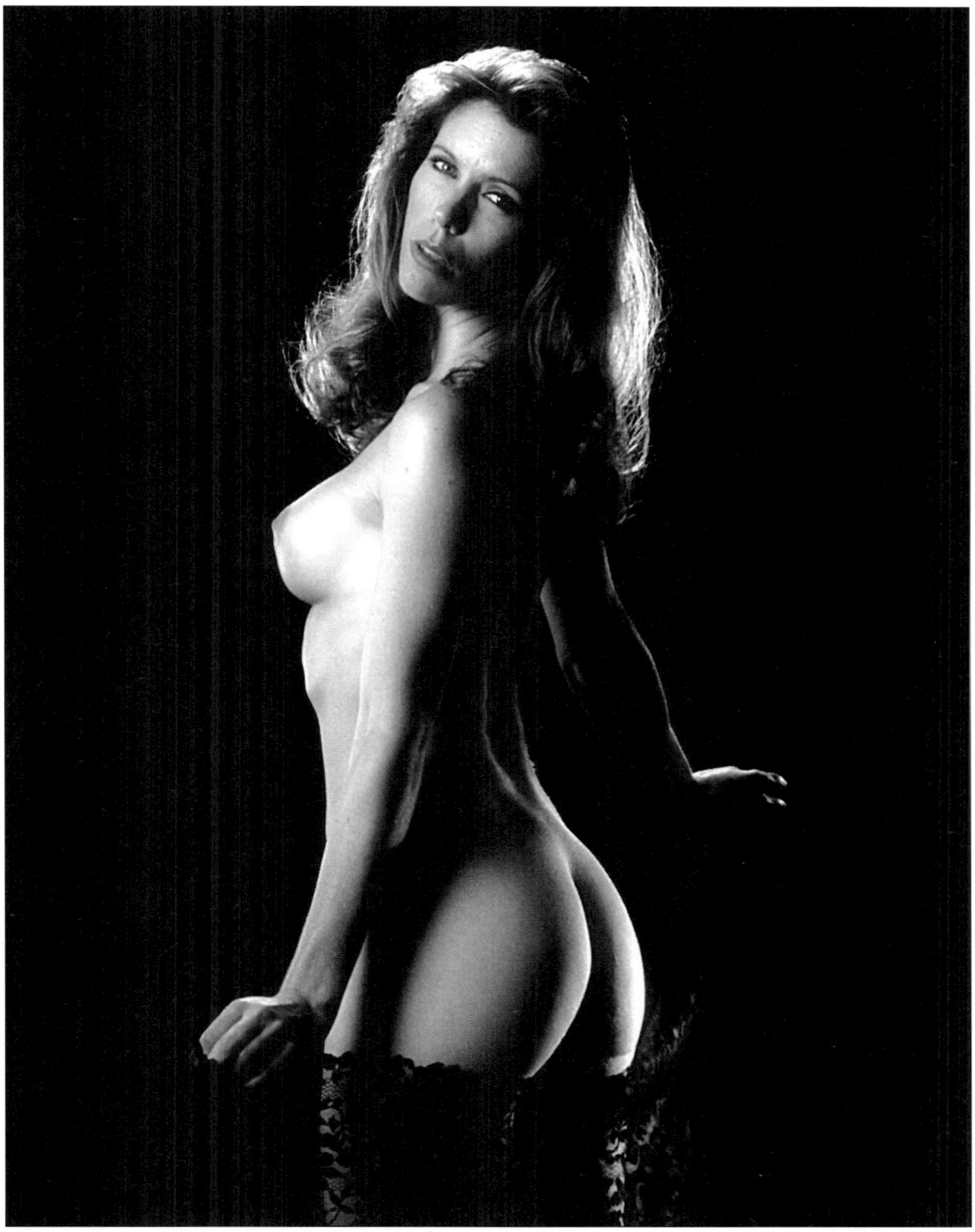

Above: *Sometimes it takes time and patience to prepare a subject psychologically for a nude photo session. However, when the photography is over and the results are seen, most subjects are anxious to become involved in further photo sessions.*

• **The best way to deal with a shy subject is to start the photo shoot slowly.**

"...more daring images and poses will be possible..."

poses. But, if they don't respond rather quickly at the beginning of your photo session, don't despair. If you think that the subject merits your extra time and effort, we suggest taking a slower approach.

Start slowly — If you have a willing but nervous model, you may have to take your time by starting off the photo shoot with guarded poses, perhaps using a bit of material covering the private body parts. Start the session more conservatively, such as doing head-and-shoulder portraits with the model fully dressed, or some combination.

However, we must advise you that this approach is very time consuming. For example, for the first 10 or 15 minutes, you'll start with a subject who is fully dressed and engage in only head-and-shoulder photography.

Following this, you should move on to the next step, to more revealing boudoir type head-and-shoulder shots, with her clothing or material draped slightly off the subject's shoulder, revealing a bit more of the subject's bust line and so on.

After this, suggest to the subject that she attire herself in a more revealing costume, such as a negligee; shoot full-length images of her in this attire. With each ensuing pose, have the subject assume just a bit more daring body position and expose just a bit more of her body to the camera than the previous pose.

After you have shot one or two rolls of film, have the subject change again, this time to an even skimpier outfit — a bra and panties or a bikini. Keep shooting more images, with each new situation being closer to a nude pose than the previous one.

The next step is to have the model remove the garments, but have her hold them up against her body so that they still cover her private body parts. Her body will still be covered, to a greater or lesser extent, but more daring images and poses will be possible. In addition, the clothing next to her body will act as a psychological crutch; she will not perceive herself as being close to a nude state.

At this juncture, if you think that the subject is psychologically ready, you should have her move the garments she is holding; have her move them away from her body and put them down but only a few inches away.

You'll often find that a subject will need to have reasonably close access to the clothing or material she had been holding, much like a security blanket, until after the first few totally nude shots have been taken.

And, once they have been taken, the subject should then be ready. She should be totally relaxed, very confident with both herself and with you, and emotionally prepared to be photographed totally nude, without the benefit of any clothing or drape either on her person or even in the near vicinity.

This approach, structured to gently ease a new subject into nude photography, is time consuming but usually works for the more cautious subjects. You'll often spend a couple of hours with a subject before actually undertaking a nude photo session.

Using this slow approach, you may even find yourself splitting the photo session and dividing it up over a period of a couple of days, doing guarded shots on the first day, and more revealing shots the next. However, all of this presumes that the subject you're working with is worth the time and trouble.

Unfortunately, some subjects never achieve the desired relaxed state that you'll be looking for and need.

This, of course, reduces your choice of prospective, suitable models, but that's okay. There are others out there, and they can be found.

You must be the sole judge as to how much training and initiation is necessary, and how much time you need to spend with any given subject.

The Preparation

As with boudoir photography, nude photography requires a subject to engage in a certain amount of physical preparation prior to any actual photo session beginning. This will usually include paying attention to such elements as makeup and hair, a suntan, temporary and permanent body marks and body enhancements.

Makeup and Hair

Although we shall be covering these two topics in Chapter 6, a brief comment is necessary here. Having a subject's hair styled and makeup applied by an expert is usually critical for nude photography. This, as we have already stated, is because a viewer's attention will often have only one place to focus upon — the subject's nude figure.

If hair and makeup are not perfect and appropriate for the type of image being shot, their deficiency will be glaringly obvious, and this could ruin an otherwise beautifully executed figure study.

Suntan

Many subjects believe that they should lie out in the sun in advance of a photo session, to give their bodies some color. This is wrong. A fresh suntan can leave skin looking reddish, blotchy, and unevenly tanned, even when the subject sunbathes in the nude. But, our experience has shown that very few people sunbathe nude, and this causes an even worse problem.

Grooming

Advise all the women who are going to pose for you to groom their bodies well. Among other areas, this should include shaving the legs and under the arms and it should be done about 12 to 24 hours before the shoot. If it is done too close to the time of the shoot, the shaved areas may appear reddened or blotchy.

Fingernails and toenails should also be neat and polished and the soles of the feet should be as clean as possible. At least 24 hours prior to the photo session, make certain that you advise them to use some sort of body lotion over their entire body. Have them apply such lotion in generous amounts and at least twice before the actual sitting. This will usually prevent their body from looking dry and drawn.

Temporary Body Marks

The wearing of a bra, panties, or other tight fitting clothing can mark or crease a subject's body. These marks or creases will usually show prominently in a photograph and can be very distracting to the viewer.

Admittedly, after a photo session, you could remove such body markings from any resulting print, but this would require retouching or airbrushing. Techniques like this take time, cost money, and often deprive an image of a totally natural appearance.

To help avoid or lessen such body marks, advise your subjects to wear no tight-fitting garments for at least 24 hours prior to a photo session. In addition, have a subject buy some cocoa butter (available at better drug and food stores), and apply this to the marked areas of her body two to three times a day, at least one day prior to the day of the sitting. Cocoa butter tends to reduce the severity of the markings and redness caused by tight fitting clothing.

Permanent Body Markings

Many subjects have some type of markings, such as birthmarks, scars or even tattoos, somewhere on their bodies. Such markings usually appear more prominent in a photo than to the eye and often detract from the mood and desired effect of an intended image.

- **Permanent body markings tend to appear more prominent in a photo than to the eye.**

As a result, you're often well advised to conceal, as effectively as possible, any such markings with makeup, lighting, a well placed prop or piece of material, an appropriate pose, or some combination of all of these methods.

Your pre-shoot conference with the subject should include questions about possible body blemishes and marks, so that appropriate steps can be taken to deal with the problem in advance of the actual photo session.

Ideally you should try to avoid becoming surprised by any such markings; you don't want to be on the set, ready to take photos, and first discover the condition. You might not be able to successfully deal with it at the last minute.

At the other end of the spectrum, you're going to come across some subjects who have been tattooed and who may be proud of the markings and want them prominently displayed in the photos. Be cautious. Most of these subjects have no idea how prominent such markings can look in a photo.

Once a subject sees the markings in an image, he or she will often dislike these markings, and will want them removed. Although this can be done through airbrushing or other retouching methods, again, such measures are expensive and time-consuming.

Our procedure is to take some photos with the body markings displayed, and the balance without. This gives us the benefit of both worlds just in case the client, or we, dislike the way the marking appears in the final photos.

Body Enhancement

If it is part of your photographic intention to add something to the subject's body, such as body makeup, body paint, baby oil, and so on, be sure to discuss this with the subject well in advance of any photo session.

You don't want to confront her with last-minute surprises and thus give her added feelings of uncertainty or give her an excuse to back out of the photo session at the last minute.

In addition, .you'll need prior knowledge of a subject's sensitivity or possible allergic response to any enhancement products you do intend to use. An actual photo session is no place to test a subject's skin for sensitivities.

- **Always have a capable assistant with you and the subject during the entire photo session.**

To avoid such problems, you may wish to give your subject a sample of the body enhancement you intend to use. Have her take this home and try it out on a small portion of her skin. In any case, and whatever you do, make certain that the makeup or other enhancement you intend to use is hypoallergenic. You should be aware that excessive application of paints and other materials, ones which may block the subject's pores and which otherwise do not allow the body's skin to "breathe," can be very dangerous.

This is especially important with products that will cover the subject's entire skin. Be very sure of your materials and methods. Consult or use an expert; one who is quite familiar with the material you want to use and its application.

In addition to a subject's physical safety, you should also concern yourself with her modesty. Therefore, and to enhance a subject's feeling of security, a male photographer should make a special point of informing a female subject that he will be providing a member of her sex to assist in applying the body enhancements.

"...obtain a signed release before making any use of the image."

In the event that you only have a male makeup artist available, then make absolutely certain that the makeup person is chaperoned; have a female (in addition to the subject) in the presence of the makeup person and subject at all times.

We'll be saying more about body enhancements later, particularly in Chapter 6, where we'll discuss how makeup, hair styling, props, and accessories can contribute to the photography of the human figure.

Legal Considerations

The purpose of the information that follows is not to make you a legal expert. It's also not to take the place of good, competent legal advice, which you can get from your local attorney. What is our intention is to make you sensitive to certain areas that could cause an unsuspecting photographer some real problems. As the trite but true saying goes, to be forewarned is to be forearmed.

The Value of an Assistant

When a female photographer does figure photography of a female subject, we consider it important for the photographer to have at least one female assistant present during the entire session. When a male photographer does figure photography of a female subject, we consider the presence of a female assistant mandatory.

Not only will a capable assistant make a sitting go faster and more smoothly but the presence of another female also makes a female subject feel more at ease. As important, the presence of the assistant will also tend to give you some vital legal protection. It affords you a witness in case a subject later claims that you made improper advances or remarks to her during the course of the session.

Even if our subject is one who has posed for us many times in the past, we would never conduct any nude photo session without the presence of at least myself, my wife and one additional female assistant. For us, the nature of nude photography is just too sensitive to take the risk of handling the situation in any other way.

The Model Release

As a general rule, you should not display, exhibit, or otherwise publish any nude photographs that you have created, without having first obtained a signed model release from the subject. Even if you cannot discern the subject's face in an image, if there is any other way the subject might be identified (by a birthmark, tattoo, bone structure, hair style, and so on), then you should obtain a signed release before making any use of the image. This is just good business.

Obviously, if you are being paid to create a nude figure study for a subject, having her sign a release may not be so important; you're creating an image for money not for yourself.

However, if you are photographing a subject for the purpose of expanding your own portfolio and expertise, or otherwise to display the image, it is important to have all your subjects sign a standard model-release form. Without having a signed release in our possession, there is absolutely no way that we would use any subject's photograph.

If you are not being paid by a subject to do a nude figure study, and the subject seems hesitant about signing a model release, or remarks that she wants to wait until she sees the photo results before she decides if she is going to sign a release, our advice is to abandon the session and find another subject.

If you go through with the photo session, and she eventually decides not to sign a release for you, your photos will be unusable.

Model release forms are readily available from most camera or office supply stores and are very inexpensive. However, before you use any general release form, we suggest that you consult with an attorney; give him a sample of the form you want to use and get his or her advice. Some standard model release forms that we have seen have not been worth the paper they were printed on; they were legally insufficient.

Although the laws on releases can differ from state to state, there are generally some common threads. One of these legal threads is an element called consideration. For a contract (release) to be valid, and among other elements, it must have good and sufficient consideration. This basically means that the person signing the release must receive something of value in exchange for her posing for you and giving you the right to display, or otherwise use, the images of her. Her mere signature on the release is not sufficient without consideration.

The something that is given in payment does not have to be money, but it needs to have some value. For example, giving the subject a print or two in exchange for posing and signing the release would usually be of sufficient value, or, actually paying her an agreed sitting fee (irrespective of its amount) would usually be of sufficient value, too. The whole idea is that without this type of exchange (quid pro quo; something for something), a signed release is generally worthless.

Photographing Minors

If you intend to photograph a minor, you should proceed very cautiously, and only under the explicit advice of legal counsel from your area. If you don't, you could be in for some big surprises and shocks. Pair this with the fact that the laws often vary a great deal from state to state on what a minor can and can not do and when they can contract in their own behalf. What constitutes a minor is often not clear cut.

For the purposes of entering into a legal contract (such as a release), the law often varies from one state to another; in some states it may be 18 years of age, some 21 years, and so on.

One thing we can tell you for sure. When it comes to minors and contracts, the law most always favors the minor. For example, consider that in most states a minor's written consent on a release is valueless. Even if you have the written consent of one or both of the minor's parents, most states allow a minor to disavow any such parental consent within a reasonable length of time after reaching the age of majority. In practical terms, what this all means to a photographer is simply this: when you deal with a minor, you often do so at your own financial and legal peril. A couple of examples should help make our point.

Parental consent — Assume that the girl you want to photograph is a minor; that she is 17 years old. Assume further that you have decided that because of this girl's natural beauty, you want to have her image on most of your advertising: brochures, business cards, mailers, letter heads and so forth.

Also assume that the girl in question, as well as both of her parents, want you to photograph her; that they are all in agreement to have her image appear on all of your advertising; that they are willing to have the minor cooperate with you for no fee whatsoever. However, you, being the cautious type, inform her parents that you will only photograph the girl if both of them and the minor sign a model release form and they accept $1,000 from you in

- **For a release to be valid, it must have good and sufficient consideration.**

payment in full for the girl's model services. They all agree. They all sign the proper legal release form; you pay the money and photograph the girl.

One year later the girl comes back to you and advises you of the following: that she has seen her photos in your advertising all over town; that she is no longer living with her parents, but with a boyfriend; that she turned 18 about two weeks prior to coming back to see you; that she has decided that the $1,000 initially given to her parents for her modeling services was not enough money; that she wants an additional $4,000 or she will sue. You promptly show her the signed release and show her the door. She thereupon sues you. Result?

She wins, at least this would be the result in most states. The fact that her parents signed a release is not permanently binding upon the minor nor is the fact that the parents were paid on her behalf. However, let's take a look at an even worse situation.

Dealing at your peril — I recall reading a particular case in law school which, I believe, is still the majority law in most states: A well-dressed, mature looking young man went into a Buick agency one day, approached one of the salesmen, and advised he was interested in trading in his old car for a new Buick convertible.

"...if you are in doubt as to a subject's age, ask for proof..."

After a couple of hours of looking around and negotiating, the customer and salesman came to terms. It was agreed that the young man would trade in his old car, pay something like $1500 down and $600 per month for the next 30 months. After a quick credit check and approval of the buyer's credit, the salesman asked for the keys to the old car, the $1500 down payment, and title to the old vehicle which was to be traded in.

The title, having previously been signed and notarized by the young man's mother (the old car was in the mother's name), was given to the salesman by the buyer along with his check in the amount of $1500; the young man left the agency driving the new Buick convertible.

Two or three months later, the buyer drove back to the Buick agency, reapproached the same salesman and basically announced the following: that he was tired of the new Buick convertible he had recently bought, wanted his old car back, wanted his $1500 returned, and wanted the agency to tear up the finance contract.

The young man had never made one car payment on the new car. In addition, the new Buick was heavily damaged at the time of its return and had over 10,000 miles on the odometer. To make matters worse, the auto agency had long since sold the man's old car. The salesman got angry and asked the buyer to leave the premises under threat of being arrested.

The young man renewed his demands and added, "...if I don't get my money and car back, I'm going to sue you; I'm really only 17 years old and you can't do this to me." The salesman ignored the young man and escorted him off the premises. A law suit ensued. Result?

The young man won. The Buick agency had to take back the beat-up Buick convertible, pay the $1500 down payment back, and tear up the finance contract. Since the agency no longer had the young man's old trade-in, they were required to furnish a car to him that was of "like kind and quality."

The agency couldn't even charge the kid with a rental fee or for the damage done to the Buick. These are severe consequences, but the law in the case was clear: when you deal with a minor, you do so at your peril.

If this is the status of the law in your state, and if you are going to photograph a minor, we would suggest that if you are in doubt as to a subject's age, ask for proof: birth certificate, passport, and so on. If you can't get proof of age, then we would abandon the photo session and look for a new subject to pose for us. Better safe than sorry.

CHAPTER THREE

Shooting Locations and Settings

Photographically speaking, a shooting location is nothing more sophisticated than a place to take photos. A setting is nothing more than a place within a place. With such broad definitions, and for seriously executed figure photography, choosing location sites and settings might seem like an overwhelming task; hundreds of locations and settings might immediately come to mind.

However, to make things simple, and for our purposes, we can confine our thinking and our discussion to four major shooting locations—a photo studio (or a studio in your home), a subject's home, an outdoor location, and a commercial location site.

Once a location has been chosen, we can then give some thought to choosing a setting within a given location.

Whatever you do, don't minimize the importance of a setting for the nude study. A setting can be as important, if not more so, than the locale which it is in. For one thing, a setting can have a definite affect upon a subject and the final pictorial result.

For example, a setting can be responsible for a subject's attitude, the time period and mood of an image, and even the mood of the subject. In addition, and to further complicate matters, settings can range from the most modest and simple to the highly elaborate.

As a result, the prudent photographer should know such things as how to control a setting, how a setting differs for a figure study compared with other types of people photography and, most importantly, how to get the very most out of any setting.

The Setting

A wide range of settings can be appropriate for figure photography: from the simplest, seamless, studio backdrop to the most elaborate setting in a mansion; from the most straight-forward to the most intriguing.

This latitude, or feature, gives a photographer of nude studies an almost unlimited choice of settings at his or her disposal. The photographer is usually only restricted by his or her own imagination, judgment, style and taste and the interpretation that he or she wishes to give to a subject.

The art to figure photography lies with such things as a photographer's camera skills and ability to light, pose, and direct. It also lies with such things as one's ability to convey, on film, the mood, and atmosphere sought, as well as a model's skill, agility, and sensitivity.

Although it's true that you can generate numerous moods and effects with different settings, your choice of these settings is generally not going to be the controlling factor as to whether or not a resulting image is art.

An improperly chosen location site or a setting within a given location site can ruin an otherwise artful nude figure study but the converse is not true. An image that has not risen to the dignity of being

"...an almost unlimited choice of settings..."

"...exhaust all the possibilities that even a simple or limited setting offers."

classed as an artful nude study will not become such simply because it happens to be captured in a well chosen location site or setting.

Control of a Setting

The photographer, as opposed to the painter or sculptor, has a different problem in the recording of a location and setting. If nothing else, settings must be controlled for two major reasons. First, control is needed to keep one's workload down to the minimum; to keep from having to move or remove too many things from a set.

Secondly, one should control a setting in order to keep from having to spend time and money correcting negatives and prints (such as by retouching, dodging, burning, and/or air brushing). The reason the photographer has more problems than a painter-artist is obvious. It's because the photographer's canvas — or the film in the camera — sees all of the elements of a scene and setting, at the same time, in one click of the camera's shutter.

This means that ideally a photographer should have a very good and pre-conceived idea of how the subject is to be presented in relationship to the chosen setting well in advance of the exposure of any film. It also means learning how to subtract unwanted elements from the setting before exposures are made.

Get the Most from Each Setting

Once you have chosen or created a particular setting, don't just take a few shots and then leave it for another one. Work it to its fullest potential. Many of us get into the habit of locating or constructing a set, taking a few shots from one favorite camera position or angle, using one lighting setup, one lens, and so on, and then moving on. So often, we fail to seize the opportunity to shoot from different camera angles, from different locations within the setting, with different lighting, different lens focal lengths, and the like. Many photographers fail to exhaust all the possibilities that even a simple or limited setting offers.

Elaborate And Simple Settings

If you are hired by a client to create a nude study, you might find yourself bound by the dictates of the person who hired you. You might have to adhere to

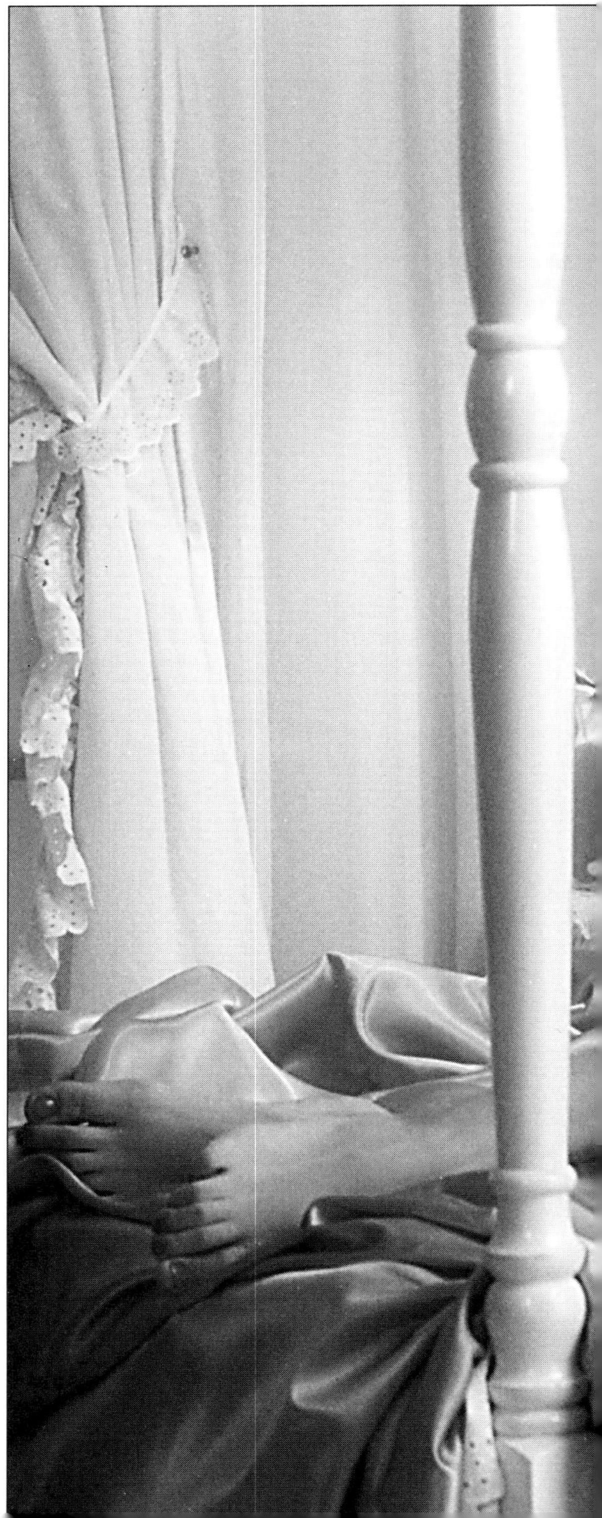

Right: *One of our most popular permanent sets is the bedroom set. It virtually reeks of femininity and it's extremely versatile. A three light set-up was used: a 4-inch snooted back light; a top light housed in a 6-inch bowl reflector; and a 3 1/2 x 7 1/2-foot softbox, approximately 45 degrees to the right of camera axis. Even though the image displays frontal nudity, the subject was able to project a quiet elegance. This fact, along with the poses, lighting and setting lead to some beautiful images.*

the setting your customer has selected, whether it is elaborate or simple. However, keep in mind that aside from such dictates, you alone are responsible for locating or fashioning a setting that will be consistent with the pictorial interpretation you wish to achieve.

Elaborate settings — An elaborate setting is not a cluttered or busy setting, but rather a setting that contains a number (usually four or more) of fairly large, appropriate elements or props in the photo scene; these will be in addition to a mere backdrop.

An elaborate setting is a developed and structured area that provides more than just a background for a photographer to shoot in. More or less, these elements become part of the overall photo composition. For example, in our studio we have a setting which we call the fireplace set. (This set is featured in some of the photographs in this book.) Within that one set, there are several areas which a subject can be posed and photographed — at or on the bar, on or near the hearth, at or near one of the windows, on the spiral staircase, and so on.

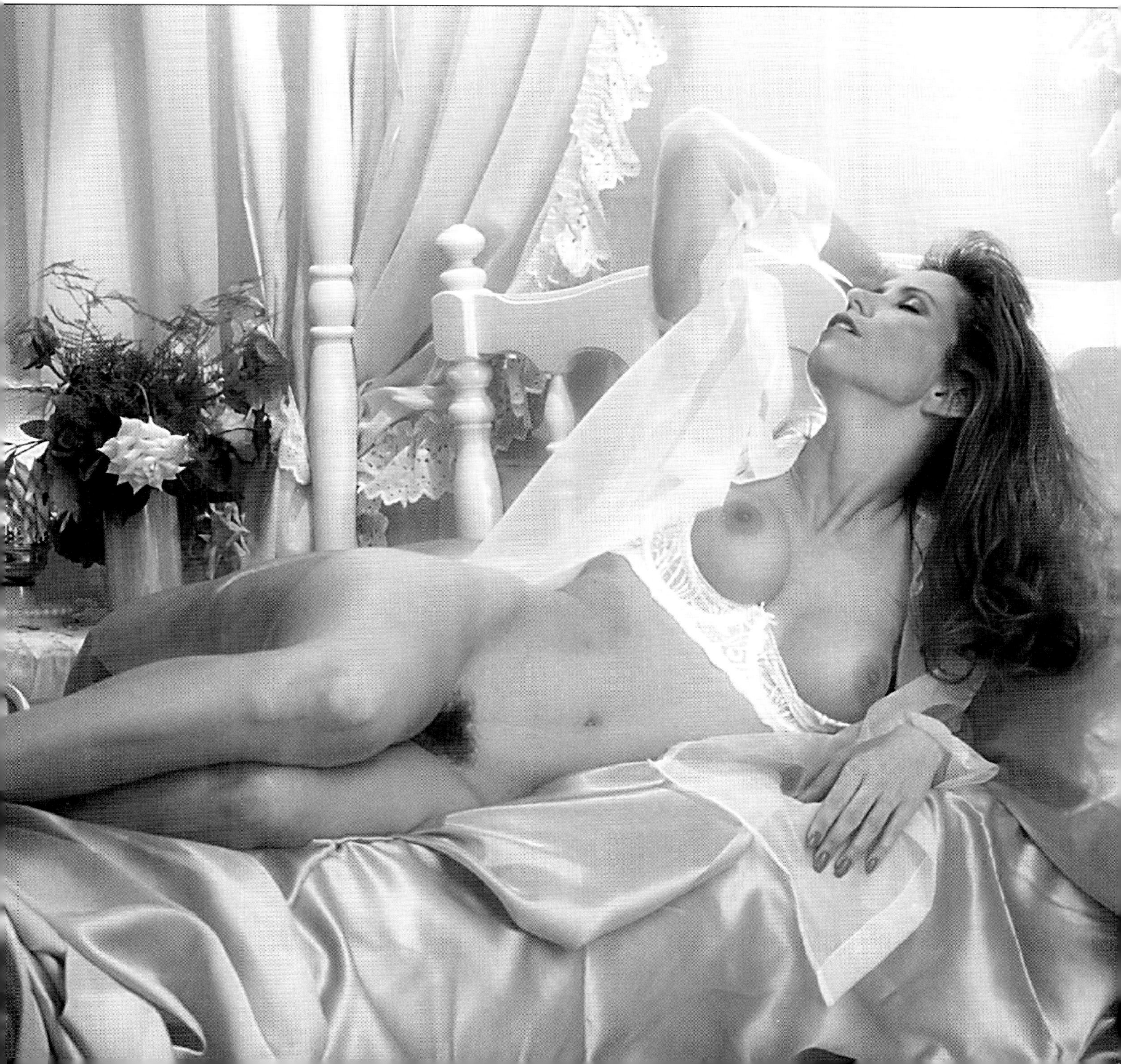

"An undraped figure can express itself much more easily..."

With an elaborate setting (such as a well furnished and decorated bedroom, living room, or even kitchen) you can usually photograph a subject in one section of the set, and then easily and rapidly reposition the model to another spot within that same setting for other poses; each repositioning should provide a different look (and sometimes even mood) for the subject and the resulting images.

Such a setting helps to provide pictorial variety, and gives both you and the model an added challenge. Such a setting is also a safeguard. Just in case the poses in the initial location of an elaborate set don't suit your subject or your taste and pre-visualized concept, re-positioning her will allow you to change or modify the poses without faulting the subject for her inability to carry out the poses properly. There is another big reason for using an elaborate setting: distraction.

Whenever a subject is less than attractive, is too overweight, or has problems with her skin, the use of an elaborate setting can be a blessing.

By having a number of elements in the photo composition, you visually give a viewer a lot to look at. This condition creates a small diversion, and directs a viewer's attention away from the problem — the subject.

Another very valid reason for using an elaborate setting is time constraints. It takes time to go from one setting to another, especially when you're on location, in the great outdoors. This is time which you may not have or be able to charge for.

If the whole reason for changing locations is to get some new settings to work in, you often can achieve the same result by simply working an existing setting to its full potential. For the above reasons, and whenever we can, we use fairly elaborate settings for our figure photography.

Simple settings — A simple setting generally provides only one posing place in which to shoot. A simple setting consists of nothing more than a seamless studio background or a plain wall; it might also contain one or two simple props.

For example, a single chair or stepladder could be added as a posing prop to enable you to shoot more varied poses on a seamless background. Even the addition of another person could be entertained as a prop for a simple setting.

Although it sounds rather limited to use simple settings for such a sophisticated thing as a nude figure study, you should not underestimate its potential power. An image photographed on a simple setting can be startling.

An attractive subject, posed against plain background paper, with well placed and appropriate lighting, can hold a viewer's total attention and yield some terrific pictorial results.

Another nice feature of the simple setting is that once you have taken the few shots that you want, you can easily abandon or dismantle it and move on to another, equally simple setup with minimal delay and effort.

Even if you don't want to move on, you can achieve an astonishing variety of dynamic images within the confines of one simple set. You do it by changes in the posing, expressions, camera viewpoint, lighting, and so on.

Subject Attitude and the Setting

Just as different types of music can have an effect on one's mood, so can various types of settings. For example, light and airy settings will usually provoke a subject into a light and sometimes frivolous mood, while austere settings will usually have an opposite affect. Again, it's not that one will be the right one to use, the other wrong, it'll all depend upon the pictorial concept you're trying to convey and capture.

In addition, and with a fully dressed subject, a photographer often has to go to great lengths and make major changes in both the setting being used, as well as the lighting, the poses and the clothing the subject is wearing, to achieve really noticeable differences from one photograph to the next. What's worse is that changing all of these elements usually takes time and during this time period a subject's mood can change drastically. By contrast, and with nude studies, a photographer need not resort to such drastic changes.

An undraped figure can express itself much more easily through subtle and yet very clear changes in just one element: body language. This means that whatever mood the nude subject has gotten into can usually be maintained while the photographer directs a subject into body position changes within a given setting.

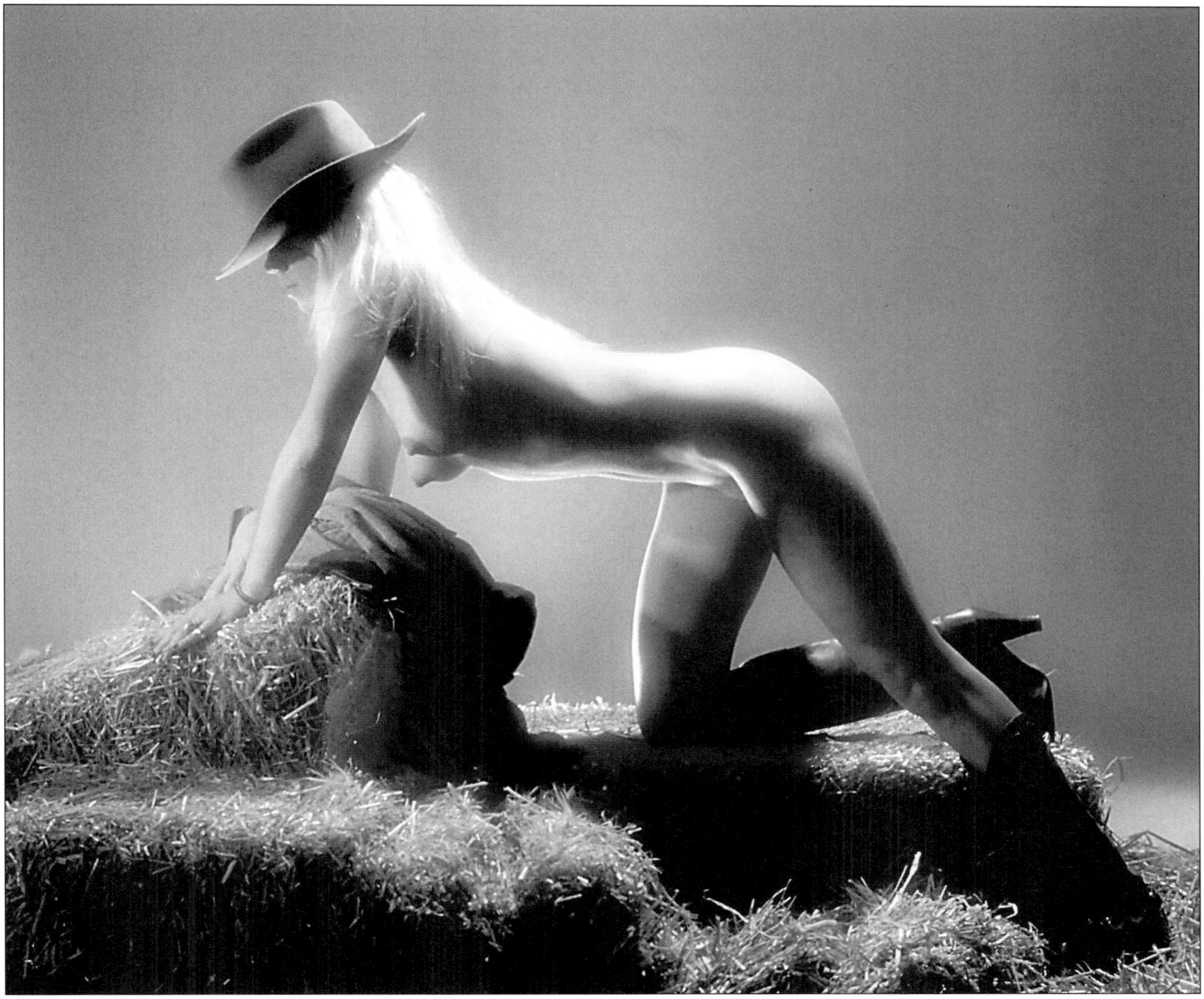

Above: *A scene such as this is so easy to set up and tear down that it is a pleasure to work with. All we needed was a few bales of hay, a prop or two such as a cowboy hat and boots — and we're ready to shoot. We started with a white background sweep. For a main light, we put a 6-inch bowl light on a boom stand, above and slightly behind the subject. We added a couple of kicker lights gelled yellow, for accent lights. One such light was placed on the floor directly behind the subject. The white background was not photographed as white because we allowed no illumination other than the spill light from the accent lights to strike it. The other accent light was amber gelled and was directed toward the face and chest. This light had its power set to an intensity of one f-stop less light than the main light. The other accent light had its power set to one f-stop more than the main light.*

Just as a face is capable of exhibiting different expressions, so also is a subject's entire body. The tilt of the head in a certain manner, the raising or lowering of an arm at a certain angle, a slight turn of a leg, a slight movement of a hand, even the posing or placement of the fingers, are all examples of the use of body language in photography.

Body language is personal expression through the use of the subject's body and can be strongly suggestive of many moods and feelings including: shyness, sensuousness, defiance, pride, strength, timidity, and so on.

Establishing a Mood and Time Period

You can inject a mood or the feel for a specific time period into any photograph, even when shooting in the simplest of settings, such as on an innocuous gray seamless paper background.

By the thoughtful selection and use of an appropriate prop or accessory, such as a large, turn-of-the-century, flowery hat, a kerosene lamp or an art-deco chair,

"...expression through the use of the subject's body..."

different points in time and moods would be suggested for the subject to adopt.

The Interrelationship of Subject and Setting

While preparing for a nude photo study, quite frequently you will first decide what kind of look you want to create — such as classical or contemporary — and then choose a setting that is appropriate. Sometimes, however, this process will be reversed. You'll come upon an attractive setting first, then decide how to fashion a figure photograph with the subject, or subjects, and posing that will be appropriate for the setting.

Whichever comes first — the concept of the kind of image you want or the setting — you must create a credible relationship between the subject and the pose, on the one hand, and the setting on the other. Just as you wouldn't typically photograph a company executive in a child's nursery, so you must be sure that the chosen

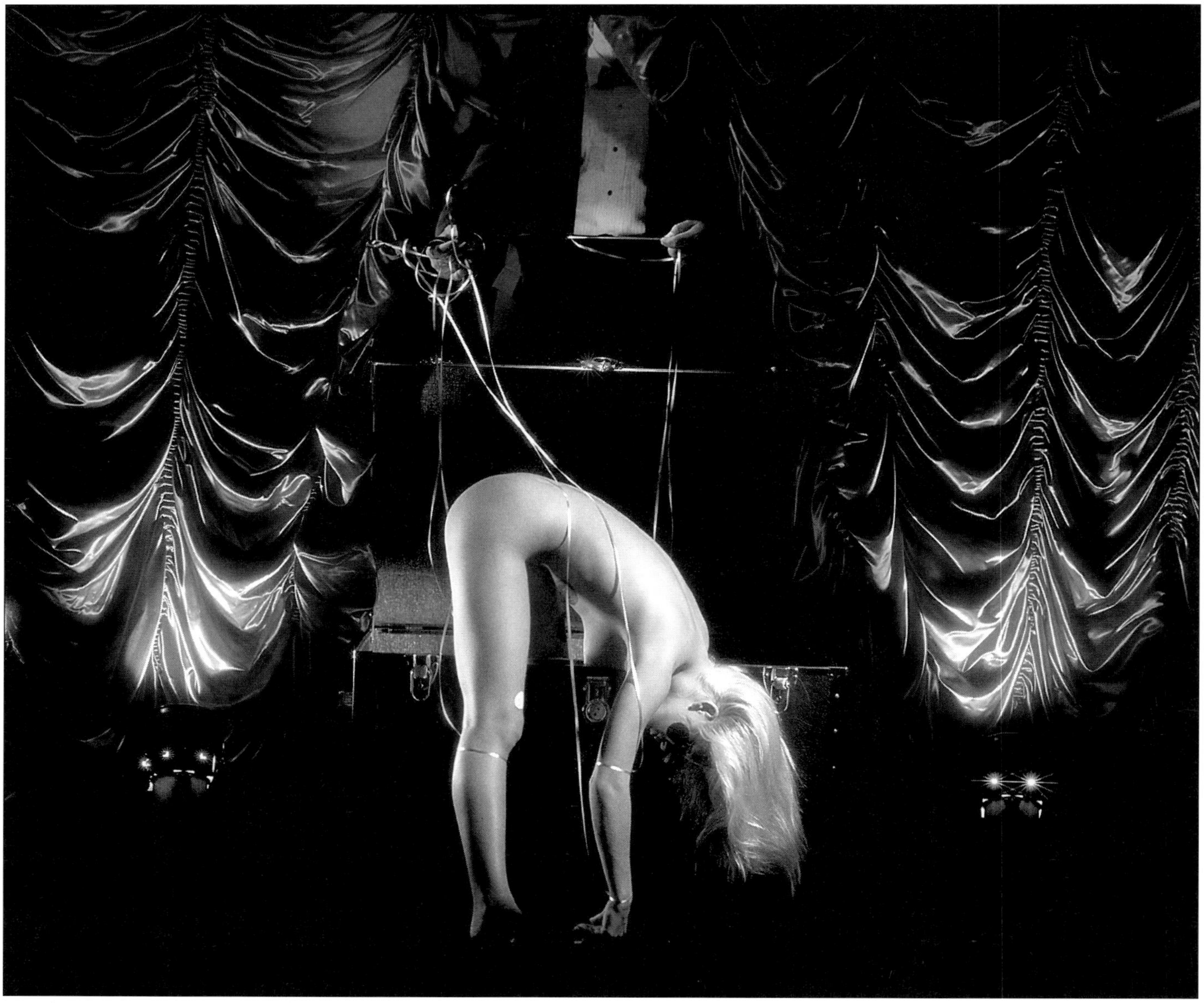

Above: *This image was created in a setting we call the "marionette scenario." This set-up was rather elaborate , involving seven lights. We attempted to create the effect that the subject — the marionette — was on stage in rather classy surroundings, including wine-colored satin drapes for a curtain with the barely-visible puppeteer wearing a tuxedo. To give the subject a theatrical and festive "marionette" appearance, we painted a couple of circles on her body. We used black and white Tempura body paint. This paint dries rather quickly and has a tendency to crack; therefore once the paint is applied to the subject, be prepared to photograph immediately. To make the puppet's strings festive looking, and more prominent, we used silver ribbons. Although top, background, and accent lights were used, we wanted to create a "theatrical" spotlight. We used an adjustable electronic flash spotlight as our main light source. It was positioned at about 45 degrees to the right of the camera position.*

model, her appearance, pose and mood, and the chosen location and setting, all make sense when blended together.

A talented and imaginative subject can often help you find suitable locations. But even without such a help-aid, often a subject's basic nature and appearance will offer you a clue.

For example, some subjects will look distinctly old-fashioned and conservative while others will look more modern; some will look vampish while others will look elegant and stately. As a result, you'll will often locate a setting that is in keeping with a subject's look.

But, this requires practice; learning how to recognize the basic, essential look of each model. Learning how to see her look and being able to capitalize on it by having it mesh with an appropriate setting will frequently be a very good guide and starting point.

Tip — Whatever you do, don't ever try to force a model — no matter how beautiful, graceful, or experienced — into a setting that is unsuitable for her, simply because the setting happens to be handy and available. If you do, it will almost certainly lead to disappointing photographic results.

Photography in the Studio

In the beginning of this chapter, we mentioned that it would be helpful and would simplify matters if you thought of locations for nude studies as falling into four major places: a studio, a subject's home, outdoors, and at a commercial location sites. It's not that one is any better than the other for a nude study, just different. We still have our preferences. Our experience has shown that if we are given a choice, we would immediately opt for a studio location first and secondly for an outdoor location.

From a positive standpoint, a studio—whether it be a commercial environment or a studio in your home—offers the greatest potential control for figure photography for at least four major reasons:

1. It ensures privacy.
2. It ensures more control over your equipment.
3. It affords one total control over the lighting.
4. It affords one control over the photo situation.

On the negative side, there are at least three major pitfalls which you should avoid to studio photography:

5. Stagnation.
6. Subjects may get overworked.
7. Subjects may become overwhelmed and intimidated.

The Assurance of Privacy

Depending upon the laws which exist in your state and because nude photography is an extremely sensitive photographic area, extra precautionary measures for the subject's well-being, safety, and security should be taken. With the exception of the subject's own home, your studio or home will usually be the safest and most private location you can find, as well as the easiest to control. Among other things, you can have some control of phone calls, as well as the people in the shoot-room area.

• **Never force a model into a setting that is not suitable for her.**

The subject's sense of privacy and security during a figure photo session is very important. Privacy is important to a subject's emotional ease. If a subject is not totally at ease while she is being photographed, the photo results can be ruined. A subject who is new to figure photography tends to be nervous anyway and doesn't need the additional concern of having strangers looking on or wondering what a stranger might do once she is posed and in a state of nudity. In fact, once a sitting starts, you should never allow anyone whom the subject has not previously met and expressly approved, to invade the shooting area, to watch, or interrupt the photo session. The only exception to this rule should be in the case of a true emergency.

Control over Equipment

Most of us who have traveled know that traveling can be a pain when it comes to packing for a trip. Not only does traveling force you to think about what you have to pack, but it usually forces you to take less than what you might want. Just as it is easier to dress for any occasion from your own home (since all of your clothing is at your immediate disposal), so it is easier to photograph out of your own home or studio rather than on location — all of your equipment is right at your fingertips.

This really addresses itself to only one form of equipment control. There is

"...you have control over your own environment."

another type to be sensitive to; one that involves theft and loss.

When you photograph in your own studio, you usually don't have to worry about equipment theft or loss; it's safe; you have control over your own environment. You can't feel this confident when you leave your studio and go on location, even to a subject's home. If you don't watch your equipment like a hawk, chances are better than even that things will get lost or stolen. And, if this happens before a photo session, and the piece of equipment was essential, it could cost you the loss of the entire session.

Control over Lighting

Periodically, during the course of any given year, Sheila and I have the pleasure of teaching seminars at various state photographic conventions across the country. During most of these seminars we put on live demonstrations. This means we actually photograph one or more subjects during the course of our seminars so that the viewing audience can see and better understand how Sheila and I work during a Boudoir/Glamour photo session. Even though we — egotistically — like to think that we know exactly what we are doing when it comes to lighting the human form, there never is a time during these shows that we are not in doubt as to the final photographic outcome. Why? Because we don't have total control over our lighting.

When we photograph in our studio, we know exactly what each of our lights can and will do. We also know the effect of using one type of light over another: using a small bowl light over a larger one, a white umbrella over and silver-lined one, a small soft box over a larger one and so on.

We are accustomed to working with our lights in our studio and know the result we are going to get within our own environment. The moment we're forced to work with someone else's lights, the photographic results become somewhat less than 100 percent predictable. The photo results are always going to look good, but they could be better by having more control over the lighting.

There is another type of control that you'll have when working in a studio compared to location photography — the control of lighting variety. It's usually impossible or impractical to take all of your lights with you when you go on location to do figure photography.

Control over the Photo Situation

When you are photographing in your own studio (or home), you control how the photo session is to be conducted. You don't have to get permission from anyone for anything. In addition, you'll usually be able to exercise better control over the model in your own studio than anywhere else.

Beware of Stagnation

Location work offers different challenges and frequently involves the instantaneous solving of problems without advance knowledge of the exact photographic outcome. Even if you have photographed in the same natural location before, time has a way of altering things. This can lead to delays and inconsistent results.

Even though studio shooting appears more desirable than location work in this respect, studio photography has at least one big drawback — the danger of creativity becoming stagnated. By consistently working in the same environment, with the same tools and lights, sameness can work its way into the daily procedures. As a result, many photographers forget to reach out and experiment; to try new and different things. Growth is sacrificed for comfort. The consequence? The photo results become technically consistent, but your photos begin to look alike, even when the subjects are different.

Overworking the Subject

- **If the model gets tired, you should end the photographic session. Tired subjects generally photograph poorly.**

No photographic session should be carried to the point where the model is fatigued. This can easily happen when you are shooting in your home or studio where you are in familiar, comfortable territory. Frequently, you might have a tendency to push a subject and photograph for longer periods of time than if you were conducting the photo session elsewhere. Don't.

Models will tire from the rigors of posing, no matter where the location. A professional model may be able to pose for many hours and still look fresh and vibrant. However, it's been our experience that non-professional subjects begin to look tired and photograph poorly if they

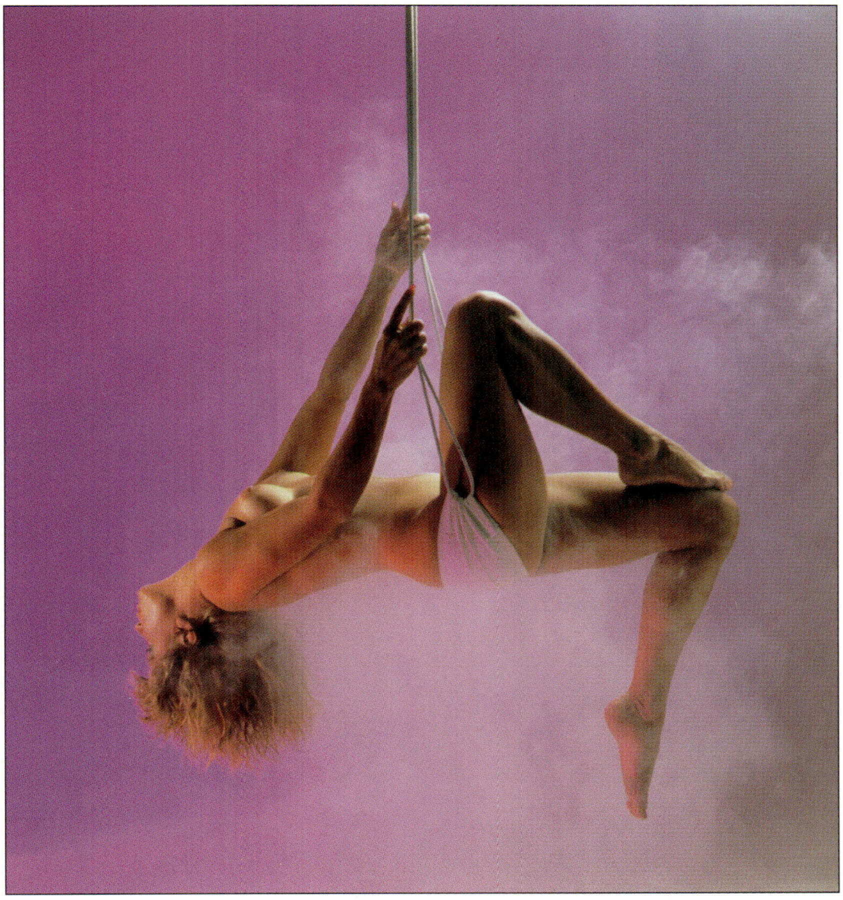

Above: *A swing is a great prop for female figure photography. In our studio we have swings with hard, wooden seats as well as ones with a pliable seat made with such material as canvas or leather. As this image depicts, a pliable seat follows the contours of the body beautifully, becoming a part of the subject. A swing suggests a light, happy atmosphere. This is why we like a white swing, bright props and a light and colorful background.*

Right: *For this image, we used moist ceramic clay, a material that was new to us. We had tested it a few days before the shoot. To save time, we only applied it to a portion of the subject. It looked smooth, clean, and great. On the day of the shoot, after applying the material to the subjects' entire bodies, we noticed that the material was drying too quickly and cracking. Every time the subjects changed poses, the material would crack and pieces would fall off. Although this was not what we had intended, we got some interesting results.*

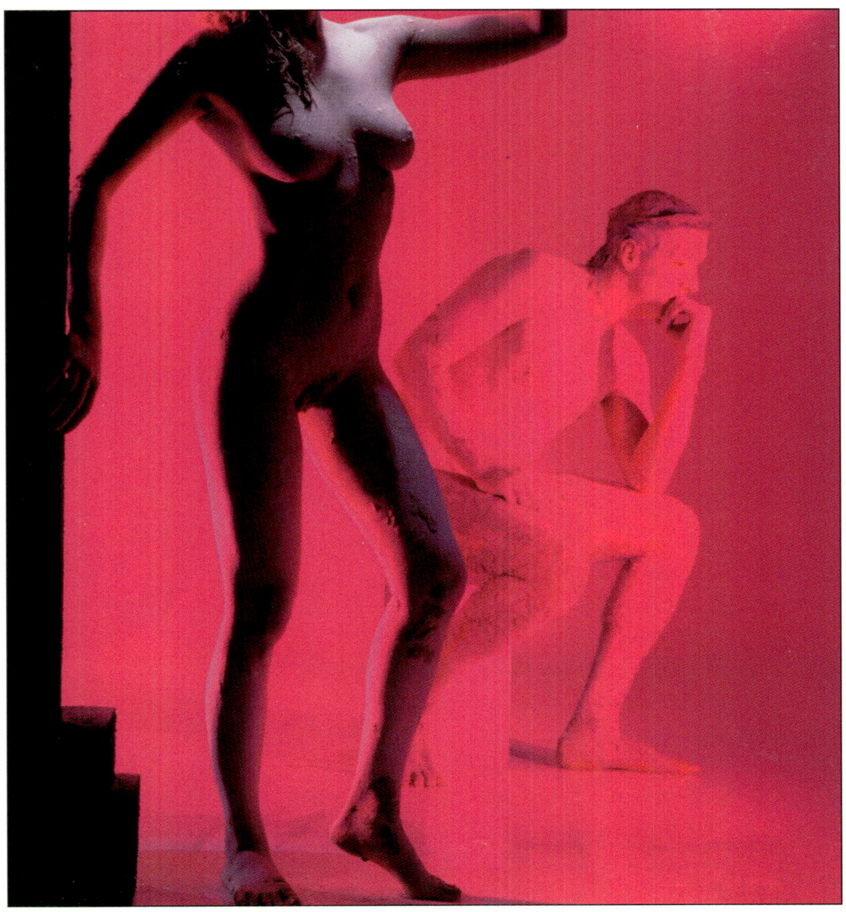

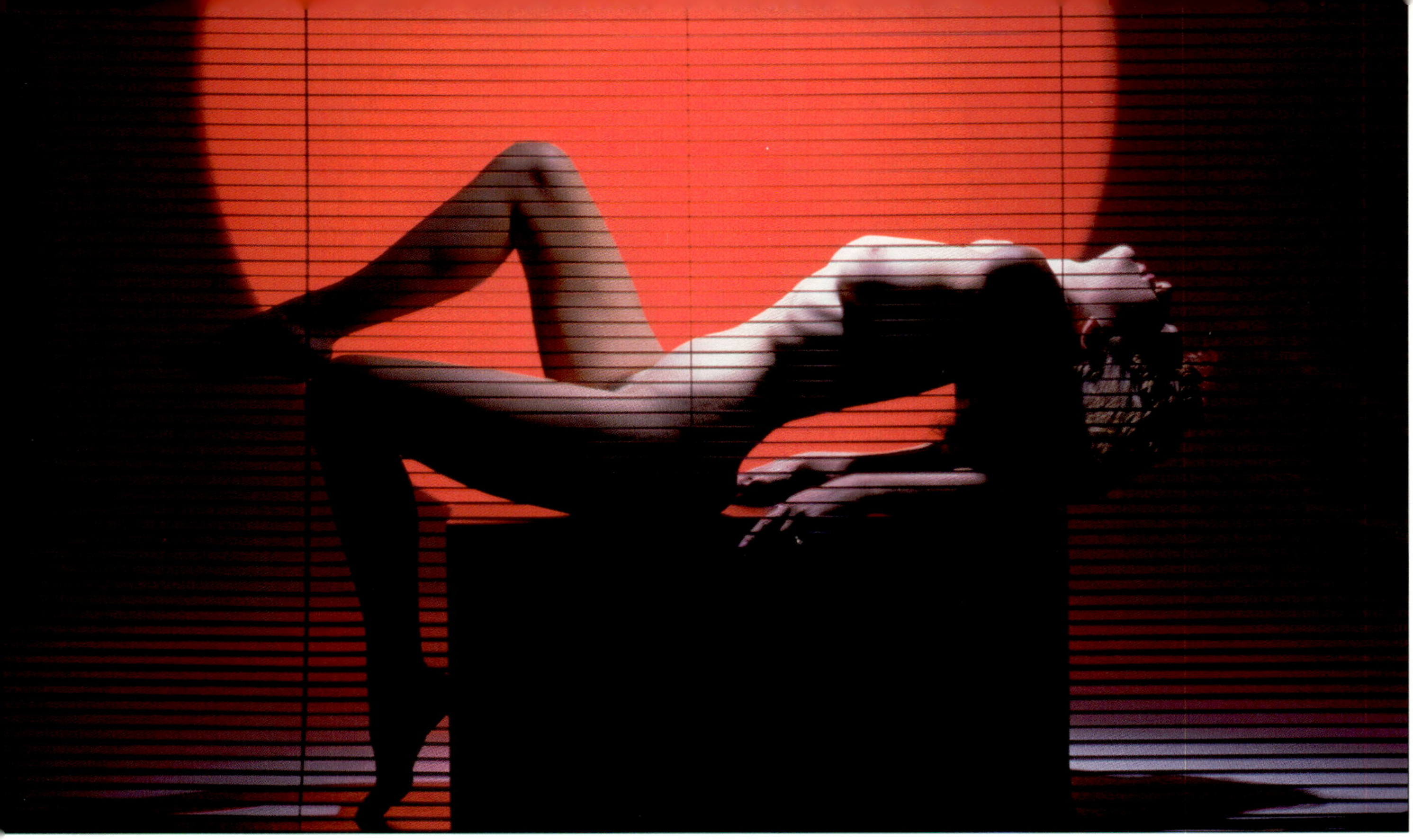

Above: *Many of our figure-photography subjects like to be photographed in silhouette. Such images can be very flattering while being less blatantly revealing than a fully lit nude. We have tried using other colors for the background including yellow, amber and green, but they all seemed to lack the "punch" we were looking for. The top main light is white while the background light was made with a Bowens Monospot with a red gel affixed.*

Right: *Mirrors are always great props for figure photography. When working with a mirror, you have three options as to where to place the point of optimum focus. You can focus on the subject, allowing the reflected image to go "soft," you can focus on the reflected image, allowing the original subject to go "soft," or you can manipulate the point of focus and depth of field to get both in sharp focus. Getting both the subject and her reflected image in focus generally leads to a more realistic "documentary" result. In this image, we chose total sharpness on both the subject and her reflection. We also chose to give slight lighting emphasis to the reflected image rather than the direct view of the subject. When setting up your lighting and calculating exposure, be sure to allow for light loss that might be caused by the mirror itself.*

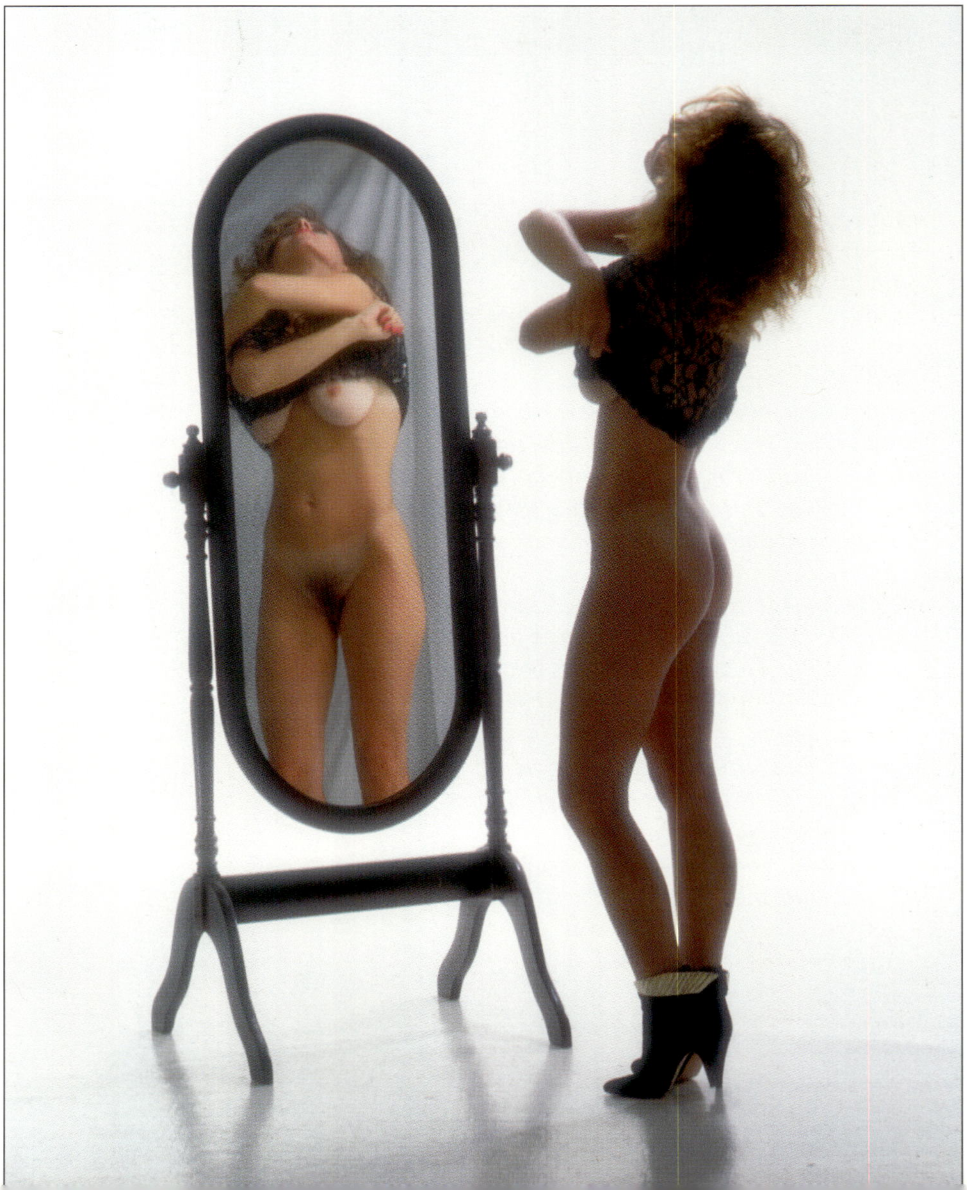

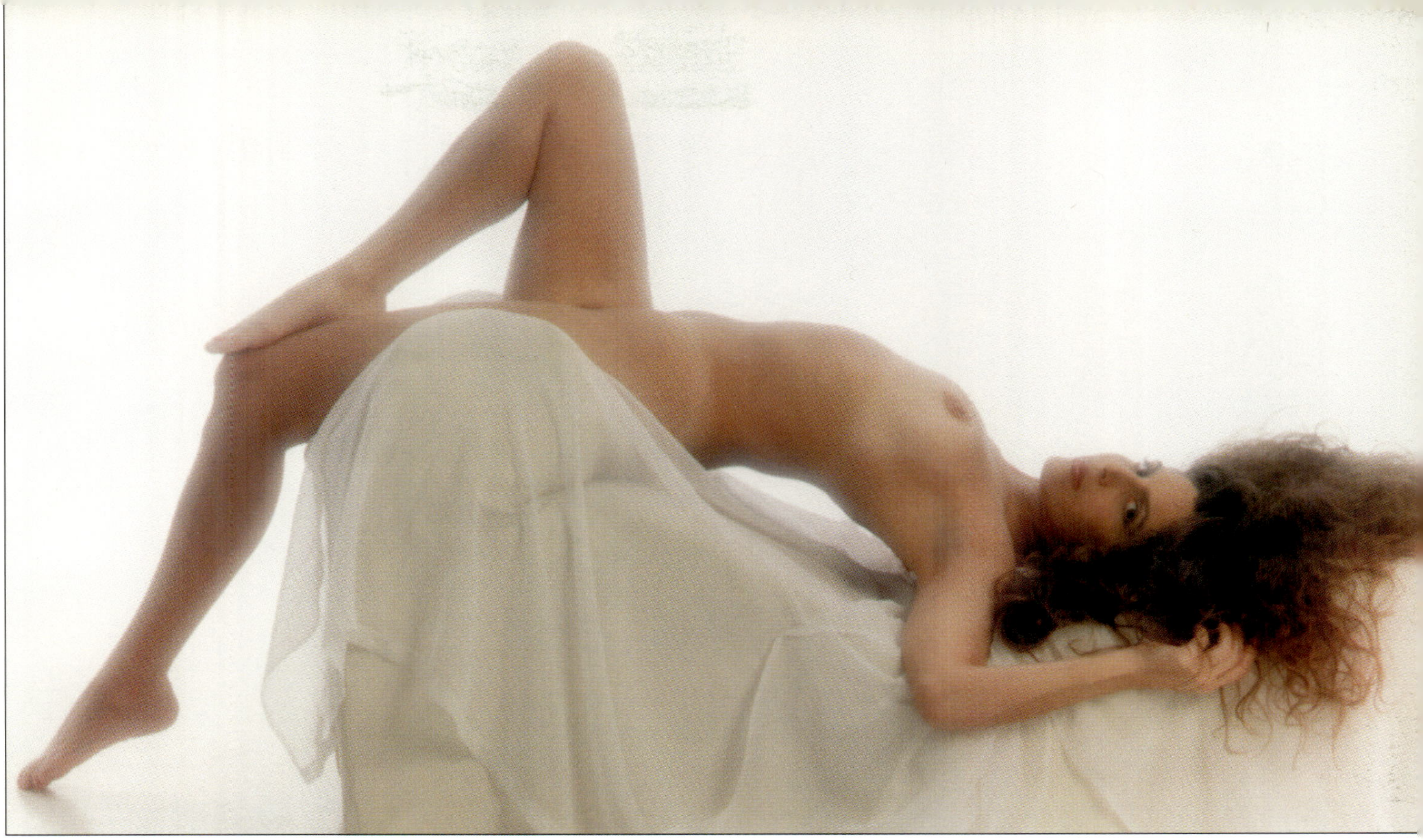

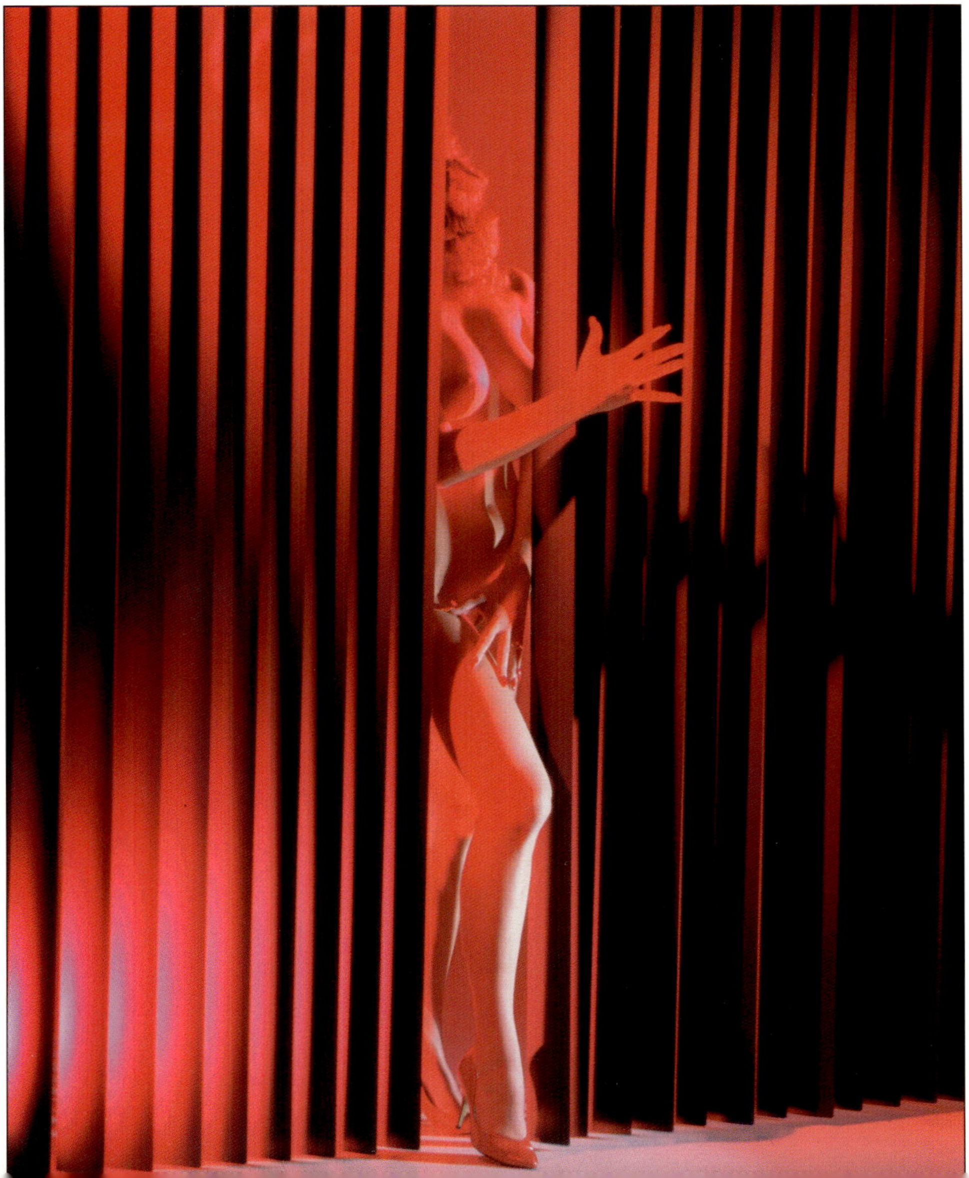

Above: *This photo was shot in a high-key setting. Although we prefer nude studies in low or medium key settings (they're more dramatic), high key is a favorite among most of our clientele. Even a simple setting such as this can produce a number of different and interesting images. Experiment with different poses, using both the personal, as in this image, or impersonal art form.*

Left: *Although we work with horizontal blinds in assorted colors and sizes, we've recently started using vertical blinds as well. When using blinds, one has considerable creative control over how it is to be presented. It can be shot as a silhouette, with no light striking it from the front; you can illuminate the wide slats from the front with either hard or soft light of various colors; or you can illuminate the slats partially, as we have done here. Notice that the frontal light on the slats need not necessarily come from the camera side of the blind. In this case, the illumination on the slats came from behind the blind, on the lower left side. We posed the subject so that some of her lines countered the vertical flow of the slats of the blind. By highlighting the subject partly with red light and partly with unfiltered white light, we have added further interest to this image.*

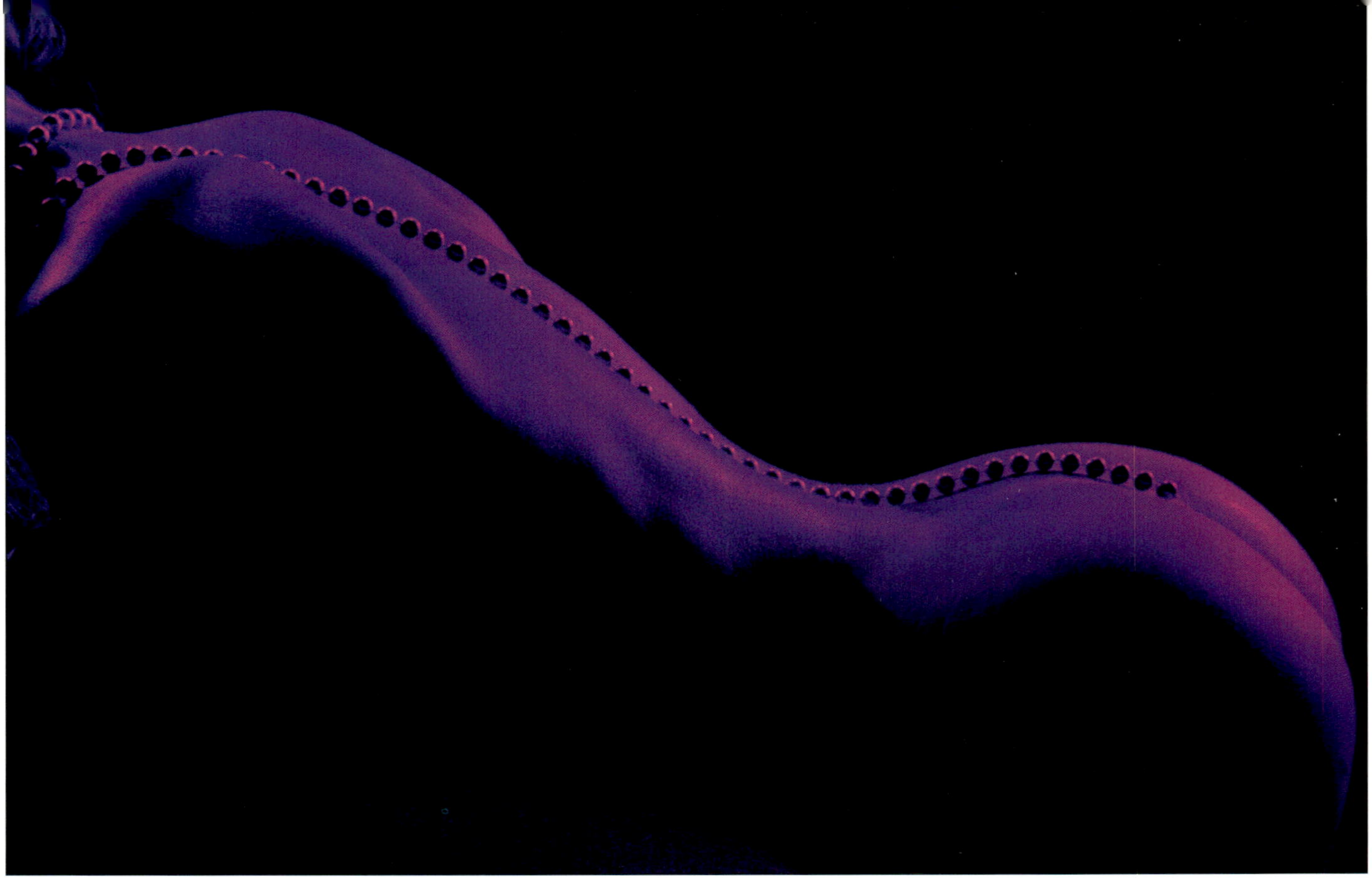

Above: *This image was taken using black and white film (T-Max 100 by Kodak). When we printed the image, we printed it two separate ways: black and white and color. We preferred the look we achieved when we printed it on color paper with our color enlarger. The print was then processed in a normal manner just as though it had been shot with color film.*
Below: *This image demonstrates another way to use mirrors as props. We like to work with multiple mirrors so that we can create multiple-image effects. With the incredible image sharpness provided by today's camera lenses and films, most female subjects are recorded much more "forgivingly" and kindly with the use of a soft-focus filter. Also, the use of soft lighting is often advisable. Without these precautions, images tend to be very stark and literal, revealing any flaws that might exist on a subject's body. Although this kind of "documentary" photography has its place, it is not one we favor for our figure work.*

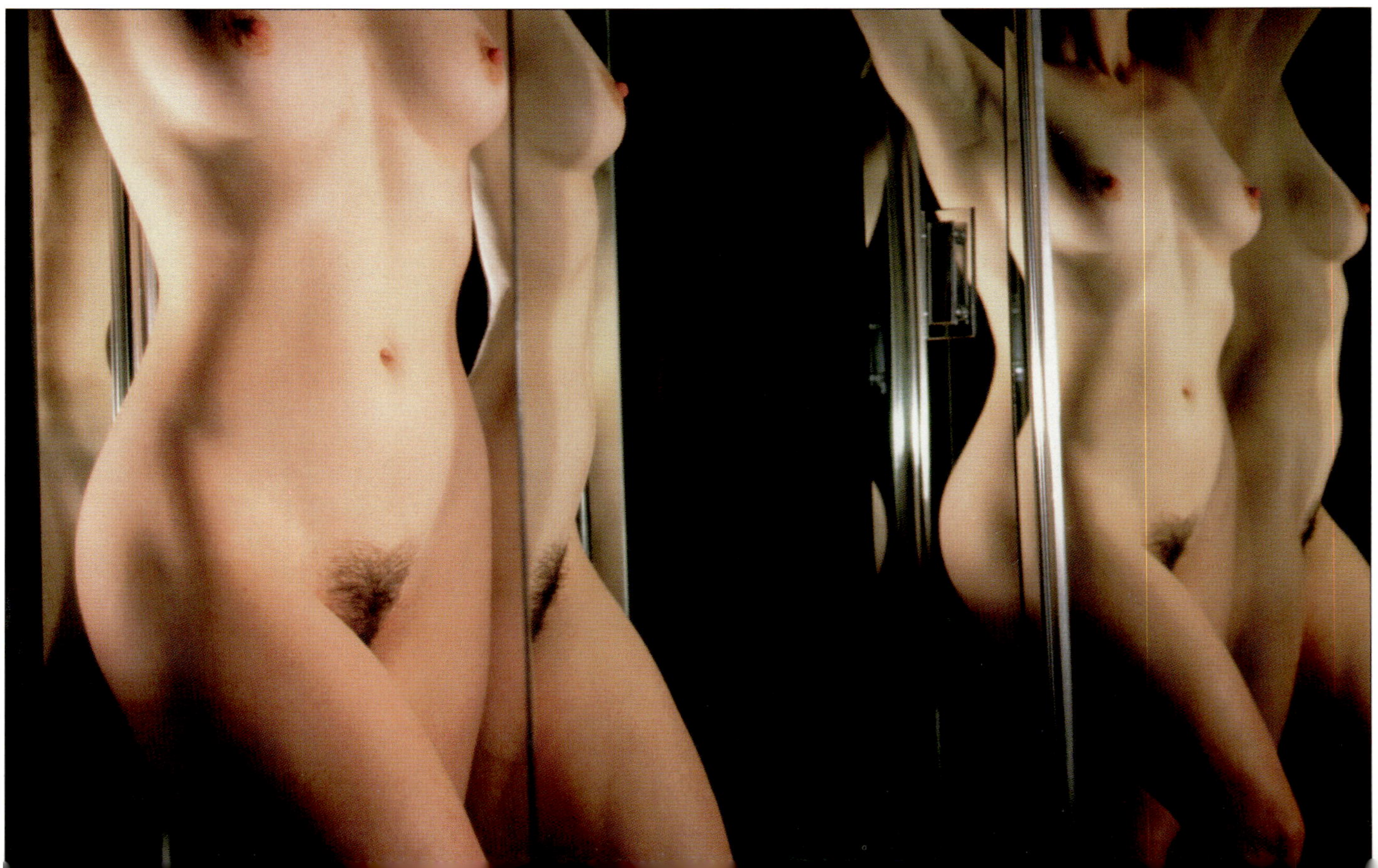

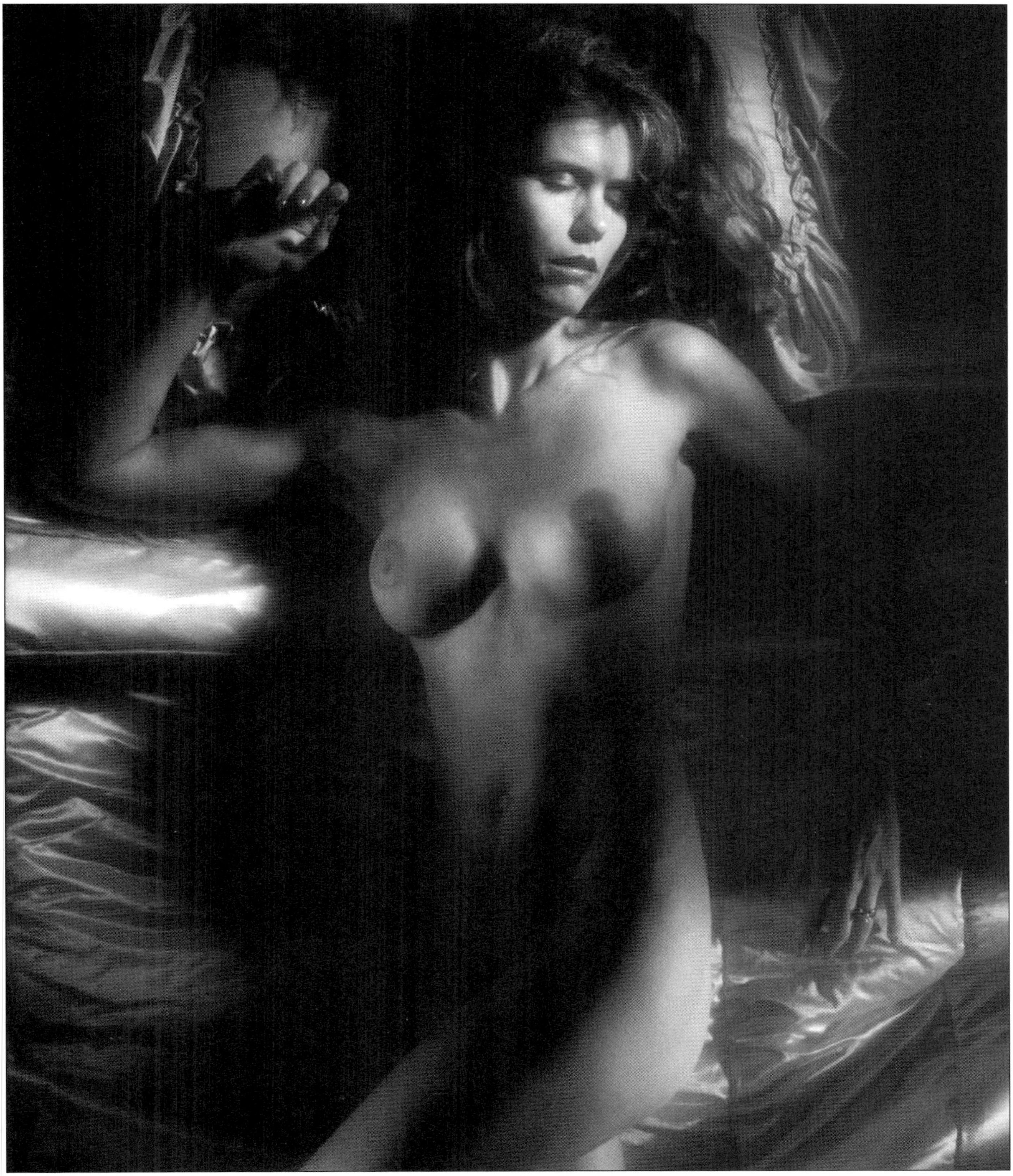

Above: *When you first look at this shot, it seems quite obvious that we were up on a ladder or scaffold and shot straight down on the subject in order to capture this image. Right? Wrong. We only have an eight foot ceiling in our studio and there wasn't enough room to shoot straight down using a 150mm Hasselblad lens. So we designed a bed that would stand up. The subject's entire body weight is on her right leg with the other leg raised just enough to give the viewer the impression that she is lying down in bed. We wrinkled the bed spread and pillow to give the impression that the body weight was causing the indentations. We also pinned her hair, in a rather flared, askew style, onto the pillow.*

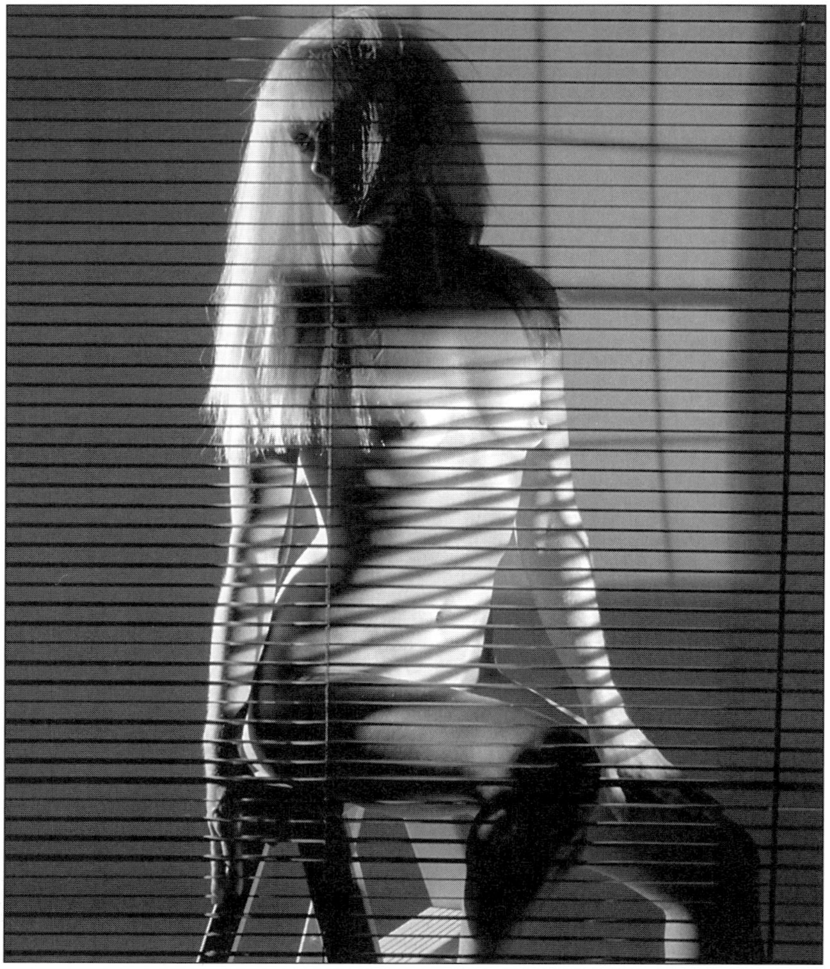

Above, Right and Opposite page: *The main light in these images was a Bowens Monospot flash, with a "window" grid pattern inserted into a holder just in front of the light. A similar light was used to direct light onto the subject. In order to keep the window pattern from overpowering the subject and distracting attention from her, we adjusted this light's output to one f-stop less light than was coming from the main light. As these photos show, once you have established the basic setting — the blind in front of the subject, the projected shadows on the subject, and the background window pattern — you have considerable scope for pictorial variety within those confines.*

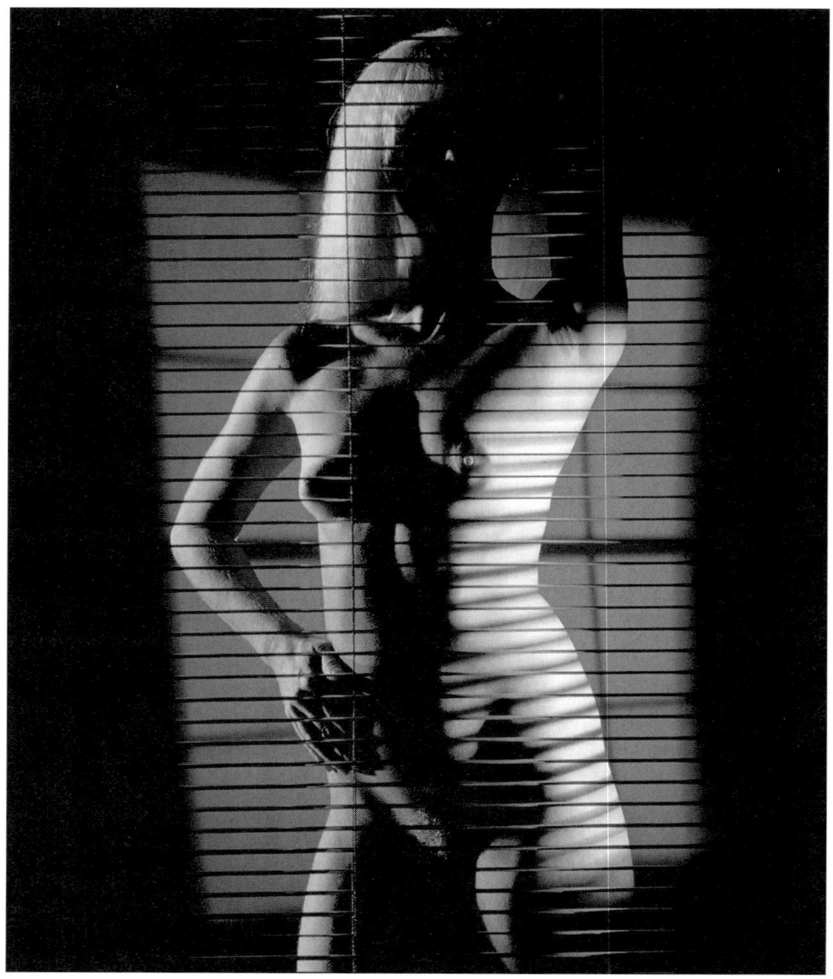

are worked more than a couple of hours at any given time.

Overwhelmed Subjects

Those of us who have a rather well-equipped studio, sometimes take such a studio for granted. We sometimes forget that lay-subjects often have no idea what type or quantity of equipment it takes to run a professional photography studio. As a result, many subjects can become intimidated by all of the props, lights, powerpacks, and other equipment.

Many subjects may not openly express these anxieties; however, you should be able to pick up on these feelings. Most people will show obvious signs of being tense or uncomfortable. In the beginning of your photographic endeavors you may ascribe such uneasiness to the fact that the subject is apprehensive about posing nude. However, with experience, you'll soon learn that many times their anxieties have nothing to do with posing; it's the sheer presence of all of your equipment and the fact that they are in a strange environment (your studio).

The best advice that we can offer you, when faced with such a situation and subject, is to stop the photo session and spend a few quality minutes talking with them. Talk about anything which they might find of interest and which might distract them from the surroundings: their husband; their children, their job, and so forth.

Photography in the Subject's Home

As with other types of location work, figure photography in a subject's home can afford a photographer a number of new challenges: new problems to solve, new settings, props and photographic concepts to work with, new lighting arrangements and poses to use, and so on. Photographing in a subject's home is also not without its problems: you'll be working in unfamiliar surroundings, the home may dictate the type of image you must capture and the element of privacy will usually be very different.

Working in Unfamiliar Surroundings.

Unlike your home or studio, a subject's home will usually be unfamiliar territory to you. You won't know, with any degree of certainty, what the exact photographic results are going to be until after you have taken the shots, or even how long it is going to take you to take the shots you want. This is not a desirable situation.

To keep disappointing results and time delays to a minimum, we suggest that you visit the subject's home in advance of the day of the actual photo session. See exactly what advantages and disadvantages the home offers. Make notes and sketches of the rooms where you will be shooting.

Several rooms may offer the potential for different settings. Note wall colors,

- **Keep careful notes and even sketches of a subject's home where a photo session will take place.**

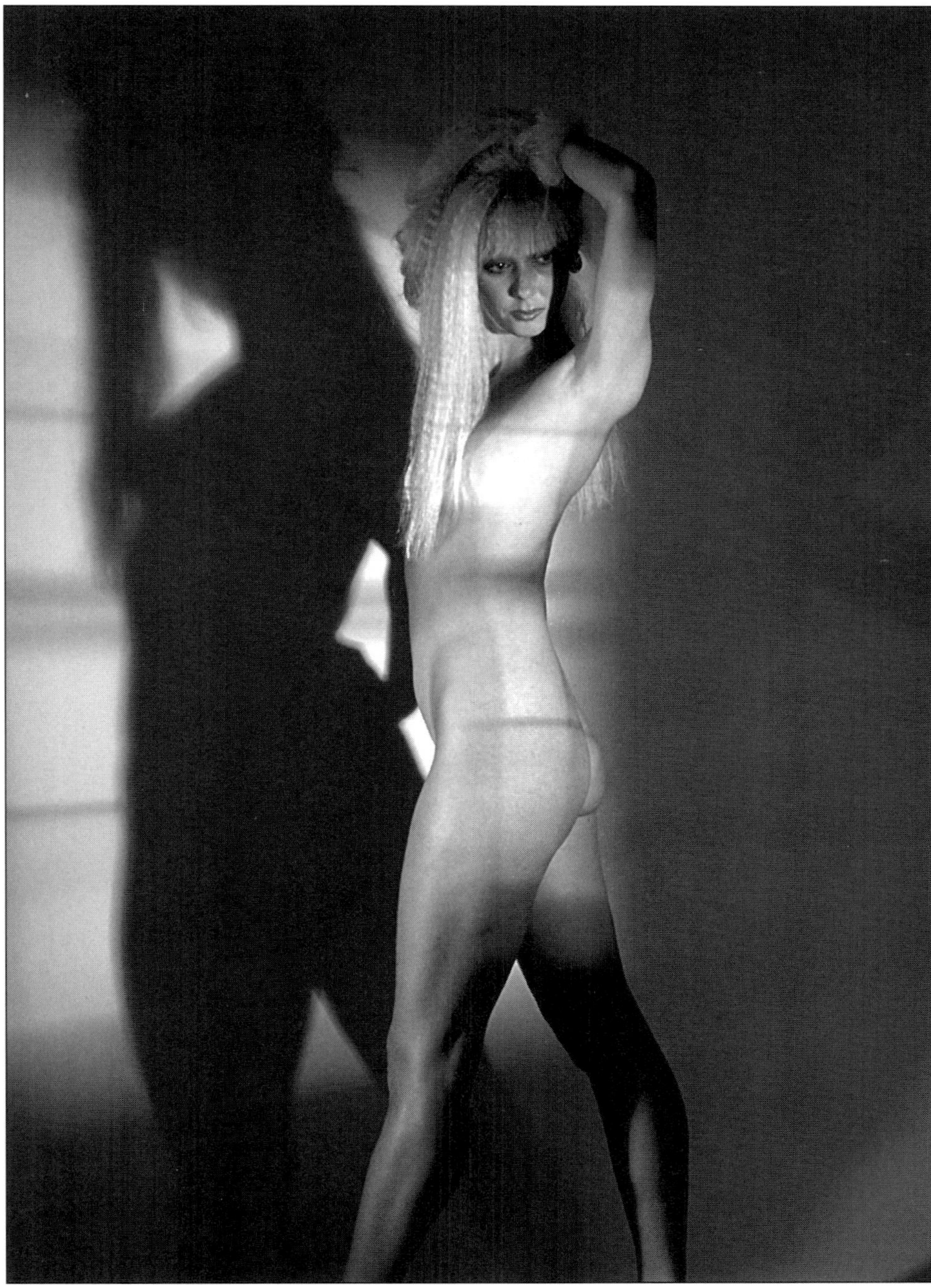

room sizes, ceiling heights, location and size of furniture, whether furniture will have to be moved, the theme or style of each room, and so on.

Spend enough time in the home so that you are familiar with the surroundings and have a good impression of what to expect when you come back to photograph. You want to know exactly where you'll be setting up your equipment and shooting, and how you are going to work with and around certain items in the home that may offer potential problems, such as large, bulky furniture.

Also familiarize yourself with the location of electrical outlets and, if you plan to use daylight, window sizes, the directions they face, and the best time of day to get the most light from them.

By taking these advance precautionary steps, you'll be better prepared to move more quickly on the day of the actual photo session. In addition, you'll be able to predict the photographic results with a better degree of accuracy.

The Setting May Dictate the Mood

Shooting in a subject's home will frequently not give you the luxury of choice. Typically, when shooting in your studio, you will first decide on the type of look you're after, then look for a subject that

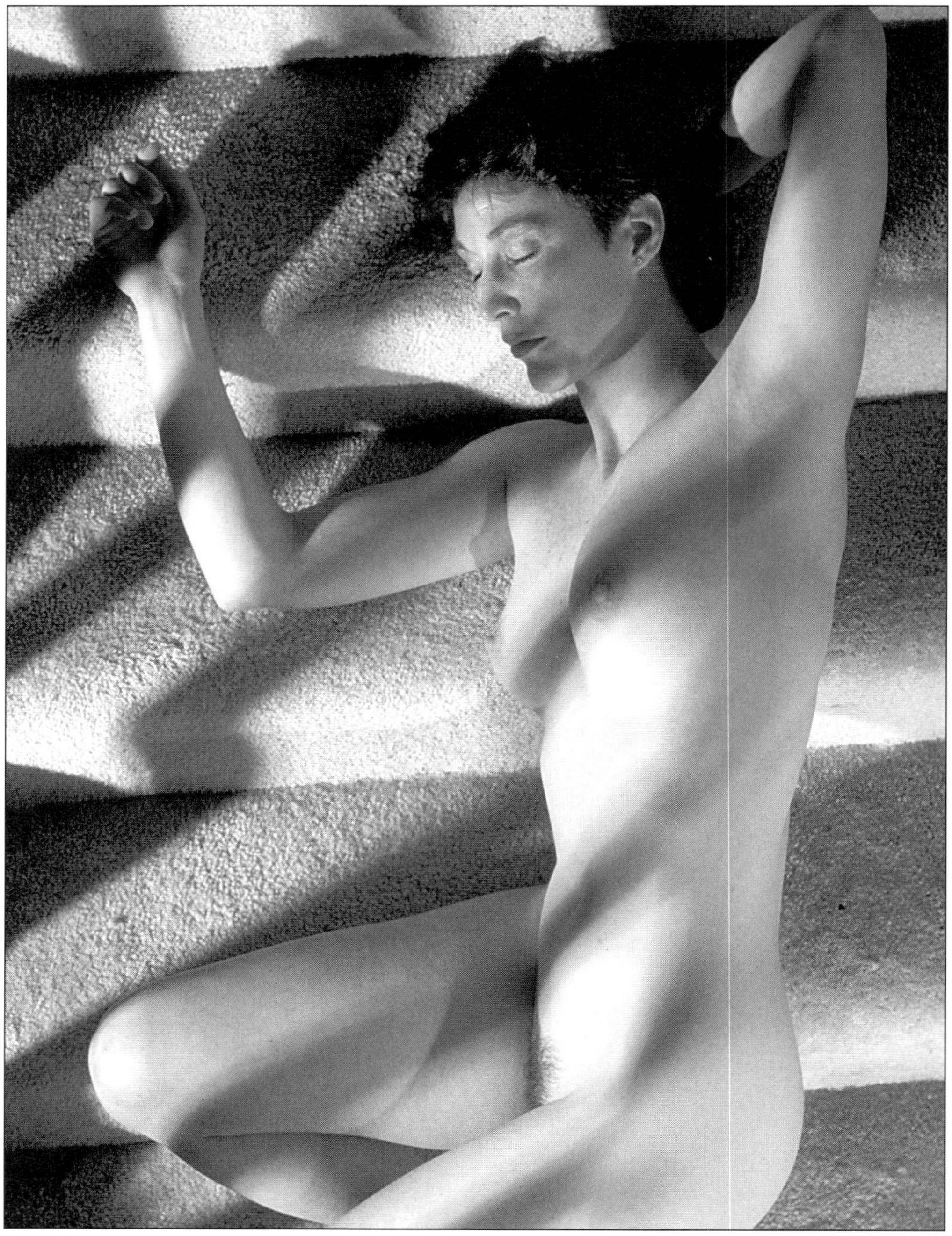

will fit into that type of concept. Next, you will fashion a setting which will be in keeping with the chosen subject and concept. However, when shooting in someone's home, things will usually be different. You will usually have little latitude for making drastic changes to someone's home and will generally have to work with the available decor as best you can.

Subject's Home and Privacy

In your own home or studio, privacy is almost guaranteed. However, photo sessions at a subject's home will not automatically offer this luxury. A subject's children, spouse, friends, or neighbors may come in and out of the shooting site with little to no warning or they may wish to just stand around and watch. This can be very disrupting for both you and the subject and have an adverse effect on the photo results.

Our best advice is to discuss and resolve these problems with your subject before the actual photo session begins. At the very least, attempt to have an understanding with your subject to keep intrusions and interruptions to a minimum.

Other Location Site Photography

You can go almost anywhere — a beach, a park, a deserted farmhouse, a forest, a waterfall, a rocky knoll, a warehouse, office, and so on — and produce beautiful figure studies.

Because of these great choices, you shouldn't automatically latch onto the first location you think of or even encounter. Visit many areas and choose selectively after giving much thought to the types of images you want to create.

Keep in mind that outdoor and location site photography is going to offer you the following:

1. New and different challenges.
2. Involvement with the legal concept of public nudity.
3. Greater concerns over a subject's privacy.
4. Greater concerns over a subject's safety and well-being.
5. Great concerns over the weather.
6. Different lighting problems to solve.
7. A requirement to get advance permission to photography.

Dealing with all of these variables might cause you to become disheartened, but don't. The end results will usually be worth the trouble.

The Challenges

Unlike your studio, each new outdoor location site you go to will be different and offer new photographic problems to solve: lighting, weather, onlookers, and so on.

However, these are all part of the special challenges to location photography; challenges which you should have planned and prepared for, long before the day of the actual photo session. If you have planned well, then on the day of the actual shoot, you should be able to go to your chosen site, set up your equipment, and pose and photograph your subject with very little delay, doubt or confusion.

However, even though this may be a sound game plan, there may be one more challenge that you might not be able to thoroughly prepare for and this will often be the subject herself.

It's one thing to ask a subject to pose in the nude, in the security and privacy of your studio (or her own home) but it's quite another to ask her to pose in public. Some subjects may initially be very reluctant to be photographed in public environments and may require a lot of reassurance before they agree — if they ever do.

For others, there will be little problems; they'll jump at the chance. This is because there is often a special attraction to shooting outdoors or in a strange location site which sparks a subject's interest: a subject may feel that she is truly going to commune with nature or

"...keep intrusions and interruptions to a minimum."

Opposite page: *Even though you may have previously scouted a subject's home and have definite ideas of where and how you are going to shoot, always keep your eyes open for other shooting possibilities on the day of the photo session. In this case, we noticed strong, graphic shadows on the stairs which were created by the sun streaming though the living room window. Working quickly, we were able to set up shot using this natural light with one electronic flash as a fill light source. It was placed to the right of the camera-subject axis and directed toward the back of the subject. It was covered with an amber gel and its power was adjusted to provide two f-stops less light than the natural light.*

"Be acutely sensitive about a subject's need for privacy..."

that she will be engaging in something that is a little off-beat, provocative or even naughty.

As many models can tell you, disrobing and posing nude outdoors can give a subject a wonderful feeling of freedom and sheer exhilaration. It can help lead to vital, exciting images, often with a wide variety of poses, in a very short time period. A subject may even project a facet of her personality that might be otherwise concealed during studio photography. Take advantage of this condition if and when it occurs. It can lead to some dynamic, stunning, and joyful images.

Public Nudity

In almost every state we are familiar with, there is some type of prohibition (some state law or local ordinance) against public nudity. These various laws are often not consistent nor in harmony as to what constitutes public nudity. In the United States, there is no uniform criminal code. There is no one law which prevails and covers public nudity (nor for most all the criminal laws) for all the cities and states.

As a result, you often have where some activity (such as public nudity) is a crime in one city or state and not in others. Or, there might be confusion over terms and definitions. In the case of public nudity, there often are problems regarding such things as what constitutes a public area? and when is a body legally nude?

For example, assume that you have positioned a nude subject on a beach, near water's edge and she is waiting to be photographed. Assume further that the beach property that you and she are on is owned by a prominent hotel chain. Is she on public property? Is she nude? Yes, to both questions.

However, is she guilty of violating the public nudity law? Maybe. A lot is going to depend upon the local ordinance or state law that exists in that particular area. It may require the existence of one more legal element before you can definitively say that a crime has been committed: the presence of at least one more human being in the immediate area (such as a nearby onlooker).

What if the land that you and she were on was in fact your own land and hence private property? Would she now be in violation of the public nudity law if she was nude? Maybe. Again, it will depend on the law in your area, how it has been written, and how it has been interpreted in the past.

As a result of this legalistic turmoil, you should check in your area to see what the law is before you go outdoors for a nude photo session. It could be tragic for you to take your subject on location (even inside a public building, such as an office building) only to have her (and maybe you too) arrested. Not only could it prove costly to you, but at the very least you could lose credibility, and probably a client.

Privacy

Be acutely sensitive about a subject's need for privacy when outdoors or at a strange location site.

When shooting in an area that could be accessible to the general public (such as at a public beach or city or state park), it's advisable to take someone along with you to watch out for possible intruders. This helper need not be a witness to the actual photo shoot, but would merely alert you about the approach of anyone who is not to be involved in the photo session. For best results, we have found that hiring an off-duty police officer is a great deterrent to intruders and onlookers. It also goes far in making the subject feel very safe.

Without such a safeguard, you might well find yourself being interrupted by unwitting and unwanted intruders. If you are, handle such intrusion politely but quickly. Also make sure to instruct your subject in advance to cover herself the moment either one of you are aware of any intruders.

Then explain to the intruders what, in general you're doing (to satisfy their curiosity), that you are taking artistic figure photographs, and that you'll wait until they leave to continue. Whatever you do, don't attempt to continue with the photo session until the intruders have long left your site. At the very least, it may

Opposite page: *Outdoor locations offer new photographic problems to solve: lighting, weather, onlookers, and so on. However, these are all part of the special challenges to location photography; challenges which you should have planned and prepared for, long before the day of the actual photo session.*

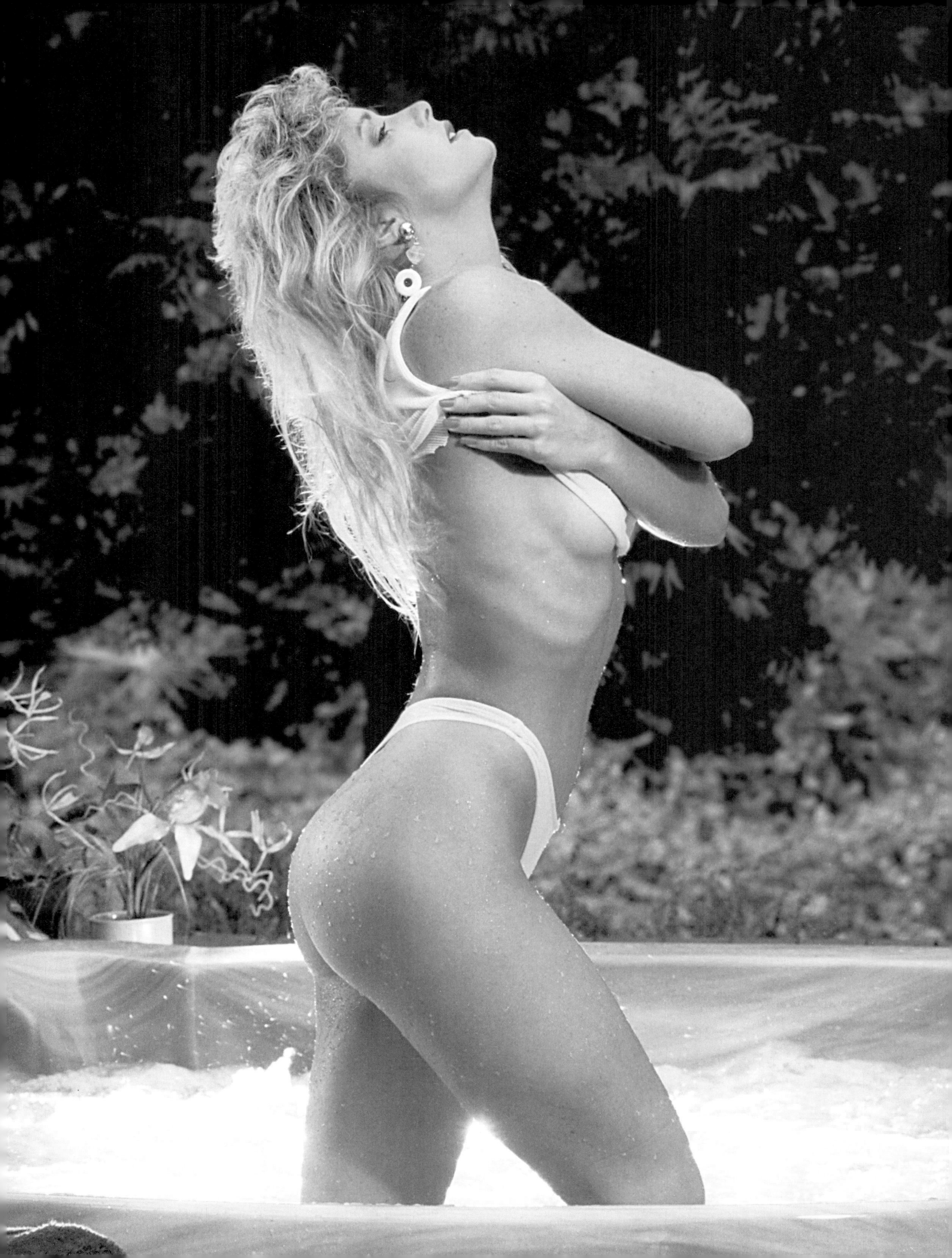

"You always want your subject warm, dry, and comfortable."

put your subject in an embarrassing situation. If the intruders don't leave within a reasonable length of time, then you should pack up, move to another location site or abandon that day's shooting.

A Subject's Well-Being

When you are doing a professional photo session for a commercial account with experienced, trained models, it is generally expected that either you or the company that has hired you will have one or more attendants available for the exclusive benefit of the models. These attendants will usually have just one major function...cater to the needs of the models.

When you are doing nude photos for your own pleasure or portfolio, or even if the subject has hired you to take photos, then you must be responsible for the comfort and safety of your subjects. Accordingly, it'll be advisable to have a personal assistant with you, not only for legal reasons, but also as a general helper.

Keep in mind, that in most states you're going to be more or less responsible for the subject's safety and well being during the entire time she is in your company. This means that from the time she has arrived at your studio through and including the time when you return from your location shoot, you're going to have some degree of responsibility (depending upon your state's laws) for the subject's safety, well-being and care.

This is especially true, and the degree of care you must take will generally be higher, if you have been hired to photograph the subject.

You should only seek shooting location areas where you feel confident, that appear, and are known to be safe, and that offer no conditions which might cause the subject harm.

The locations chosen should pose no threat to your subject's feeling of well-being. You cannot afford to have strangers looking on, intruding or posing any type of threat during a nude photo session, have the police harassing you because of your public display, or even have your subject trekking over precarious natural or man-made obstacles, all in the name of art's sake.

Avoid having a subject become overly exposed to heat, cold, dampness, high wind, and insects or any other undesirable condition or thing. Apart from all other considerations (including legal), any discomfort caused in such ways will usually reveal itself adversely in your photo results.

In order to help ensure the comfort of a subject when on location, it's a good idea to take along a supply of creature-comforts; items such as makeup, a hair dryer, baby oil, baby powder, rain gear, a robe, blankets, an umbrella, towels, hot or cold beverages, and snacks, just to name a few.

During the course of actual photography, it would be ideal if you could have your assistant constantly attend to the needs of your subject. You always want your subject warm, dry, and comfortable — at least between shots. You also want to assure her that you are concerned for her welfare and safety. Gestures such as these go far in having a subject work very hard for you and this, of course, is what helps to produce stunning imagery.

You'll also find it very beneficial if you can take a van on location, rather than a car. If there is no other spot on site suitable for your subject to retire to, a van is a great private place for her to prepare for the photo session, to disrobe, get dressed again, freshen up during the course of the day's shoot, and rest and relax between shots.

Weather Conditions

Many ardent photographers are accustomed to going to great lengths to capture an image. More than once we have braved a storm, photographed in the rain, hung from a tree, perched precariously off the side of a hill, all in quest for the "great photo."

This course of action is all well and good when the subject matter is an inanimate object or scene. We might even expect the same type of commitment when we work with experienced, professional models who are being paid to help us accomplish a certain photograph. However, when working with inexperienced, non-professional subjects, especially in figure photography, one needs to be a lot more considerate.

Since weather conditions are just another one of those factors which you will not be able to control when on location, the subject should be prepared, well in advance, to have you cancel the photo session at the last minute due to bad or inappropriate weather.

Without such advance notice, the subject may not be so willing to go along with your canceling the session if the weather starts to deteriorate. This too may influence your future business dealings with your subject.

In addition, you have another big concern: your equipment. In our opinion, you absolutely never want to put any of your equipment in harm's way and otherwise expose it to any sort of adverse weather. Accordingly, we always travel on location with a quantity of large (16x20 inch and larger) plastic bags. The moment there is a hint of moisture in the air, we will stop shooting (at least temporarily), cover all of our equipment with the plastic bags, and seek shelter. Here again is where it is nice to have someone with you to help. While you protect and take care of all of your equipment, your assistant can be caring for the subject, or vice-versa.

Illumination

When doing photography outdoors, one of the things you'll have little control over is the natural lighting. The prevailing weather will play a big part in the type of lighting you will be facing and it may not always be as you had hoped or planned. These conditions merely give you more challenges and is one of the reasons that location (outdoor) photography is so interesting.

In our area, Southern Florida, it could be raining heavily one minute and bright and sunny the next. Accordingly, we usually prepare for a number of different lighting conditions and rapid lighting changes. Both we and our subjects must be easily and readily adaptable, so that we can quickly change between different types of photos and atmospheres and moods.

If we went on site with just one photo concept in mind and the weather changed on us while we were shooting, we would be out of luck. That's why we advise preparing for different photo concepts: one that would be appropriate in a rainy atmosphere, one for a gray-sky day, and perhaps, one for a sunny day.

In Chapter 7, we'll discuss lighting in more detail.

Official Approval May Be Needed

If you have any doubt about the private or public nature of the outdoor site you have chosen to shoot, seek out the owner of the property in advance and get permission to photograph on the property. This need for permission, incidentally, includes the national and state parks.

The situation that you want to avoid is one where you have made extensive preparations to shoot, have arrived at the designated site, spent time setting up all of your gear and preparing the subject, only to learn that you are trespassing and are forced to quit. Not only does this waste time but it may cause you some embarrassment with your subject. What's equally as bad is encountering an unexpected cost simply because you failed to inquire, in advance, whether you needed permission to photograph.

For example, we know of a situation where a photographer, his two assistants and the subject went to a remote and apparently abandoned farm house to conduct a photo session. Since the farm house was obviously deserted and had been for sometime, the photographer thought that it would not be necessary to find the owner and ask permission to shoot on the property. About 40 to 50 minutes into the photo shoot, the owner of the property showed up along with a deputy sheriff. The owner acknowledged that had the photographer sought permission to shoot on his land beforehand, he probably would have granted it free; however, the owner demanded $300 or else he was going to have them arrested. The photographer paid.

"...get permission to photograph on the property."

CHAPTER FOUR

The Shooting Session

There is definitely a need to prepare and plan for a nude figure study photo session. Without a game plan to follow, photographic results would be left too much to chance.

"Chance" photography is really a type which should be reserved for the non-professional. Why? Because chance photography is an approach which generally leads to inconsistent, unpredictable and, in the end, poor results.

Preparation Before a Shoot

Although many preparatory aspects for figure photography are discussed in depth throughout this book, in this chapter it's important for you to consider the following:

1. Planning.
2. The best time for a location shoot.
3. Preparing the shoot-site in advance and then testing it.
4. Equipment and props.
5. Preparing an outline.
6. Preparing a pose list.

Planning

Some years ago, while studying with a very successful New York still-life-product photographer, we had an opportunity to learn a valuable lesson: good photography is planned for.

During our tutelage, we were with him when he got an assignment to photograph three rather bland and innocuous looking cans for a national company. We carefully watched as he spent almost two full business days planning and preparing for the shot. He made sketches, arranged the product dozens of times, changed cameras, lenses, angles, lighting setups, exposure, and so on, until he had the combination that he thought would produce the image he had originally conceived in his mind's eye.

Then, on the third day, he finally took his first shots. Although his preparation took him almost two days, the final shots only took him about 30 minutes to execute. The results were exactly the way he had wanted.

We know that you won't be spending two or three days preparing a subject for a nude shot. But you could easily spend many hours, if not several days, thinking or planning how you are going to photograph a subject, in thinking about a given setting or even in preparing a set.

The Best Time for a Location Shoot

When doing location photography, the time selected to take photos is often critical. Don't assume that you automatically know what the best time of day will be — it can vary from location to location, week to week and, of course, from season to season.

"Visit the area a few days in advance..."

Visit the area a few days in advance of the planned photo session and view for yourself the conditions of the light at the time of day you initially have in mind. Depending upon the hour you have chosen and based upon your examination of the site, you may have to change the intended hour of your shoot to a time more suitable for the type of image you are seeking.

Many of the photographic books we have read have indicated that there were only two preferred times of the day best-suited for outdoor photographs of people: when the sun is low in the sky, either very early in the morning or late in the afternoon.

This statement might be true when you are thinking of taking mere portraits; however, for nude photography the statement is false. The best time of day to capture nude images is any time of day you think is best. It will all depend on the type and character of lighting that you're seeking.

Another of our mentors — an excellent scenic photographer — told us that he often spent several days scouting an area. During this period, he would study the light as it changed and played upon the various elements in the scene before he would even think about taking a single photo.

Then, of the dozen or more shots that he would eventually take, only a few would actually represent the scene as he had pre-visualized it. To him, spending many hours per day, for several days, just to study the light, was not only normal but necessary.

But, (and he would stress this point) the time of day which he had chosen to take his photos might not be suitable for us; we might opt for different times of the day and different types of lighting, depending upon the type of image and photographic statement we sought.

In this respect, doing nude studies on location is no different. You must select the time of day that will best serve the types of photographs you are planning to shoot. For one situation you might need a hard, overhead light with lots of contrast. This type is usually found on a cloudless afternoon.

On the other hand, a soft, gentle light that is more typical of evening may be better suited for another subject. Whatever the type of lighting you need for the type of images you intend to create, don't rush it nor compromise it. Don't choose just any type of light to take a few quick shots. Choosing the right type of light (and this means both time of day and weather conditions) is as important as choosing the correct subject.

When you are outdoors, you cannot move the natural light source about; you must adapt to it. To adapt, you must be familiar with the nature of the movement of the sun through the sky at various times of the year.

It's one thing to read about lighting conditions in a book and quite another to experience them. You must know for yourself what the conditions will be in your chosen area, how long the type of lighting you seek will last, and what effect it will have on your subject, the photographic concept and the photo results.

Advance Preparation

Whether you are shooting in your studio or on location, don't wait until the last moment to ready the shooting area for photography. Non-professional subjects, who are usually nervous anyway, might become even more anxious if they are required to wait too long while you prepare a site for photography. In addition, be sure that the site is workable, both from a physical as well as a purely photographic standpoint.

"...be sure that the site is workable..."

For example, one of the permanent sets we built in our studio is a shower set, with real hot-water capability. When it was first tested, we found ourselves faced with a series of problems. We got no hot water from the shower head; the shower head and floor leaked in several places, flooding a portion of our studio; certain lighting setups could not be employed because they produced hot spots or unwanted reflections on the tile in the shower.

Although the shower set was initially completed and ready for use late one Friday evening, it actually took us about two weeks of additional time, ironing out all of the problems, before the set was workable and ready to be used for a serious photo session. Had we used this new set on a paying client when it was first done, without first testing it fully, it would have led to an interrupted session, a disgruntled subject, and some rather disastrous photo results.

When shooting on location, especially in the outdoors, it even becomes more critical to ready the shooting area in advance and test it. Why? Because you have much less control and predictability than a setting in a studio atmosphere. Therefore, it becomes especially important to make

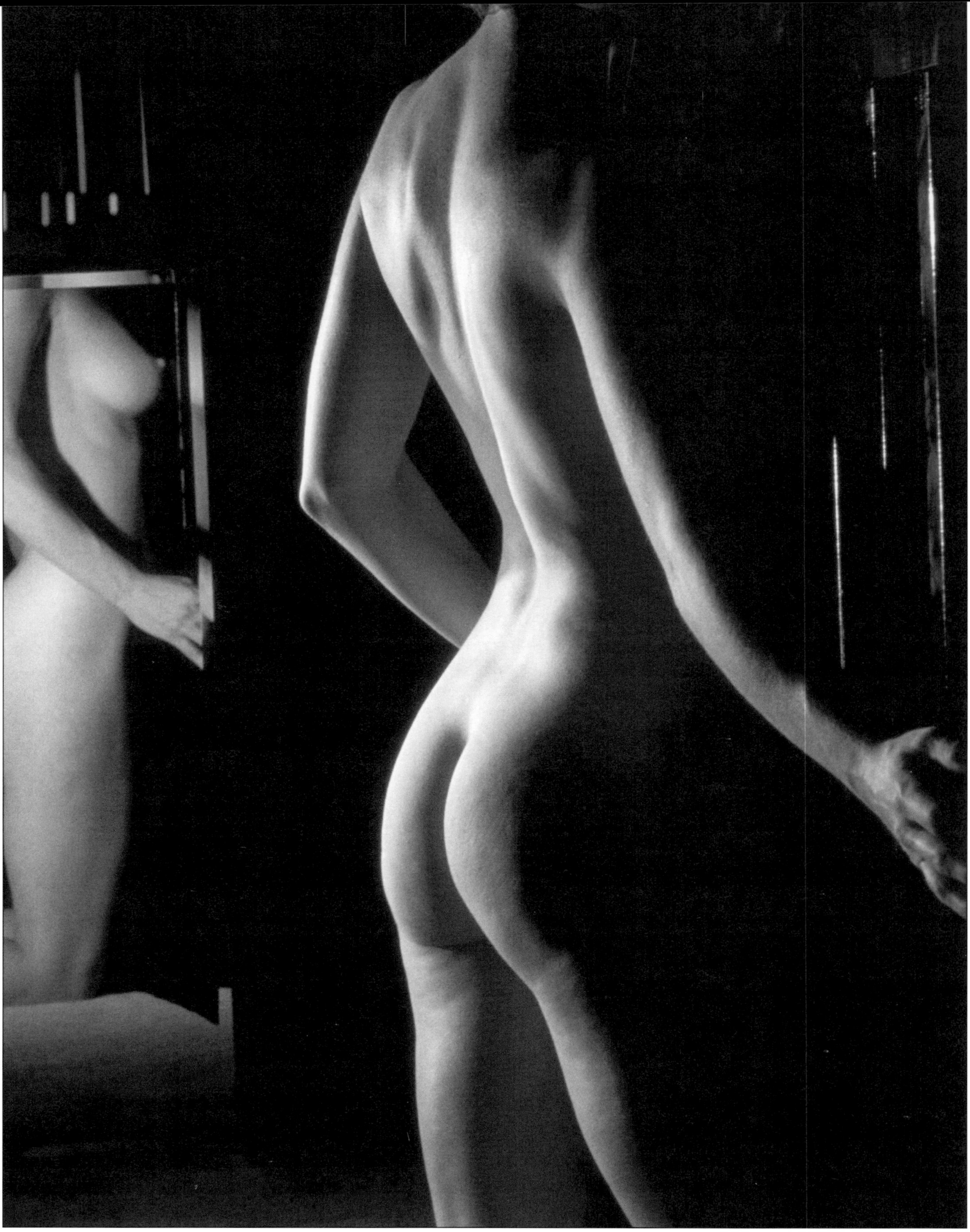

Above: *A home environment can offer many potential settings for nude studies. A game plan is essential to get the most out of these potential settings. We love working with mirrors — however, there are some precautions. First, make certain that you see no part of your own reflection in the your camera's viewfinder. Also be sure that none of your lights or lighting equipment are reflected toward the camera. This will require choosing the light locations carefully, bearing in mind the basic rule that the angle of incidence is equal to the angle of reflection. If light strikes a mirror at a 20-degree angle, it will reflect from that mirror at a 20-degree angle.*

plans, preparations, and tests before actually starting serious photography.

Equipment And Props

Just as your location site and setting should be readied before you start to shoot, so also should your equipment be fully checked and prepared. You should know, with reasonable certainty and in advance, which cameras, lenses, meters, filters, lights, and other pieces of equipment are going to be used.

Check to make sure this equipment is clean and functioning properly. In addition, pack or lay out your equipment so that you know exactly where to find each item with minimal delay. An actual photo session — whether on location, in a studio or a home — is not the time or place to start searching through camera bags, looking for a much-needed filter, lens, or accessory. You should know exactly where everything is and everything should be at your fingertips.

There is another concept to be aware of: familiarity with equipment. Unless you and the subject are aware that the session is to be a purely experimental one, an actual shoot is not the right occasion for testing equipment or lighting, or for using new items. You must know which items of equipment are compatible for use with each other, and the results that each item you intend to use will achieve.

Of course, you must also know your basic photographic rules, regulations and techniques. If a session calls for some special technique or approach with which you are not familiar and comfortable, brush up on it well beforehand. Make some practical tests, if possible.

Backup equipment — Most photographers have good reason to believe in Murphy's Law: if something can go wrong, it will. Therefore, it's just good business to always have backup equipment immediately available.

This means having enough equipment with you that would enable you to complete your photography, even if all your primary equipment had failed. For example, you should have at least two cameras, lenses, spare lights, extra batteries, additional sync cords, and power cables. You will also be well advised to have a good selection of props with you.

If you have constructed an entire photo session around a simple, single prop, such as a feather boa, and before or during the shooting it suddenly becomes lost, soiled or damaged, the session would have to be abandoned. Being prepared with alternative props (as well as picture concepts too) will help to avoid such a dilemma.

In order to help us be better prepared for an outdoor photo shoot — at least when it comes to having equipment with us — we always think and ask ourselves, what if? What if some of our equipment breaks or doesn't work during a shoot? Do we have backups? What if the place is dirty? Do we have cleaning materials with us? What if the lighting is too blue? Do we have colored gels or filters, to correct the lighting?

Admittedly, one could go on forever with speculations and worries such as these, but it is important to be as prepared as possible, to ensure that the job can be completed with the least amount of time and trouble.

Make a checklist — Until equipment and prop needs become second nature, it's a good idea to prepare a checklist of all of the equipment and props needed for any location shoot.

This will help ensure that equipment and related items will not be forgotten. Eventually, after you have prepared a number of equipment checklists for a number of location shoots, equipment needs will become automatic.

Work from a centralized spot. — To help you avoid forgetting anything you might need, we offer an additional hint: work from a central location.

Once you have made your equipment checklist, and hours before (if not the day before) you are to leave for a location shoot, go back and physically put every item on your list in some very obvious and central spot in your home or studio: on the floor near your front door or next to the door of your garage, and so on. The whole idea is to have just one spot where all of your equipment is set; you'll have only one spot to check just before you depart for your location shoot.

Prepare An Outline

We have repeatedly stressed that effective preparation is an essential element in seriously executed figure photography. To help you attain your goal, (at least in the beginning of your endeavors) prepare

"...everything should be at your fingertips."

- **Always have backup equipment immediately available.**

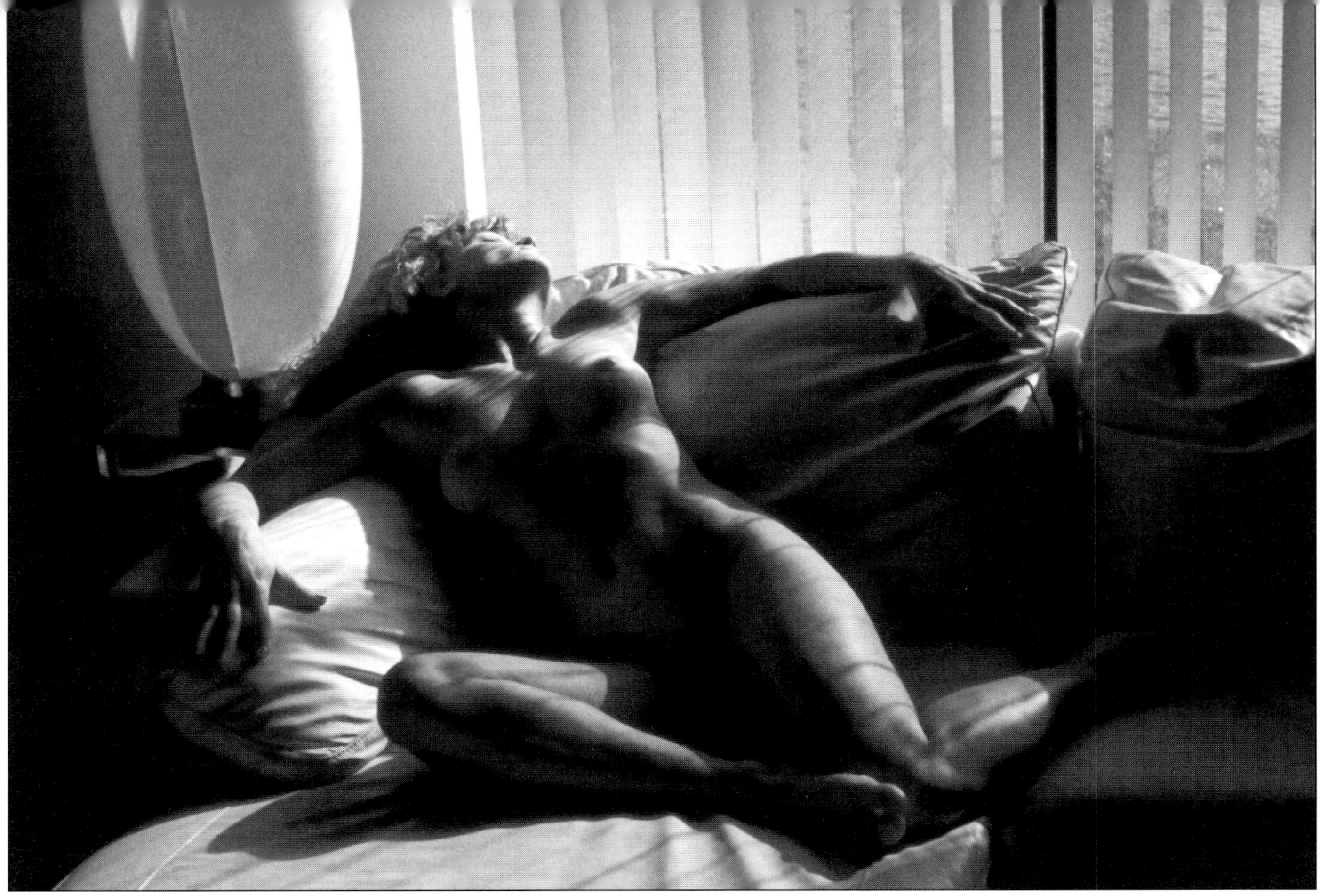

Above, Below and Opposite page: *Once you find a suitable location where all the elements work for you, exhaust the setting's photographic potential before moving on to another location. After the "obvious" shot has been taken, change your camera angle, lens focal length, camera-to-subject distance, lighting, props, filtration, cropping, and so on, to achieve different looks.*

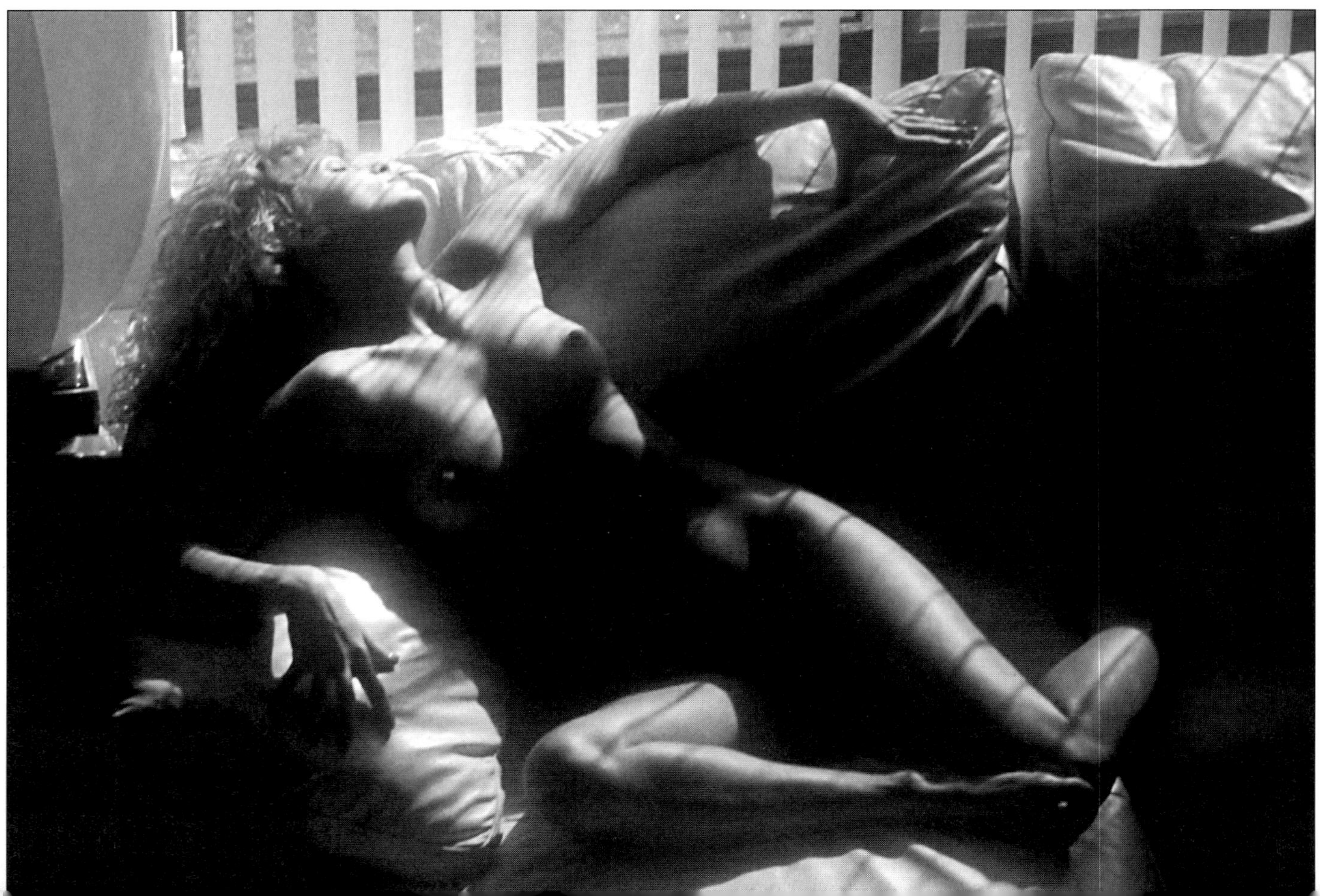

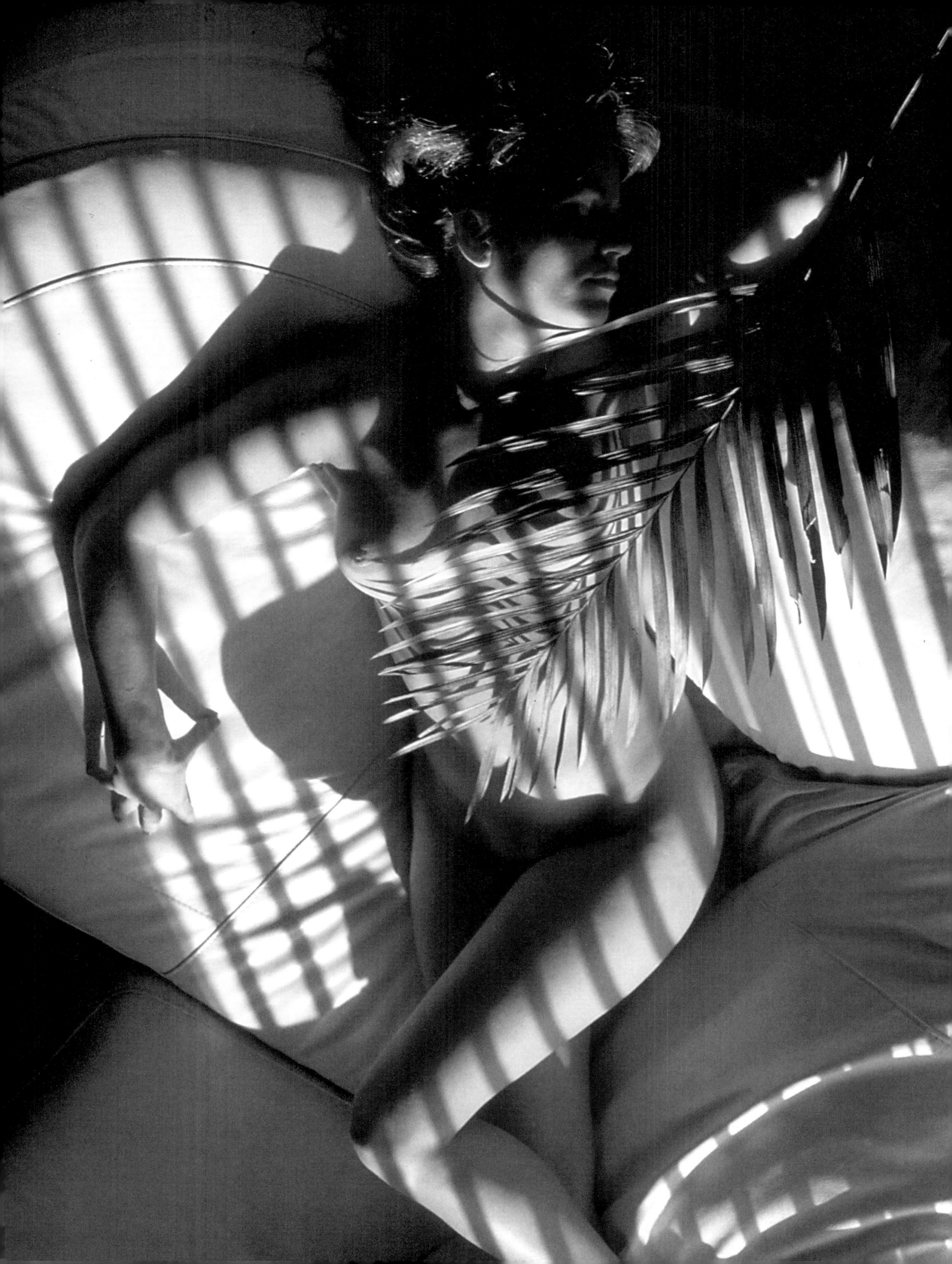

"...the outline will serve as a general plan..."

• The game plan for a photo session is very important for successful photographic results.

an outline of what you hope to photographically accomplish with a subject during any given photographic session. This does not mean to say that you cannot deviate from your plan during the actual course of your photography. You can, and often should. Be flexible and open for other ideas that come up.

But the outline will serve as a general plan to your intended sequence of events while you're behind the camera. The outline should be like the notes used by a speaker. It will serve as a guide or reminder of what you have to do and when.

It should contain information—in general terms—about poses, settings, props, accessories, and lighting setups.Not only will such an outline benefit you in increasing your efficiency during any photo session, it will also go far in building credibility with most any subject.

During an actual photo shoot, you never want a model or client to think that you are not sure about what you want to do next. Such an impression could damage your credibility, and the outcome of a session.

Prepare A Pose List

At the time you prepare an outline (which should include generalized information about a forthcoming photo session), you should prepare a rather detailed pose list.

It will help make your photo session go more smoothly and efficiently. Whatever you do, make certain that the pose list you prepare contains more poses than you could reasonably expect to cover during any given session. This will keep you from running out of material (poses) during the course of any sitting. You'll never have to waste time thinking about what pose to do next while the subject stands idly by.

Poses beget poses — Don't be surprised if you start a photo session with a certain number of poses and end up having more poses than you started with.

During the course of actual photography, the subject might naturally adopt a number of different positions (poses) you had not thought of, but are extensions of your basic poses. Photograph them.

Keep in mind that it's creative to think of new and different poses to use during a session, but it's also creative to be able to recognize new poses when they happen spontaneously.

Posing, Lighting And Mood

Many photographers make the mistake of first setting up lighting and then constructing a setting without paying due regard for the lighting. Or, they will set up lighting for a subject and then trying to get the subject to adopt a pose which looks good, based upon the pre-structured lighting setup.

Both are wrong approaches. With seriously executed figure photography, the pose, intended mood, and the setting or scene should determine the lighting and not vice versa. For example, if you created an elaborate 19th-century setting indoors, it would often be inappropriate to have the subject illuminated by complex contemporary standards. Lighting that would simulate a simple and soft "north" light, or light simulating the light from a gas lamp might be most fitting.

The Game Plan during a Photo Session

There are certain tricks and secrets we have picked up over the years that have helped us conduct a figure study photo session.

1. Discussing creative goals.
2. Building a rapport.
3. Courtesy, tact, and language.
4. Working quickly.
5. Experimentation
6. Avoiding physical contact.
7. Controlling the duration of a photo session.
8. Awareness of the psychology of nude modeling.
9. Dealing with a subject's attitude.
10. Taking Polaroids.
11. Potpourri.

Discussing Creative Goals

Before any photo session begins, spend some time with your intended subject; explain the results you are seeking and how you intend to achieve them. After all, your model is going to be the vital, central part of the final image.

This also allows your model to express ideas on some possible poses or even settings and shots.

Even though your subjects may know little about photography, they might still

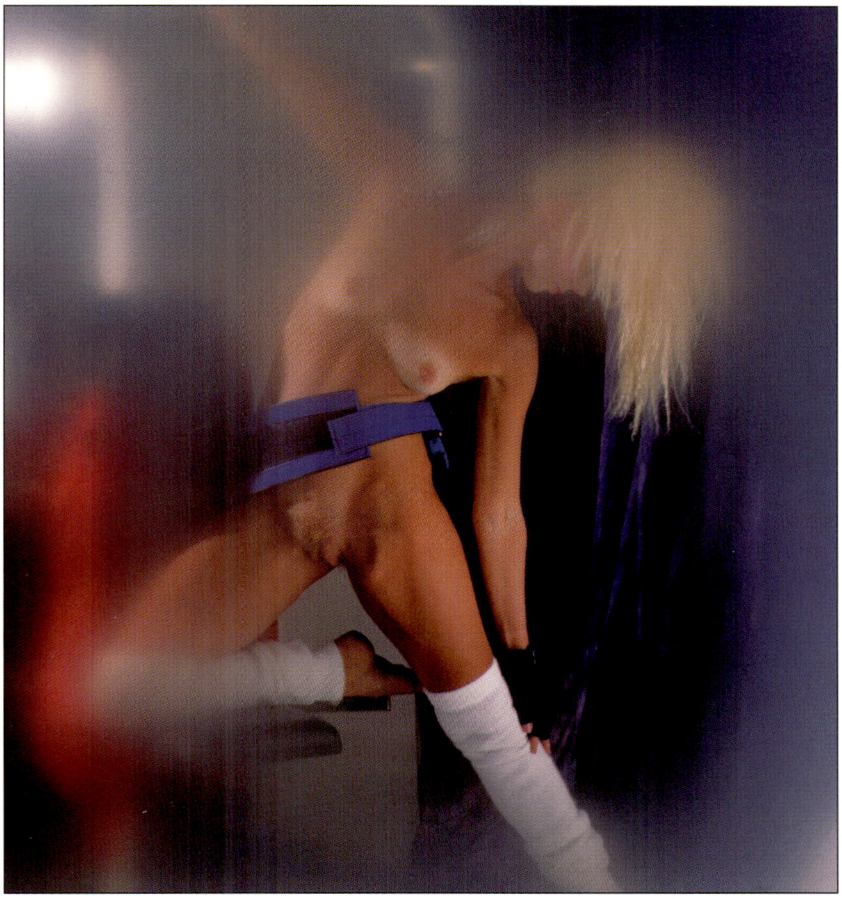

Above: *We burned a small hole in the center of a small piece of a plastic drop-cloth and placed it over the camera lens. The effect produced images in which much of the subject was in focus while the remainder went soft. The thin, plastic material we used is available from most paint-supply stores and costs less than one dollar for a 9 x 12-foot sheet.*
Right: *The imaginative photographer of the human figure can use all kinds or props and settings. The device we used to get the effect for this image was nothing more than a simple shower curtain. When you shoot through a textured material such as this, be sure that the subject's pose is such that the various parts of her body are distinctly recognizable. In addition to careful posing, this also usually demands fairly bold lighting. Notice the highlighting with unfiltered white lights of parts of the subject against an otherwise red background. The background lights were covered with red gels. No soft-focus filtration was needed for this shot.*

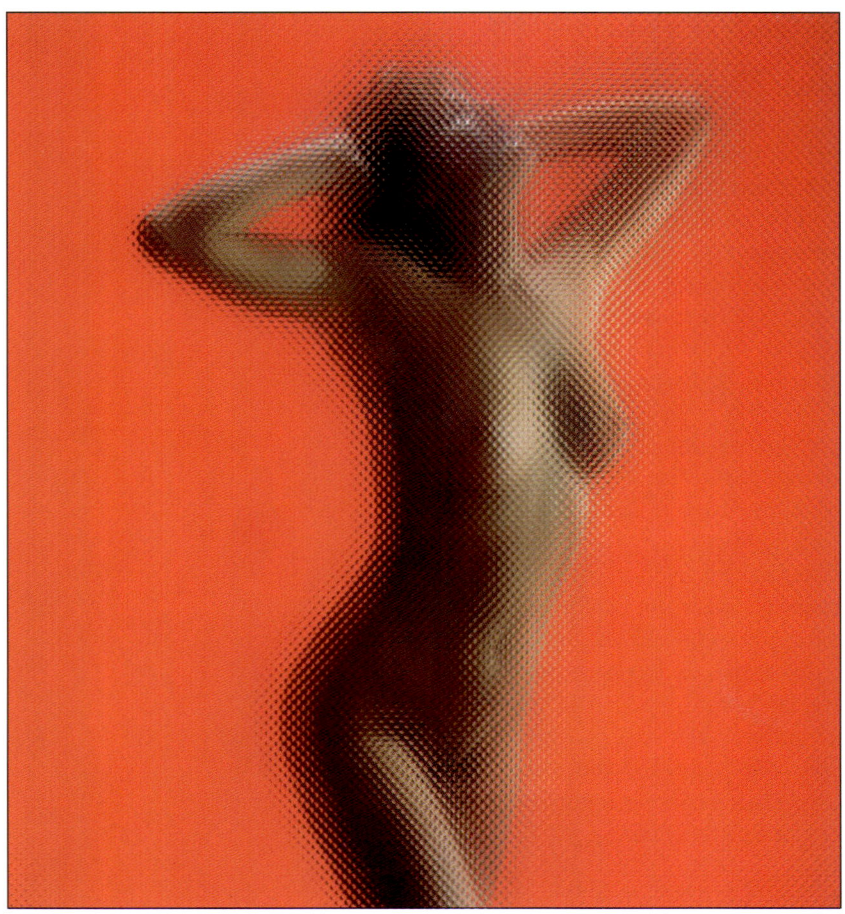

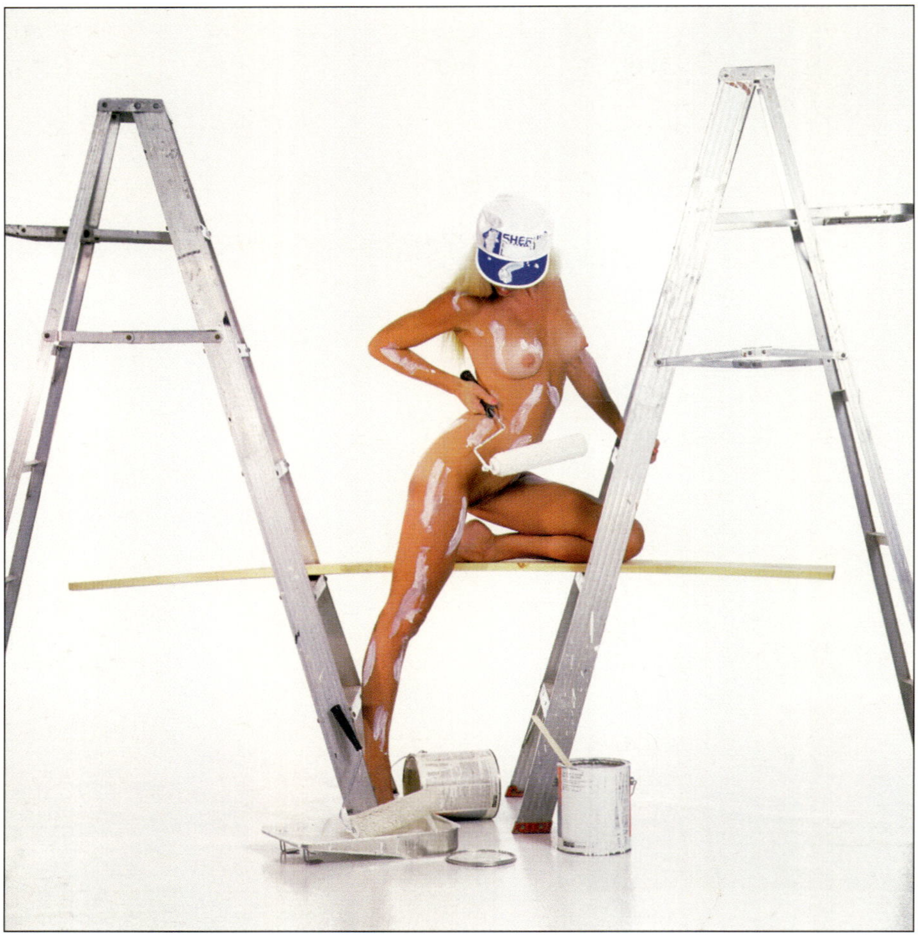

Above: *The subject in this shot, like all of our delightful and talented models in this book, was an untrained, non-professional model. The setting and props were simple and the entire low-budget shoot took no more than a couple of hours. Even though it was a low-budget shoot with a simple setting, there were many photographic possibilities. In a high-key setting of this kind, we're able to achieve about 20 totally different poses without changing our lighting or having the subject leave the general area.*

Right: *When we use colored lighting, we normally like to have white, unfiltered light illuminate at least some portion of the subject's body. In this case, the snooted accent light, to the right of the camera, was not color-gelled. Although the resulting rim light on the legs is not white, it is not as deeply magenta as other areas. The subtle color variation is achieved by carefully balancing the power of the various lights used. This variation adds further life and vitality to this image.*

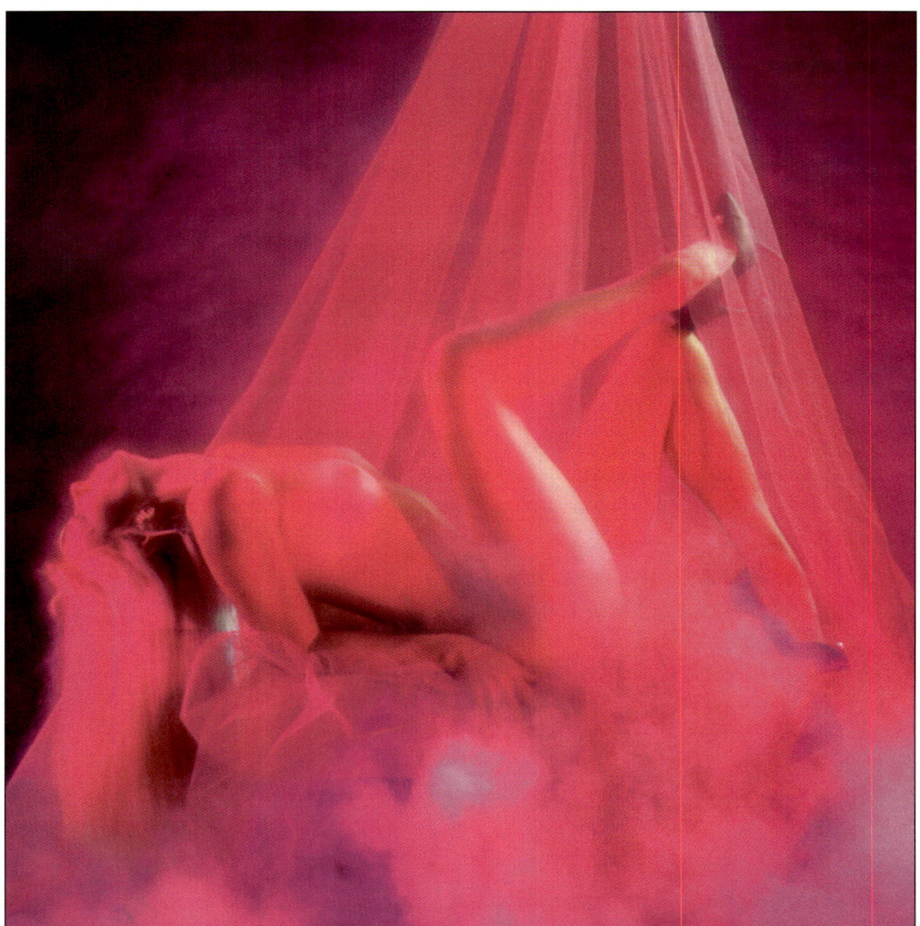

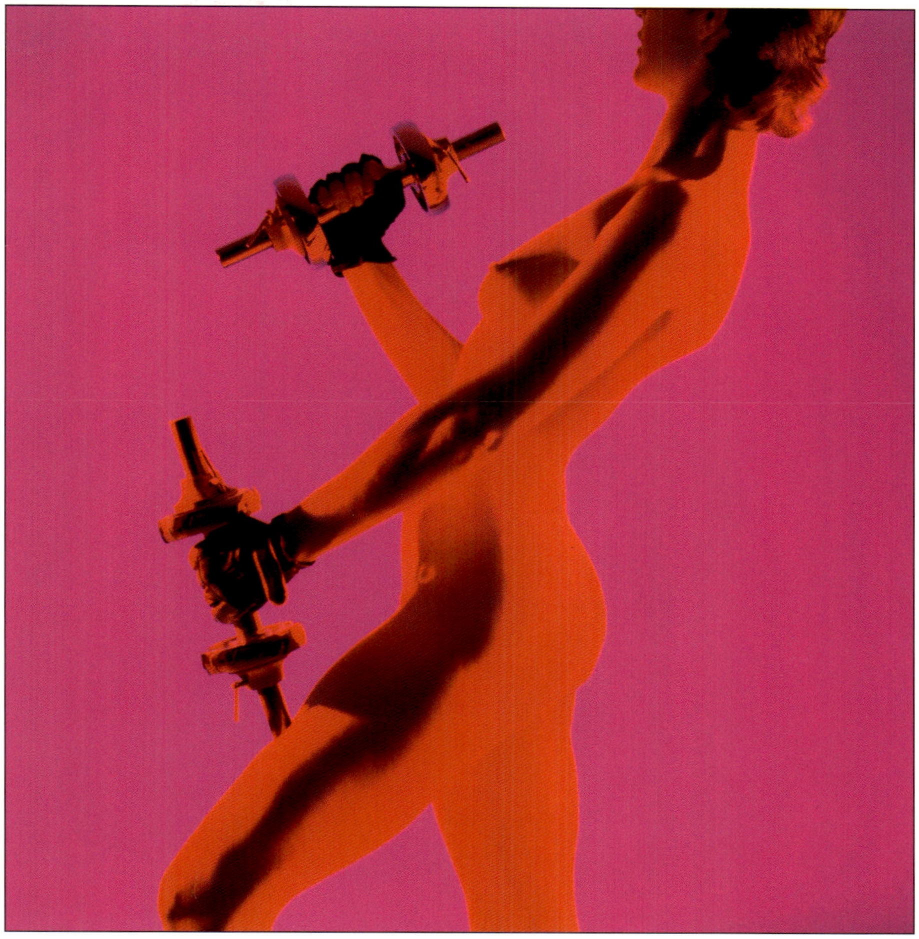

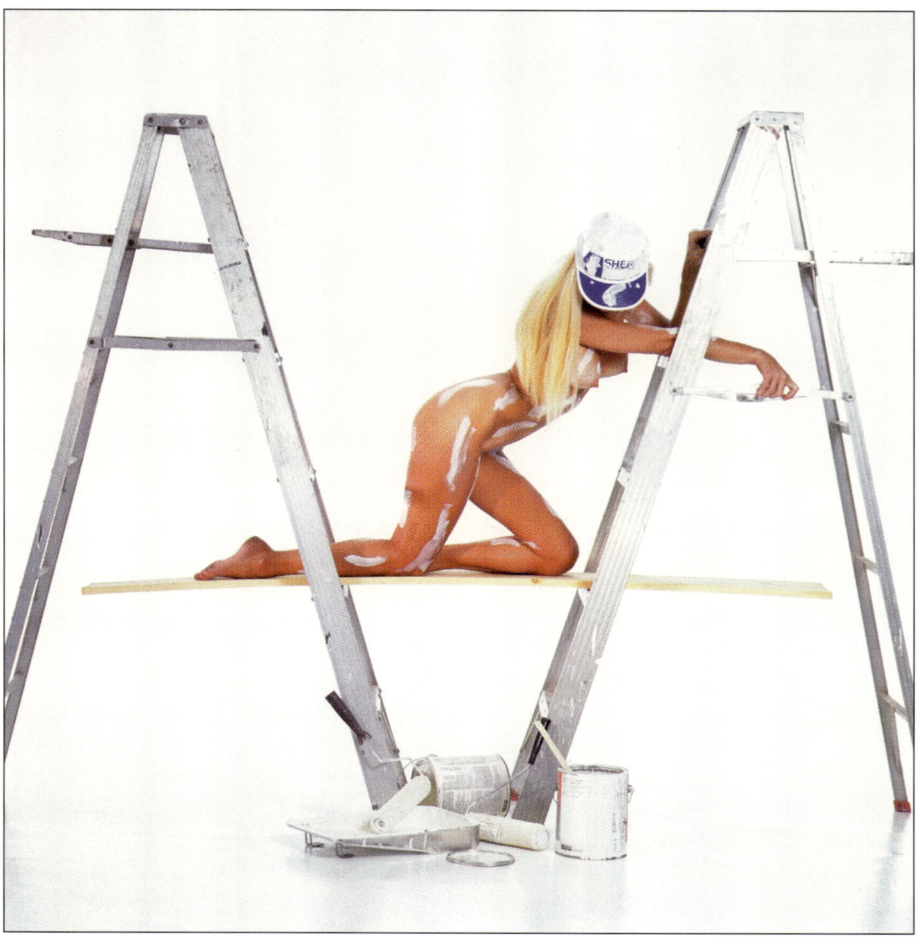

Above: *Most manufacturers of gels provide dozens of different colors to choose from, and often several tone and hue variations of each. For this image, a deep magenta gel was used on the background lights and orange-red gels were used on the main and fill lights. These colors were chosen to suggest energy and vitality. The discord between the colors helps to suggest the strain and effort of the physical workout the subject is engaged in. Don't be afraid to experiment with gels; be bold and don't hesitate to mix colors, even if the mixture seems to violate the "normal" rules of color coordination.*

Left: *This image was taken during the same session as the one on the opposite page. The inexpensive props helped to make this a low-budget shoot. A couple of old ladders, a paint roller or two, a couple of empty paint cans, a plank of wood, and a bit of white paint for the subject's body helped us to capture some dynamic high-key images. The body paint used was Tempera — a water-based, non-toxic paint, available at most art stores.*

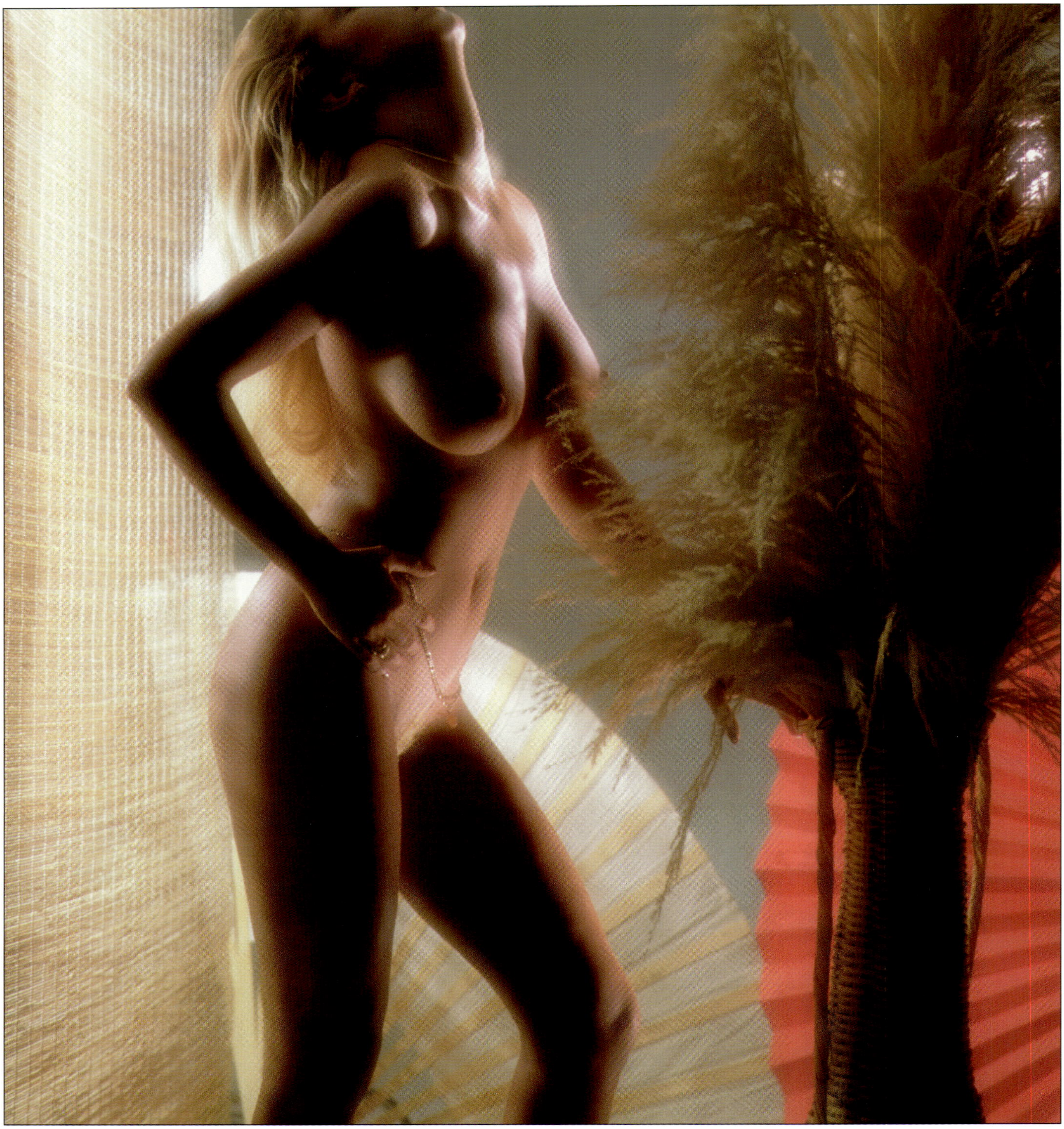

Above: *When shooting through a shoji screen, you should keep props to a minimum. However, when shooting with the screen to the side, as depicted in this image, we could afford to be more generous with our propping. We gave much more prominence to the plumes and basket than if we were shooting through the screen. We also thought that the colorful fans and the lines and texture of the screen itself were good items to either mirror or contrast with the texture, lines, and curves of the subject's figure. You will note that the props around and behind the subject are fully lit, while the subject herself is in low-key lighting, with only selected body parts accented by light. This gives the image added depth and dimension. Although this image was originally shot as a full-figure shot, the image looks better when it is cropped to include only the torso but not the head as you see in here. Usually all of our studio shots are well thought out in advance. Accordingly, we generally crop in the camera rather than after the shoot, in the printing stage. This procedure forces us into a discipline to see exactly what we want before we shoot, rather than manipulating our images at a later stage. Nonetheless, sometimes we will find, after a shot has been taken, that a particular image will look better if it is printed or presented in a more cropped fashion. Such was the case with this image. By eliminating the subject's face from the image completely, much more emphasis is placed on the body. The dramatic lighting provides beautiful modeling to the subject's body. Overall, these factors make this a lovely and stunning nude figure study.*

offer a suggestion or two which might spark an idea.

Building a Rapport

It's essential for a photographer to establish and maintain a good rapport with his or her model. In the beginning of your relationship, this might be hard to do: the model-photographer relationship is, quite naturally, at its most delicate and fragile posture at this point. To ensure the model's trust in a photographer's ability, motivation and intentions, among other things, we would suggest the following.

Get to know your subject — We strongly believe that consistently excellent photographic results cannot come about unless you can communicate with your subjects.

Before you ever get near your camera, spend some quality time with each of your subjects: talk about why they want to engage in this form of photography, which features they think are their best ones, whether they have specific poses or shots in mind, if there are certain body parts that they want concealed or emphasized, and so on. Usually this will take no longer than a few minutes—just long enough for you to get to know the subject to some extent. Your objective should be to gain some insight into each subject's personality before an actual shoot ever comes about.

This is also an excellent opportunity to have your subjects learn a little information on how you intend to take the shots, what, in general, is going to be involved and how you plan to solve certain specific problems that either you or your subject might think exist.

Give the subject an idea of the chain of events. In any case, try to avoid mere chitchat since clients usually see through that facade.

Also keep in mind that no matter how many people you may have assisting you during a photo session, there are just two key people: you (the photographer) and your subject. The best photographic results will come about only when you and the subject have a common understanding and share a common goal.

Use a long lens — I prefer using a long lens (150mm or longer) whenever we do figure photography. First, I like the way the human form records on film when I use a long lens, compared to the normal or even wide angles lenses. Secondly, by my using a long lens, a subject feels a degree of privacy and security. With a long lens on my camera, I'm able to keep the camera and myself at a relatively far distance from the subject. As a result, neither the camera nor I are intimidating; they won't feel as though their space is being invaded.

Discuss poses — Before you actually photograph a subject, discuss the poses you have in mind, at least in a general way. Inform her why you are choosing certain poses and what result you hope that each pose will yield.

Advise her that some of the poses you'll be choosing might be rather difficult for her to assume; some she may not be able to get into at all. Whatever you do, reassure her that such a condition is okay and expected. Inform her that not all subjects are able to get into all poses nor will all poses look good for all subjects. Such advance precautionary words will go far in maintaining rapport with the subject.

Demonstrate poses — Once the session starts, you or your assistant should demonstrate each pose that you want the subject to assume. Or, if you have illustrations or other photos available that show similar poses, show them to the subject. Such visual aids are usually very helpful and go far in expediting a session.

Courtesy, Tact, and Language

Courtesy, respect, consideration, and tact are perhaps more important in the sensitive area of figure photography than in any other photographic area. As a result, and at no time should you or your assistants make any remarks or gestures regarding a subject's body or physical attributes that could in any way be misconstrued or taken as a slur, an off-color remark or as a come-on. Figure photography is a sensitive field, demanding the utmost in respect for the people who make it possible.

Working Quickly

Once you're on the set, endeavor to work fast and efficiently. Using an assistant (preferably of the same sex as the subject) will help you accomplish this goal. Professional models may be accustomed to working for many hours in front of a camera, but their non-professional counterparts are not. Your subjects may

- **Establishing and maintaining a good rapport with your model is essential.**

"Once you're on the set...work fast and efficiently."

"Try to maintain this flowing pace throughout the entire shoot."

not openly express it, but within an hour or so after you start your session, the rigors of posing will usually begin to show in their faces and in their inability to easily or quickly assume the more demanding poses.

Typically, once a well planned photo session gets under way, the pace will usually build quite automatically. With each ensuing pose and shot, a subject will relax more and more. She'll begin to respond better to your direction and the session will begin to flow at a nice, steady pace. Try to maintain this flowing pace throughout the entire shoot. Keep moments of inactivity and of indecision to a minimum.

For a subject who is posing in the nude, even short periods of lag time — the time it takes to change such things as lighting, camera viewpoint, props or scenarios — can seem like an eternity. It might take you 30 or 40 minutes to build a solid momentum, but it only takes seconds to loose it.

Experimentation

Just as a dress rehearsal is essential to ensure the quality of a major stage production, so are practice and experimental sessions vital to ensure good figure photography. Such sessions will help you learn what to do, when, how and what photographic tools you'll use so that you don't have to guess during an actual, client-paying photo shoot.

If a session is to be an experimental one, and the subject is a non-paying client, tell him or her in advance that you're going to be experimenting during the session.

If you don't, and when they later find out, you might find them becoming very antagonistic. They might have worked very hard for you during the course of the shoot and once they discover that you were merely practicing or experimenting (especially if the photo results are poor), at the very least, they'll be extremely disappointed.

They might never pose for you again or, worse, they might bad-mouth you to others in your community. If they are paying clients, the rule is very simple: experiment during the course of a serious photography session only after you have photographically captured the images you have been hired to take and then only after you have first warned the subject of what you intend to do.

But, there's another way to practice besides using a live subject and going through the actual steps of taking photographs. And, it's a method which we favor. It involves mental practice; thinking. An example of an actual situation should help point out its value.

Several years ago, we read an article about a well-known northern university that had conducted a very interesting and informative experiment.

Using two separate, but relatively equal control groups, their Psychology Department showed that if people actually practiced a specific physical task, their proficiency improved. Surprised at this result?

No; neither were we. However, the university was not satisfied with just this result; it took the concept further. It conducted a test in which a control group was directed not to perform a task but was instructed only to think about performing all the steps in the same task. The results were very revealing.

After several practice thinking sessions, the control group was then instructed to actually perform the physical task. The results showed that this group closely approached the same level of proficiency as the ones who had actually practiced the real task.

Avoiding Physical Contact

In our studio, I almost never have any physical contact with a subject during the course of a shooting session. If Sheila and I think that a pose should be changed, a prop or drape moved, or a light, which might be near the subject, relocated, Sheila or an assistant does it. In addition, when I do need to come close to a subject, I make certain that the subject is informed of what I am going to do before I ever make a motion toward her. Such conduct makes the subject feel comfortable and secure, as well as appreciative of the consideration.

On the rare occasion when I need to personally make a fine adjustment in a pose, to slightly move a subject's hand, arm, a foot or leg, or to adjust the tilt of the head, I not only announce my intentions beforehand, but also make certain to use only the fingertips of my little fingers to make the correction. I have found that this gesture is generally acceptable to a subject. Of all the digits on a person's hand, the little finger is perceived as being the least threatening.

Controlling the Duration of a Photo Session

The amount of time it will take to complete a typical figure-study session will depend on many factors: your experience, the nature and complexity of the images you're trying to create, the number of poses you intend to use, the ability of the subject to follow directions, the complexity of the lighting and so on. Sometimes you may spend just an hour or so photographing a subject; at other times you may be at it for a full day. If you are well-prepared, and have practiced in advance, you should have a very good idea how long the subject will be needed. However, whatever amount of time it takes, don't rush it. Your results are bound to suffer if you do.

Whatever you do, and well in advance of the photo session, don't forget to inform your subject about the amount of time the shoot is likely to take. What you need to avoid is having your subject press you to rush or ask you to abandon the session because not enough time has been set aside.

Some months ago we decided to do a nude study in which a subject's body was to be entirely covered with a material that was to make her look like a statue. We knew that it was going to be an involved shoot and one which would last about five or six hours—two to three hours to apply the body paint and another two or three hours to conduct the photo session. We made all of the necessary preparations in advance, got all of the makeup ingredients we needed, had the concept all planned out, chose our subject carefully, but forgot one small detail: we forgot to inform the subject exactly how long her services would be required on the day of the shoot.

Then, on the day of the photo session, while the subject was having the special makeup applied (she had been in our studio for about one hour at this point), she casually asked if we knew how long she would be needed. Before we could answer, she informed us that she had an appointment and had to be somewhere else in less than two hours. Since we needed a minimum of one more hour to finish the makeup, at least another two hours to shoot, and another 30 to 60 minutes for her to clean the makeup from her body, it was obvious that not enough time remained. As a result, the entire session had to be postponed. Since her shoot was the only one we had scheduled, our day was wasted.

There is another important reason for knowing how long an intended photo session is going to take: the subject's stamina. You should be able to anticipate how long a non-professional model will be able to pose for you. If, during a shoot, you notice that a subject is obviously getting tired, or if she tells you so, heed the warnings. Don't continue shooting. Let her take a break or reschedule the session for another day. Pursuing the matter further and pushing a tired subject is not only unfair and inconsiderate, it defeats your purpose: you're not likely to get good photo results.

Awareness of the Psychology of Nude Modeling

- **Be prepared and aware of the psychology of nude modeling.**

Even though a subject may initially agree, and appears eager to model for a nude study, your model might have second thoughts on the day of the actual photo session. After subjects have had a couple of days to reflect, they might not be so anxious. This is quite typical. Even the most willing non-professional model may find it difficult, at first, to be photographed without clothing, in front of total strangers.

At the time of the actual photo session, it will help if you keep the atmosphere light: have music playing; keep a light conversation going; have a bright, airy studio, and so on. In addition, reassure the subject that it will be fun, and a pleasant, rewarding, as well as challenging, experience. In any case, you should be prepared to handle such last-minute pangs of indecision; it "comes with the territory." This includes becoming sensitive and observant to such a state of affairs since many subjects may not always voice their fears and doubts. Many subjects will show their feelings in a more subtle way; in their general attitude or demeanor: they may become very stiff while posing; they will seem openly tense; they will answer questions with quick, short, abrupt answers and so on. If

"This negative attitude can appear in many ways..."

you can spot these anxieties the moment they surface and can deal with them quickly, do it. Don't wait until the indecisiveness gets out of hand; it might be too late: the subject might change his or her mind.

Dealing with a Subject's Attitude

Many of the non-professional models we have worked with perceive their figures as looking great in an evening gown, sports clothes, sleep wear, or even a bathing suit. However, few consider themselves perfect in the nude. Many are sensitive about revealing what they perceive as problem areas of their bodies. Many subjects think (correctly or not) they have thighs which are too heavy, a buttocks which is less than firm, sagging bust lines, and so on. All of these things can cause a subject to adopt — consciously or not — a negative attitude. This negative attitude can appear in many ways: antagonism; resistance to instruction; and arrogance to list a few.

From the time a subject first agrees to pose for you, up to the conclusion of the shooting session, you must constantly but honestly flatter the subject. Spend time bolstering her ego as your shoot unfolds. For example, frequently reassure the subject that she is an excellent candidate for this form of photography; that she has an ideal figure for the type of shots that you are going to execute; that she is following instructions well; that she is quick to pick up and execute the poses you have directed her into; and that she looks quite beautiful. All of this will help bolster her confidence. Whatever you do, however, never flatter dishonestly.

Taking Polaroids

Although we use Polaroid film for some photographic situations, we never take, use, or shoot Polaroids for a nude figure photo session. There are two reasons.

First, our clientele is mainly comprised of non-professional models. Consequently, if we set up a pose, light the subject and setting, then take a Polaroid, we are faced with a dilemma. If, based upon the Polaroid, we like what we have created, we will never be able to get the subject back into the same exact position as in the Polaroid in order to capture the shot again with regular film. Something will be a little different: her body language; her expression; the tilt of her head; something. It all might look very similar to an untrained eye, but it will never be the same.

The second reason is that every time we have set up a shot and taken a Polaroid, we have had problems with our client; she has picked it apart: she didn't think her hair looked just right; she thought her thighs were too heavy, her breasts too small, or that she looked too fat. By the time we got our subject rehabilitated and ready to continue with the session, the mood had usually changed and we had trouble getting the subject back into a proper frame of mind.

Even if we took Polaroids and waited until after the photo session was concluded to show them to our subject, the procedure has not worked for us. Every time we've tried it, the subject has felt that we were hiding something. This resulted in the subject tensing up or holding back until finally shown the photos.

Potpourri

1. Before a photo session, introduce your subject to any assistants you intend to use or have in the shoot room area.
2. Inform the subject that you do not intend to allow any one into the shoot room area that have not previously been met and approved of.
3. Be sure the subject has a clean robe to wear when you are between photographic scenarios or taking a break. In addition, make certain to cover (or at least offer to cover) or drape her unclad private body parts when you are between shots or moving props, equipment, or lighting around and not shooting.
4. Once a subject is in your shoot room, never lock the door to the area unless you have told the subject what you intend to do in advance. Also make certain the lock that you employ is very simple and easy for the subject to open. You don't want her to feel trapped. The whole idea of locking the door is to have the subject feel safe from outsiders and thus fostering a feeling of privacy.
5. Have refreshments and beverages available during the entire session.
6. Begin a session with simple, more guarded poses, and work up to more difficult and revealing ones.
7. Make all your photo sessions fun. Let the atmosphere be light and pleasant.

8. Never lie to a subject. It's better to be silent than to lie. You will gain nothing by saying everything is great when in fact it isn't. If there are inferior photographic results, after being "puffed up" by your remarks, they'll feel foolish and maybe even conned. They'll have good reason to question your credibility, if not your ability and motives.

9. Take periodic, short breaks during the photo session.

10. Have a hand-mirror, makeup, brush and comb handy so they can readily be used if the subject has need.

Once the session is over and the photos have been processed, another way to enhance your model's confidence is to show her the results. If you are both pleased, there will be no harm in making minor criticisms to ensure that your next shoot is even more successful. However, be sure to make any critique session a two-way affair; allow the model to present views, suggestions and feelings, and listen to them.

After the Session

Many photographers forget that any figure photo session is comprised of three separate and distinct parts: the events which take place just before a shoot, the shoot itself and the events that follow after the photo session. All three are very important. Even though these three parts are distinct, they share a few things in common.

For example, the events which take place before and during a photo session have two common aspects. One aspect is technical and one is practical.

The first aspect requires that a photographer have a certain working knowledge or technical expertise in photography — knowledge of set selection, composition, lighting, choice of lenses and film, posing and so on.

The other has nothing to do with photography per se, but involves the more practical consideration of salesmanship, or, as it is sometimes called, public relations. This means that a photographer must be able to sell a client on such things as his or her studio, talent, abilities, even the photographer him or herself.

Which aspect is more important? We've attended a lot of seminars where they've taught that all of photography was comprised of 90% salesmanship and 10% technical knowledge. Others say that the rule involves some other proportions such as 60%-40%, 70%-30% or even 50%-50%. But, the real answer is, who cares what the numbers are. The important

"It's better to be silent than to lie."

• **An important facet of after the photo session is public relations, or salesmanship.**

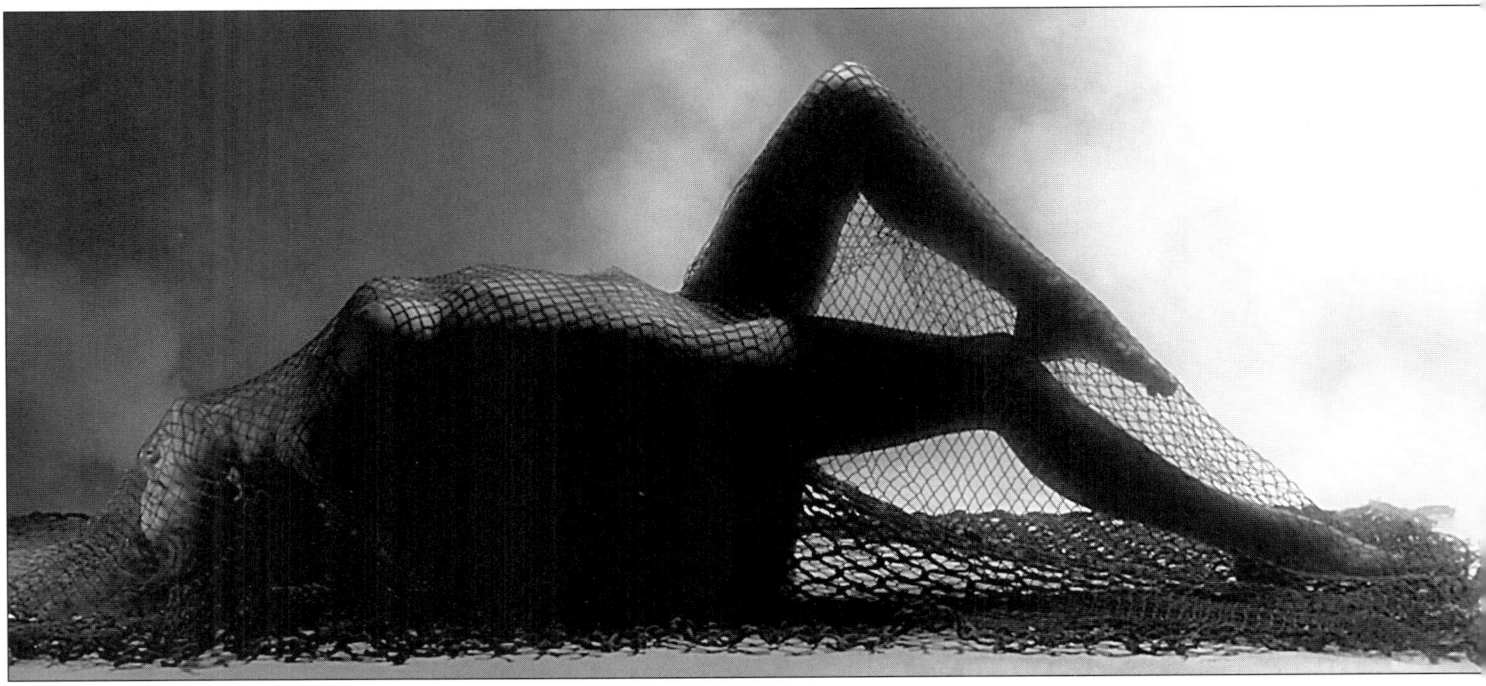

Above: *One aspect of photography is the practical consideration of salesmanship, or, as it is sometimes called, public relations. This means that a photographer must be able to sell a client on such things as his or her studio, talent, and abilities. This is important to remember when you finish the shoot — take time to talk with your subject after the session. It is just good business.*

"...a certain amount of salesmanship or public relations work must be engaged..."

thing to learn is that there is a certain amount of technical knowledge that one must have to turn out consistently good photographic work, time after time, day in and day out. And, there is a certain amount of salesmanship or public relations work that must be engaged in with any subject (client) in order to sell product (photos) and thus stay in business.

But what about the third area? What about the events which take place after the photo session? Although it's an important area, most photographers we know either completely ignore this third part or have little to no quality contact with the subject after the photo session. Although this involves absolutely no photographic technical expertise whatsoever and involves strictly public relations, it's an area that is often missed or overlooked.

The other day we were doing a nude photo session of a woman whom we will call Sandy. Although this was the first time we had photographed her, she was not a total stranger. On a prior occasion both Sheila and I had spent some time with her, here in our studio, during a pre-shoot conference. Consequently, and during the photo session which followed (which lasted about two hours), things could not have gone better: she was cooperative; she was following directions well; and the photo session was moving at a brisk pace.

At the end of the sitting, Sheila thanked her and promptly excused herself from the shoot room area. I, thinking nothing of it, followed suit: I thanked the subject, told her she did great and excused myself so that I might attend to other matters. However, the subject didn't want this; she wanted to talk.

Although she had been relatively quiet during the photo session, this soon changed. As we walked toward the dressing room, she became more and more verbal. She began telling me about the times she had been photographed up north; that she didn't like the experiences and hated the photo results; that she loved photography and enjoyed the way my wife and I worked together and that she looked forward to our photo results. By this time a few minutes had gone by and I realized that we had broken one of our own rules: We had failed to learn as much about this subject as we could before the shoot. In addition, once the shoot was over, we had failed to spend an appropriate amount of time with her, praising her posing effort.

I quickly cured this oversight and started to talk with her. I spent the next 15 minutes engaged in talk that I knew she wanted to hear: how good she was at posing; how great the photo results were going to be, and how great she looked in some of the lighting we used. I did not patronize her. If I didn't think there was at least some measure of truth in what I was telling her I would not have said anything. As a result, we finally parted company with her apparently happy with Sheila and I (and our studio). That's the way we like to end all of our photo sessions. It's just good business.

Chapter Five

Makeup, Hair, Props, and Accessories

As we've noted in a prior chapter, the primary ingredients for good figure photography are a well-chosen subject, appropriate poses, good and effective lighting, and competently executed photography. However, simply because these are referred to as primary doesn't mean that the secondary ingredients are any less important. Secondary ingredients are also important for achieving excellent end results.

They are like the frosting on a cake since they usually serve to enhance or modify a subject's appearance, a mood, the composition, the interpretation or the theme. These secondary ingredients include makeup, hair styling, props, and accessories.

The Secondary Ingredients

While the primary ingredients are absolutely essential for any serious photo nude study and must be present, the secondary ones need not be used all of the time. The experienced photographer knows that the secondary ingredients — makeup, hair styling, props and accessories — can be used individually, collectively, or in any combination, all depending on the end photographic result sought to be achieved. They are important, but sometimes not critical.

Facial Makeup and Hair styling

During the course of a nude study photo session, there might be times when it's desirable to intentionally conceal all or part of a subject's face from the camera's view. Why? For two main reasons.

Primarily this is done for drama's sake. A photographer may want a viewer's attention drawn to a subject's figure rather than to her face for aesthetic or other artistic reasons.

Secondarily the technique is used for practical considerations; when a subject's face is less than perfect due to weight or facial blemishes. The technique is usually achieved in one of three ways: careful lighting (by placing a subject's face in deep shadow), careful posing (by turning her head away from the camera's view), or selective in-camera cropping.

Involve a professional

It has been our experience that most non-professional models have little to no talent for properly selecting or applying makeup to their own face. Most women can do their own makeup and style their own hair for normal, everyday life. However, few know how either one should be properly done for best photographic results. This is why we encourage all of our subjects to have their makeup and hair styling done by professionals, immediately before the photo session. But, a word of caution.

Simply because a person is a professional is no guarantee that he or she is competent at makeup or hair styling for specifically photographic purposes. Be sure to see some examples of the chosen experts' work in advance of your shoot to

"They are like the frosting on a cake ..."

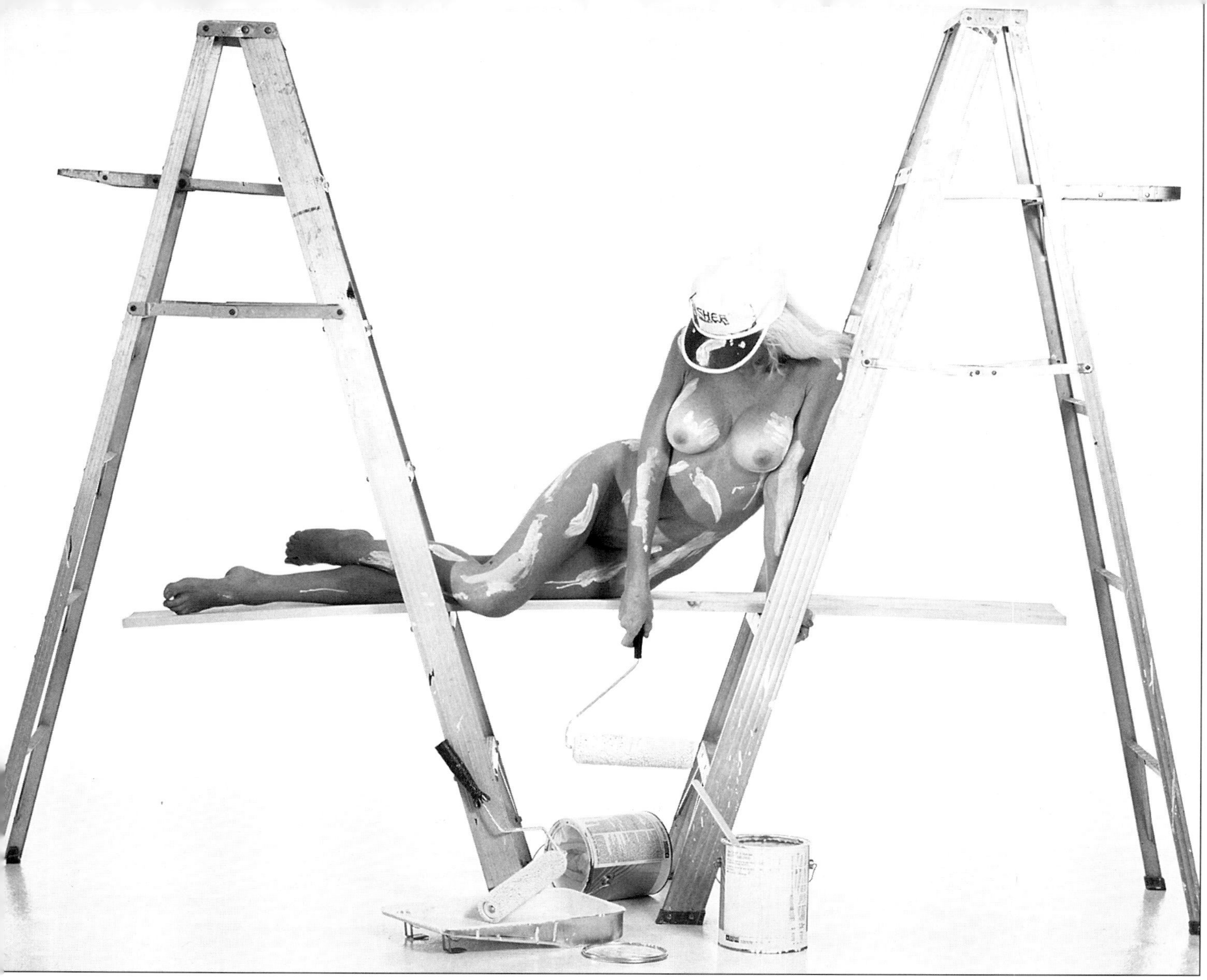

Above: *In this image, the setting and props we used were extremely simple. The entire low-budget shoot took no more than a couple of hours. In a high-key setting, we were able to achieve about 20 totally different poses without having to change our lighting. To give credibility to the concept that the subject was painting, Sheila dabbed white paint on the parts of the subject's body. We have found Tempera — a water-based, non-toxic paint, available at most art stores — ideal for such body applications. It is inexpensive, easy to apply and easily removed with soap and water.*

determine their suitability for working in the context of your photography and its special requirements.

If you do not have advance knowledge of how the subject's makeup or hair styling is going to look photographically, and your photo results are deficient as a result, the subject may fault you and hold you responsible. At the very least, this will result in a dissatisfied subject. You might even be asked to reimburse the subject for the charges of the makeup artist or hair stylist.

Makeup done at the Site

We prefer to have makeup artists and hair stylists come to our studio or to the location site. That way we can monitor the results. If necessary, we can ask for on-the-spot changes. If it's done on site, we'll have some control over the pace at which the artist works.

For example, before a makeup-hair stylist starts to work, he or she is informed that we need to have our subject readied within a certain allotted time. We usually allow 30 to 60 minutes for makeup and hair styling.

If the subject has her hair styled and makeup done elsewhere, we have no control over the time factor. This could lead to a subject arriving very late for a photo session, or to a less than acceptable makeup application and hairstyle.

In the event that the subject arrives at the shoot-site with a hair or makeup result that we don't like, we are prepared for the contingency. We usually have our own makeup artist on standby just in case we have the need; minor makeup or hair-style corrections can then be made on an as needed basis.

Make Some Tests

Prior to engaging in any serious photographic session, especially if you have to hire a subject as a model and pay her a substantial fee, be sure to shoot some test rolls of film with the type of makeup she intends to wear during the actual photo session. If need be, test a subject wearing different brands, types, and amounts of makeup.

It's important to realize that not all makeup types and brands are suitable for photography, and that color film does not respond to all of them in an equal or favorable way, or even in the way the human eye sees them.

We have learned that there can be a big difference in the types of makeup typically sold in drug or department stores from the types that are available from special, beauty supply houses. The supply houses often carry the special types of makeup that are primarily designed for television, stage, and photographic purposes. These are the ones we prefer to use.

A word of caution about makeup. Even though you may be using the correct type of makeup, it might actually respond differently with different film types, as well as different illuminations.

One makeup may look better under tungsten lighting; another may respond better with electronic flash. Some makeup will look best when using black-and-white film, some with color film. Only through experimentation will you learn what types and quantities of makeup will work best in a given situation.

Obviously, whenever experimentation is involved, it pays to be consistent once success has been achieved. When you know precisely what makeup works best, on which film type, in what amount, and applied in which manner, make a note of these facts and stick with the tested and proven combination unless there is a good creative reason to do otherwise.

Body Makeup

In normal portraiture, makeup for a subject is primarily and usually employed only for the face; secondarily it is sometimes used for a subject's neck area, arms and hands. In figure photography, where the entire body is exposed, makeup might be necessary or desirable over a much larger area.

A word of caution — Body makeup can be either cosmetic, to cover blemishes, enhance the skin's tone and the like, or it can be creative, to produce designs and patterns and other effects. Whether you use makeup cosmetically or creatively, be careful. Before you use any body makeup, we suggest that you consult various theatrical supply houses for their advice and also contact the manufacturer of each brand you intend to use.

Use Makeup that's Water Soluble

We suggest you use makeup or paint brands that are water soluble. This will expedite cleaning up when the photography has been completed. It'll also make it easier to do on the-spot corrections as the makeup is being applied or later, if the makeup starts to look less than fresh during a long shoot.

- **Use makeup or paint that is water soluble.**

The Time Factor

In our experience, it usually takes about an hour to do one side of a subject's entire body with simple body makeup; longer, if some sort of elaborate design is to be fashioned. In any case, allow yourself plenty of time.

Application Choices

If only small sections of a subject's body are to be covered with makeup, or only small designs are to be applied, having an artist perform the task by hand is usually acceptable. For more extensive body coverings and body design work, airbrushing water-soluble makeup onto the subject is faster and usually leads to better, smoother, and more professional looking results.

Other Body Treatments

In addition to regular body makeup and paint, there are other body treatments that can be used on a subject. For example, applying baby oil and water can be very effective and attractive. Apply regular baby oil to the subject's skin, and then use a spray bottle to spray warm water onto the subject. The water will bead up on the subject's body and this will create

"...there are other body treatments that can be used on a subject."

a wet look that can lead to very dynamic figure photographs.

Another body treatment that can be effective — although we don't particularly favor it — is the application of non-toxic, water soluble, ceramic clay. Once the clay has been applied to the subject's person, her body will take on the semblance of a statue. The initial effect can be great and can lead one to some very interesting photos.

However, it's not an easy substance to work with. It takes about two to three hours to apply, is very messy, and leaves a residue — a very fine powder — on everything within the immediate area of the subject: lights, camera equipment, and the floor.

Getting Body Makeup Applied

Applying body enhancements is not a do-it-yourself job. It's virtually impossible for a subject to apply body makeup or paint to her own body. Ideally, a female subject should have the job done by a professional of her own sex. If your own female assistant can do a competent job, that's acceptable.

Psychological Effect

Body makeup can change a subject's whole attitude. Once a subject has had body makeup applied to her entire body, you'll often notice an interesting change. Many subjects will feel dressed even though they are nude. This is because body makeup seems to promote a feeling of security in a subject. For this reason, many initially timid subjects will feel quite at ease in a nude session from its very beginning when some kind of covering has been applied to their skin. Take advantage of this condition. It can often lead to some dynamic photographic results very early in a photo session.

"...don't use props that are likely to overpower the major point of interest..."

Props

If you do use some type of props or accessories for a nude photo concept, it's important to choose and use them prudently. For example, and as a general rule, don't use props that are likely to overpower the major point of interest — the subject's body. But, this rule is not cast in stone. As in all artistic endeavors, this is a rule that may sometimes need to be broken.

As a point of reference, do you recall the Avedon photo of Natasia Kinski who is posed lying on a barren floor with a large snake coiled about her body? In that photo one might be hard pressed to decide which one of those two elements — the nude subject or the snake — was the main subject matter and which the prop. This is because both elements had been given equal weight in the photo composition.

On the other side of the coin, props can sometimes represent an actual setting. For example, a vase of flowers could be just a prop, but having a subject reclining on a bed of flowers would change the whole concept. The flowers would become a setting. In addition, a prop might be so closely involved with a subject that one might not even think of it as being a prop. If you were to photograph a nude under a cascading waterfall, the waterfall would most certainly be a prop; however, a viewer of such an image might not perceive it as such. A viewer might think of the cascading water as just a part of the overall setting. In any case, don't be tempted to use props just for the sake of using them. The setting, the subject, and the mood should enter into the decision of whether to use a prop. Keep in mind that a prop might easily distract from the directness and simplicity of your intended photo scene.

Propping is an Art

Effective propping can give a setting or subject a complete or finished look, while poorly handled propping can ruin an entire photo concept. Propping is so important that many professional photographers turn this responsibility over to an expert; a prop stylist. In general, the primary function of a competent stylist is to stylize; to decorate a photo scene or setting. This usually entails a stylist locating, choosing, and then applying, appropriate props to a given photo setting, in keeping, of course, with the photographer's theme, intentions and instructions. This might involve bringing a mere vase and a few flowers onto a set, or something more elaborate such as decorating an entire room from ceiling to floor. Whatever it is, a good stylist can be worth his or her weight in gold, but a good stylist does not come cheaply. If you can't afford, or don't really want this type of

Right: *You don't need a lot of props in a photo scene to produce a stunning figure study. In this image, a simple Edwardian-type chair, a strand of pearls, one earring, and a bit of material were all the props used. This lack of props forces the viewer's eye to the major element: the subject. The pose is somewhat traditional, very flattering, and almost timeless. We used only one light: a 3 1/2 x 7/1/2-foot softbox. The light was positioned approximately 45 degrees to the camera's left.*

Below: *The pose in this photo is less guarded and more daring than the image to the right. Therefore, to keep it from being too blatant and at the same time to give it an air of mystery, we enshrouded the subject with a bit of white cloth (like cheese cloth). Because of the manner in which the subject is wrapped, it is difficult to tell if the cloth is the supporting prop and the subject the main element or vice versa. The same large, single light source used for the photo to the right was used. The only difference was that the main light was positioned about 70 degrees to the left of the camera axis.*

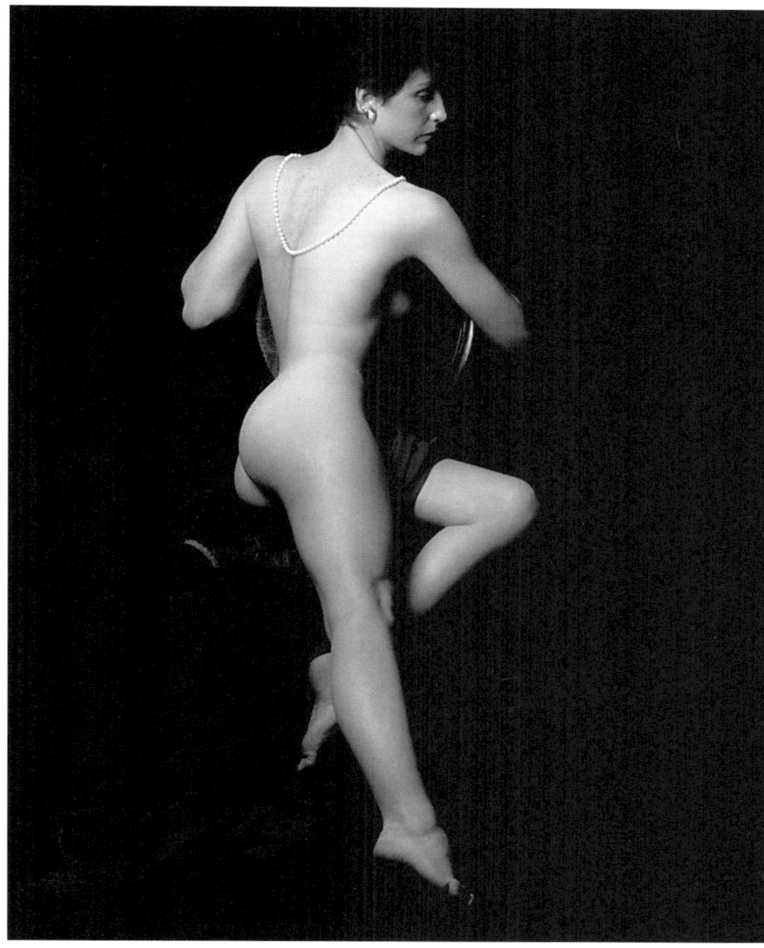

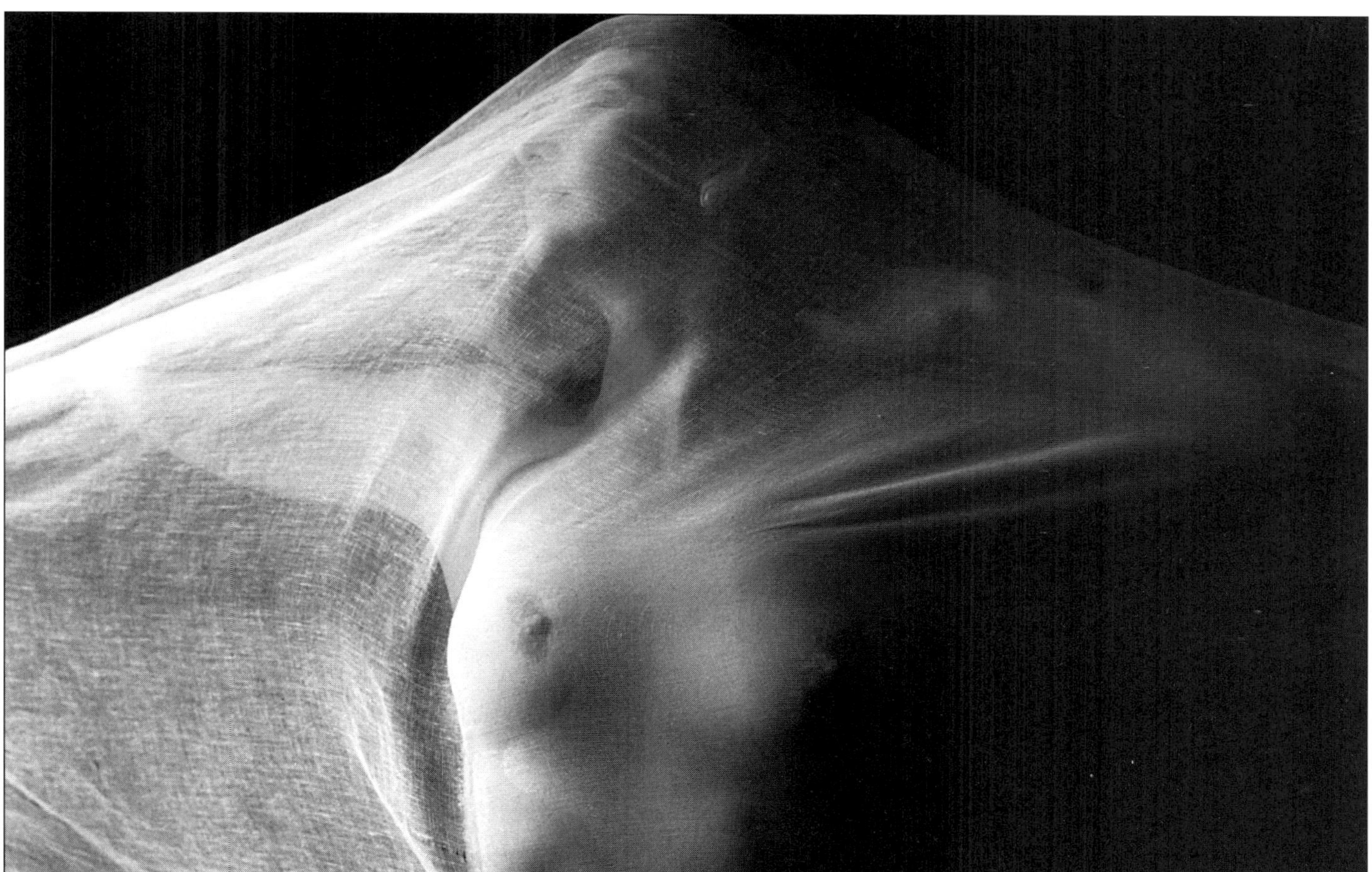

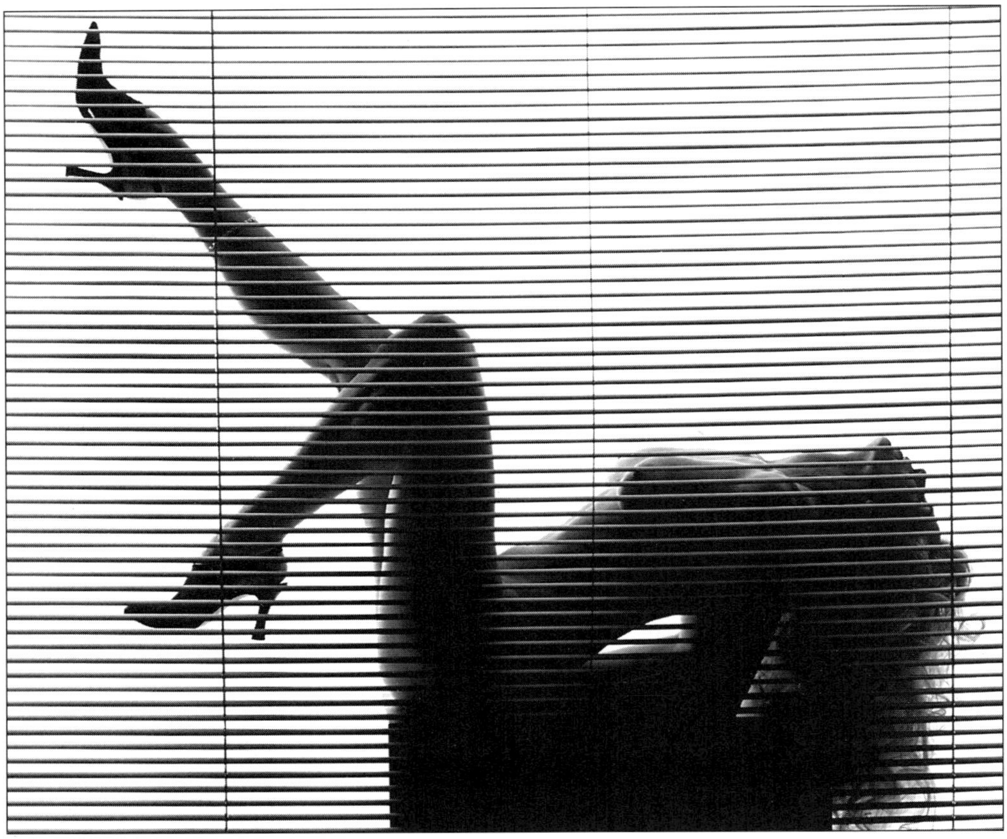

***Above and Below:** These images are examples of partial silhouettes. A high-key setting was used. The background was evenly illuminated by two 4-foot silver-lined umbrellas: one on either side of the background. The third and main light was housed in a 6-inch bowl reflector, supported on a boom stand immediately above the subject. Its power was adjusted to emit f-22 light. The background lights had their power adjusted to emit three f-stops of more light than the main light. The camera was set to f-16. The blinds were black and nine feet wide; they were supported by center stands on both sides. The point of focus was on the subject, not the blinds. No filtration was used for these photos.*

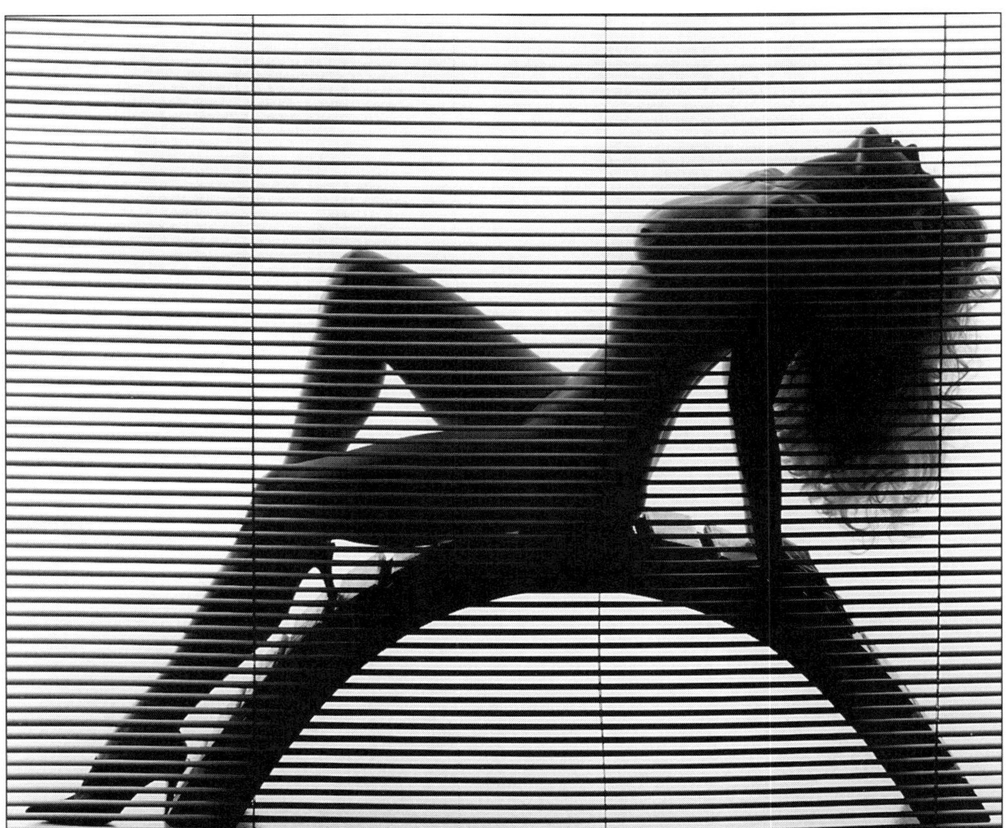

professional help, then you'll have little choice. You'll have to become proficient in selecting props and styling a setting.

It might help to develop a friendship with a good interior designer or decorator. Such a person can be useful when you are hard pressed for ideas.

National ads are another good source for ideas. Examine national photo advertisements closely; pay attention to how "the big boys" prop and stylize any given setting. Other valuable sources of inspiration are window displays; they can give you insight on how effective propping can enhance a setting.

If you are ever in doubt, fall back onto the KISS Principle: Keep it simple, stupid. Props should be used with respect and restraint; they can be a very powerful influence, for better as well as for worse. Make your visual statement decisively, but whatever you do, avoid overstatement, understatement, and misstatement.

Where to Find Props.

Some of the best sources for props that we have found are flea markets, junk stores and second-hand furniture shops. Whether you are looking for pieces of material, certain types of clothing, decorative household items, furniture, or just plain bric-a-brac, rummaging through stores of this type can serve two purposes. As well as giving you ready access to the various and sundry props that you might need, usually at very reasonable prices, they can also give you some great, creative ideas.

Accessories

Here we're not talking about photographic and camera accessories, such as filters, tripods, and lens shields. We're speaking of personal accessories that could be used and worn by a subject during a photo shoot. Examples include a strand of pearls, earrings, gloves, a hat, a scarf. Any accessory should help give a subject (and the photo composition) a more finished look.

And, like props, accessories should be consistent with the theme, setting or mood you are intending to create. In addition, they shouldn't be so large or prominent as to dominate the subject or to distract a viewer's attention from the main point of interest — the subject's body.

Once the basic theme and setting have been established, step back and see the scene in your mind's eye. If the setting or subject seems to be lacking something, think of some props or accessories that could be used to fill the void. However, as with props, add accessories sparingly. Nothing should be added without a specific purpose and design in mind, and only then with the intention of making the primary subject matter — the subject — stronger in representation. If a prop or accessory doesn't add something very specific to an image, don't use it. If it doesn't do any good, it will almost certainly do some harm to the basic visual concept you're trying to convey.

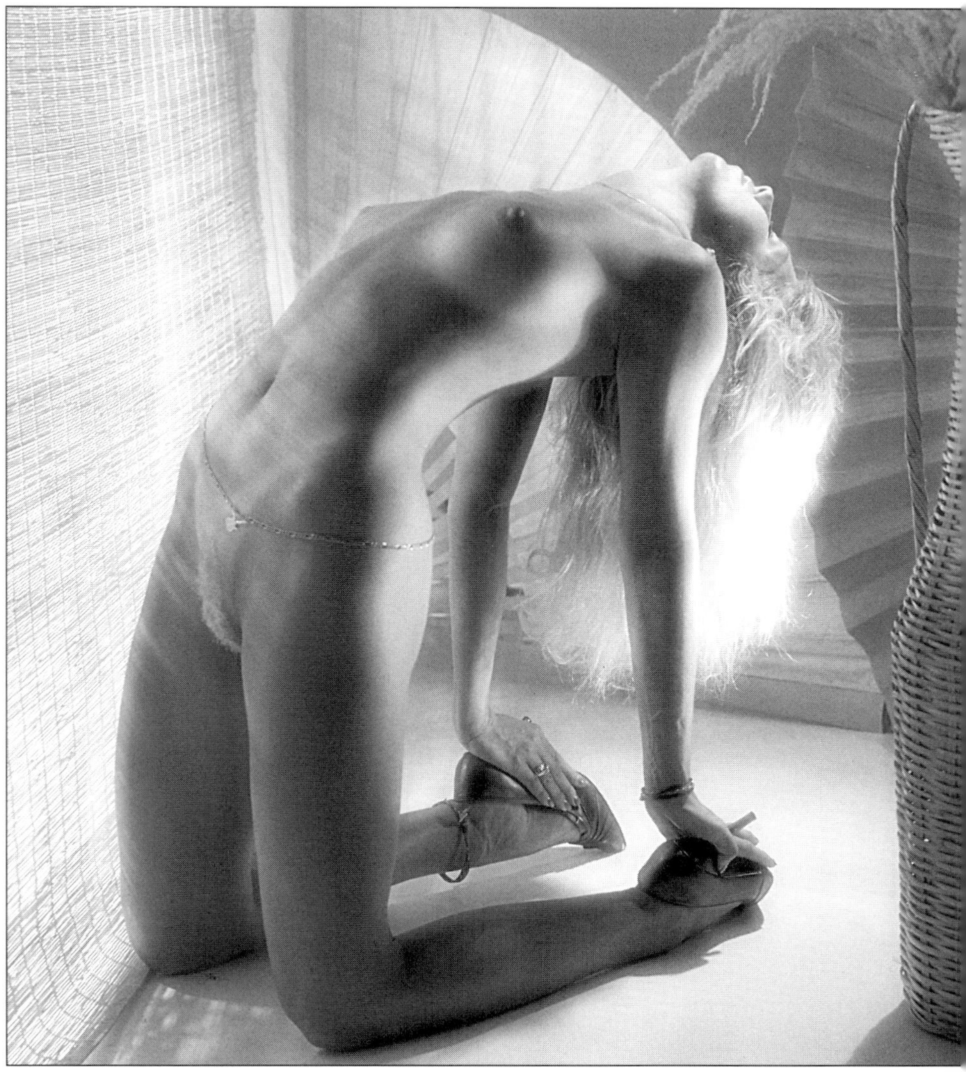

Above: *Sometimes a prop can lend strong support to an image. Such is the case with the shoji screen we used for this image. This roll-up screen is available in a number of different colors and sizes from many import stores. It is not expensive and can be set up and moved easily and quickly, making it a pleasure to use.*

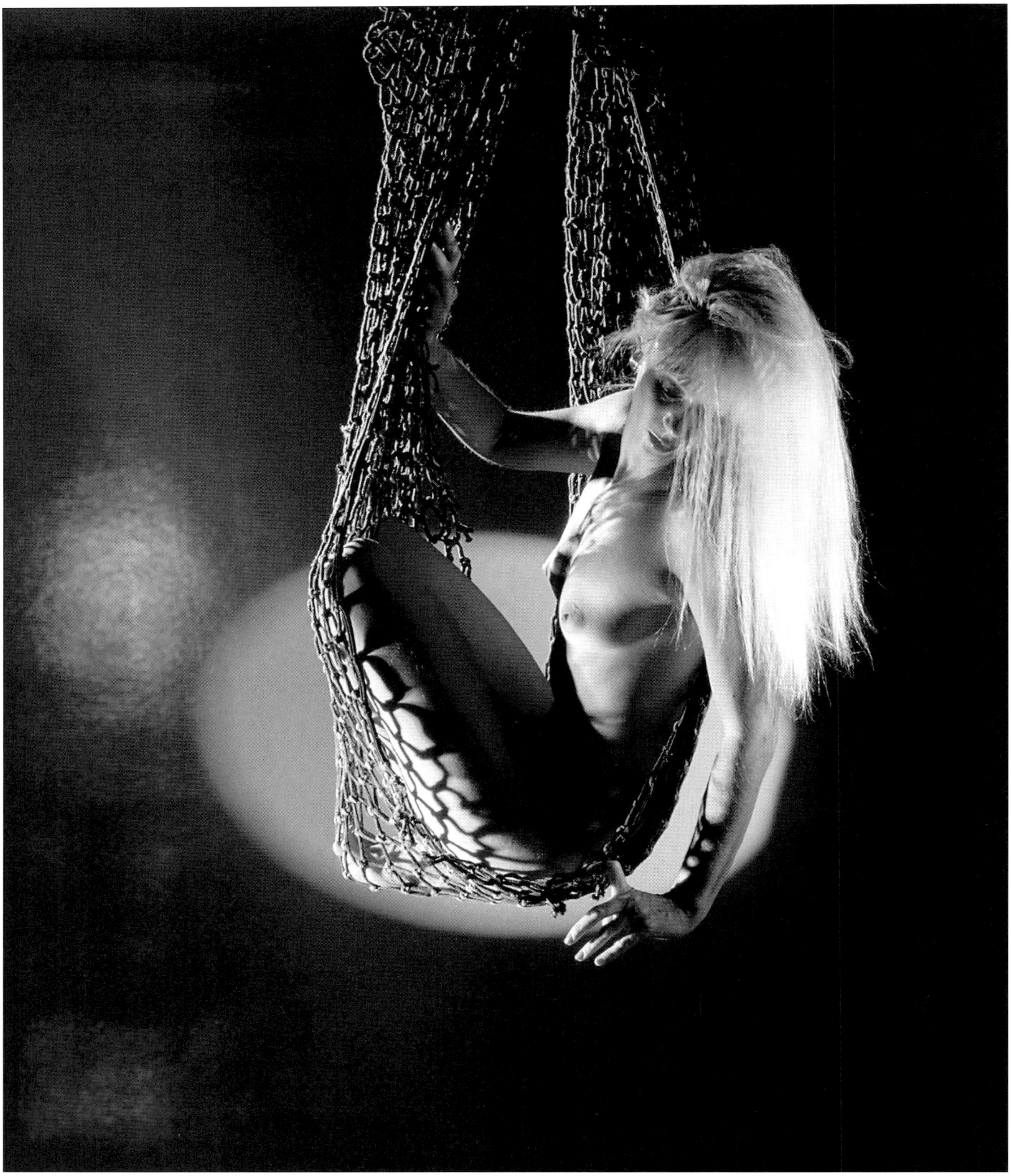

Above and Opposite page: *You should carefully think out what you want to convey in your figure photographs long before a subject is chosen and actual photography begins. In these two images (above and next page), we wanted to give the viewer a feeling of metamorphosis or transition. We wanted the viewer to sense that the subject was moving or evolving from one state of existence into another. Images with such a concept in mind would have failed totally had the subject been wearing clothing. Notice how the background lighting was designed to help tell our story of transition.* *(Continued on next page)*

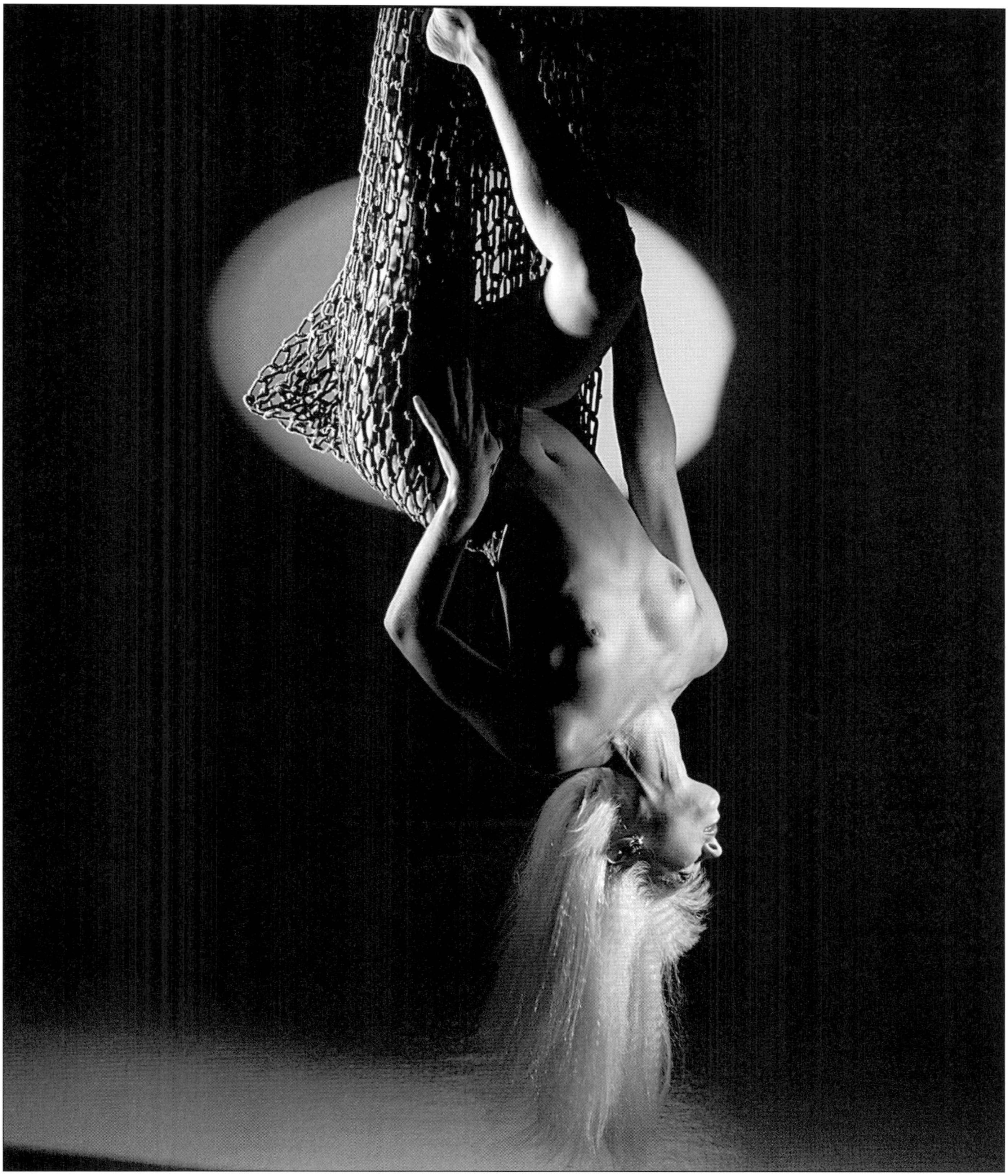

If the circle of illumination had been large enought to encircle the entire subject, it would have suggested "containment" rather than "transition." The much smaller circle, concentrated around the subject's lower half, was strongly suggestive of an emergence from a "pod" into a larger world. Of course, these photos would not have been able to convey our concept without the help of the net as a prop. We had two very large hooks securely anchored in our studio ceiling. We tested the netting to make certain that it would hold our combined body weights before the subject was allowed in the netting. The subject should always feel completely safe.

Chapter Six

Equipment

Owning a large amount of sophisticated photo equipment is no guarantee that you'll be able to produce great photographs, no mater what the subject matter might be.

The process is much more involved than this. Pieces of photographic equipment are but tools to be used to accomplish a specific end result: to capture a photographic image.

Note, if you will, that we did not say that given the proper tool, the photographic image that one could capture would be great, good, or mediocre. Why? Because any tool in the hands of a Master can lead to masterful results.

There will be no one piece of equipment that you must buy in order to make your photos great ones. This is because photographic equipment does not take photos, people do.

"...photographic equipment does not take photos, people do."

Therefore, if you have been taking fair to poor photos with limited, inexpensive equipment, owning a lot of expensive equipment will still yield you the same fair to poor results.

If you're just entering the field of figure photography, don't make the mistake of rushing out and buying a lot of expensive equipment. Or, for that matter, don't rush out and buy a lot of inexpensive equipment. You are much better off beginning with limited amounts of good, reliable pieces of equipment that are easy to work with and which you can master in short order.

As your knowledge, proficiency and needs increase, you can always purchase additional equipment to meet that growth and those needs.

Too much photographic equipment, in the beginning of your photo career, could act as a hindrance to your creativity. You could be so preoccupied with thoughts of which pieces of equipment to use, or how various pieces of equipment work, that you'll fail to devote the needed time and thought to your subject and the creation of artful photos. You'll be too busy being busy.

Basic Equipment

Any photographer can produce stunning nude images with nothing more than a 35mm camera a 50mm lens, natural window light, and an in-camera exposure meter. However, if you're doing photos for hire, we don't suggest that you be this basic.

At a minimum, we suggest that you be a bit more expansive and have some backup equipment too.

For example, you should have at least one good camera body (preferably two), at least two high-quality lenses of different focal lengths (e.g., and for a 35 mm camera we would suggest a 100mm Macro and a 35mm lens), a sturdy tripod, a couple of different soft-focus filters, a warming filter, a couple of reflectors (white, gold or silver; preferably one of each), and two good hand held exposure meters (one for backup; use the type that will take both reflected-light and incident-light meter readings). This amount and type of equipment will not permit you to be abundantly creative, but it will allow you to create some lovely natural light photos.

Buy the Best

You get what you pay for, so buy the best equipment you can afford. Cheap equipment is often unreliable and will not withstand the rigors of constant use. Also, it's often difficult and surprisingly expensive to have cheap equipment repaired or serviced.

In addition, avoid, if at all possible, equipment that is unnecessarily heavy, bulky, and awkward as well as those pieces which are hard to work with. In the long run, such pieces of equipment are not cost efficient.

Growth Potential and Versatility

Seek out equipment that will afford the possibility of growth; that will allow you to grow into it or to expand the use of the item. What you should avoid is buying something that may serve your needs today but, in a short period of time, become obsolete.

For example, when we first started we were lead to believe that owning a relatively low power, 500 watt-second, power pack would be more than sufficient. We would never need more power than this.

Unfortunately, such advice was very wrong. As a result, we have six 500 watt-second power packs (and 12 lamp heads which are designed for and only work and fit those 500 watt-second power sources) which we have not used for over 15 years.

By contrast, we have a number of 2,000 watt-second power packs which, when purchased 15 years ago, afforded more power than we then needed; however, as we developed and grew, so did our power demands and requirements.

Today, it's common for us to use 2,000 watt-second power sources (or more) for all of our photo sessions. However, even if we don't use any one of those power packs at its full 2,000 watt-seconds of power, we are still in good shape.

All of the lamp heads which we purchased and which work exclusively with the 2,000 watt-second power packs are interchangeable; they work with all of the power packs regardless of whether we are using such a power pack configured at a low 125 watt-seconds of power, 2,000 watt-seconds of power or any power output in between. That's versatility.

Don't Copy Others

Don't buy equipment just because another photographer, whose work and style you admire, owns the same type. His or her success is due to his or her skill and artistry, not his or her hardware.

Equipment selection is also a very personal matter. What suits and works for others — even experts and professional photographers — won't necessarily suit or work well for you. You need to find equipment that makes you comfortable.

"...buy the best equipment you can afford."

Camera Format

Even though figure photography is possible with most camera formats (from 35mm to the large view camera sizes), one format is usually far better than another. Why? Because each format has certain advantages, disadvantages, and has certain limitations.

For example, we have found that we do most of our nude studies with primarily the 2-1/4-inch-square format and sometimes a few photo sessions with 35mm camera equipment. Since we most often work with non-professional model-subjects, we rarely shoot nude images with our view camera.

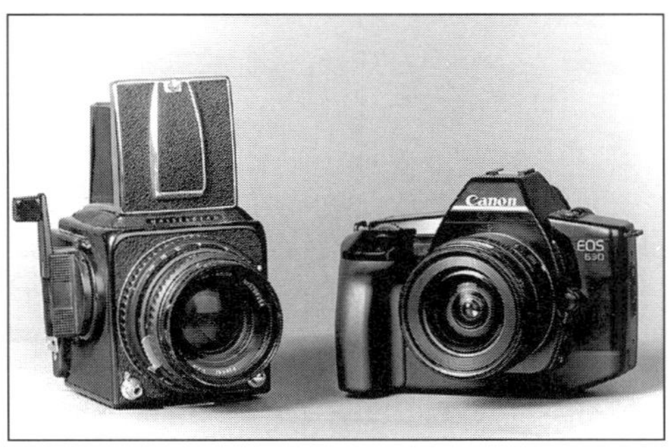

We generally use the medium format (2-1/4-inch) camera like the Hasselblad (pictured left) for our nude studies. We also use a 35mm camera such as the Canon EOS (right) for a few photo sessions.

Advantages of 35mm

With the advancements made in recent years in the resolution capabilities of both lenses and films, the better 35mm SLR (single lens-reflex) cameras can produce high-quality images, capable of considerable enlargement.

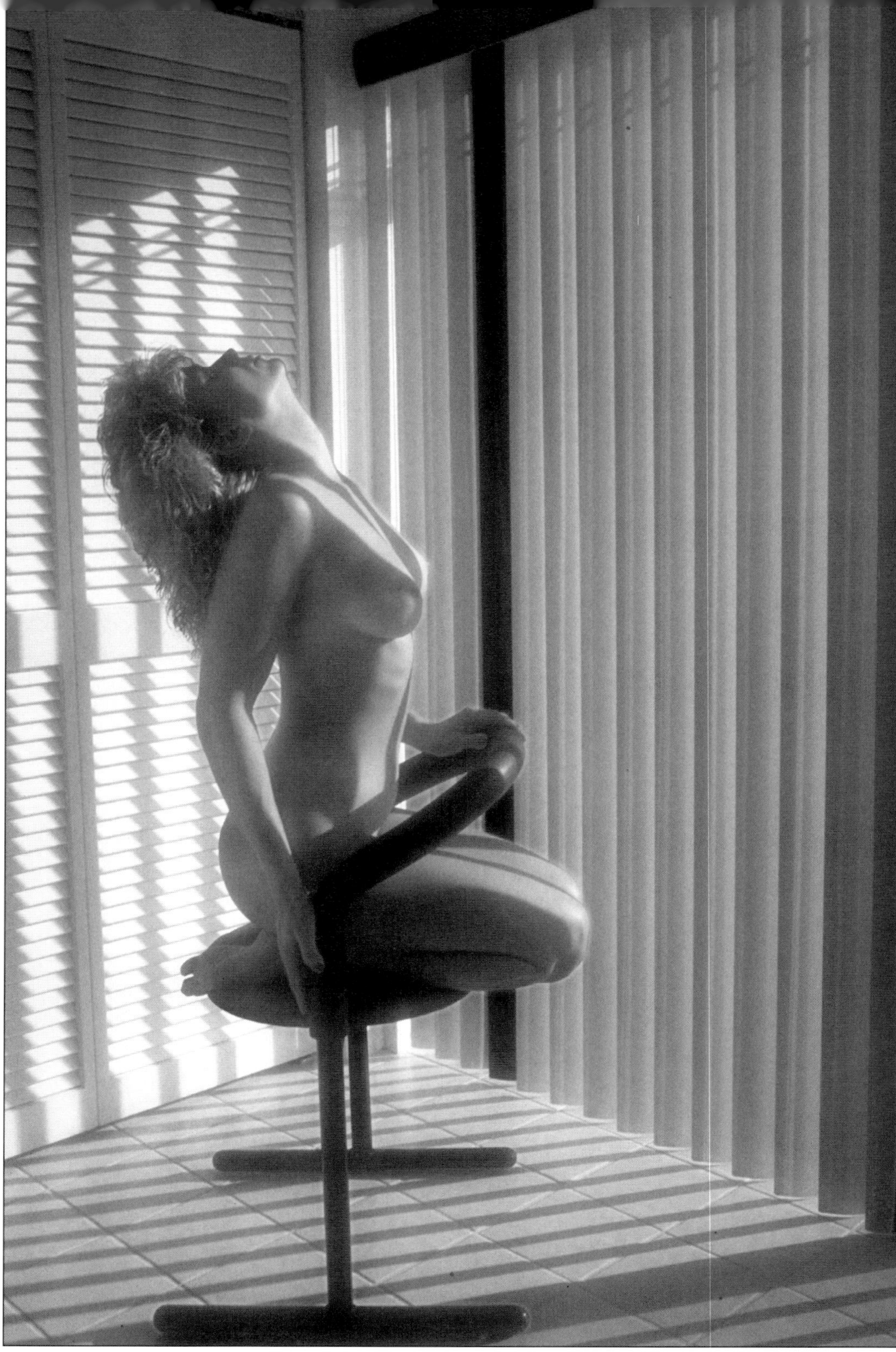

Above: *This image was taken with a 35mm camera and a 100mm macro lens. Daylight through the blind was the only light source. A white, 3x4-foot foamcore reflector was used to lighten the shadows to a greater or lesser extent. The subject's neck and upper chest area, above the bust line, have been singled out.*

These cameras are usually light in weight, portable, fast, and easy to work with. Most incorporate excellent viewing and focusing features as well as interchanging lenses.

Because of their small size, 35mm SLRs are unobtrusive and present little or no intimidation factor to a non-professional model-subject.

In addition, the 35mm camera can be used hand held, allowing one to work quickly, from many angles and often in tight quarters — such as may be encountered when working in a subject's home.

Compared with the other camera formats, the 35mm format is economical where film cost is concerned. This gives one the freedom to shoot more liberally.

Disadvantages of 35mm

Notwithstanding all of the positive features of the 35mm format, there are some disadvantages that cause us to steer away from it most of the time. Because the 35mm film frame is small, evaluation of negatives, contact sheets, and slides can be relatively difficult, especially for our non-commercial customers.

Generally we, as well as our customers, are forced to evaluate such film using some kind of magnifying device: a loop. Although we are accustomed to working with 35mm confines and evaluating the film using a loop, many of our customers are not; they become frustrated when having to view such small-sized film through a viewing device. In addition, because of the small film size, retouching an image on the film is most often impractical if not impossible.

Further, with really high image magnification, such as in 20x24-inch or 30x40-inch enlargements, overall sharpness and quality are most often noticeably better when made from a larger negative to begin with, such as a 2-1/4-inch-square, than from a smaller, 35mm negative.

Lastly, 35mm SLR cameras, typically, will not synchronize with flash at all shutter speeds. This factor alone keeps it from being the format of choice when we're photographing outdoors; this feature acts as a hamper to creative lighting control.

The 2-1/4-inch-square Format

Cameras of this format, as well as their lenses and accessories, cost more and are heavier and less maneuverable than their 35mm counterparts. They also tend to be more intimidating to some subjects because of their larger, more imposing size and nature.

However, the larger film size makes it all worthwhile for us. It makes evaluation of positive and negative film much easier and frequently yields print enlargements of a better quality than the 35mm format. The larger film size also makes film retouching less problematic. Like the 35mm SLRs, these cameras also offer the ability to change lenses.

Another feature is that because most 2-1/4-inch-square cameras have leaf shutters rather than focal-plane shutters, most will sync with flash at all shutter speeds. This feature gives us much greater lighting control when shooting outdoors and trying to balance flash with ambient light.

There is one final advantage to the larger, 2-1/4-inch format which can not be overlooked: snob appeal. Many years ago, when we first got started into professional photography, we made the mistake of shooting a wedding (our first) with 35mm camera equipment.

During the course of our photography, the father of the bride approached us and said, "...I have camera equipment just like yours; if I had known that my daughter was going to hire someone with the same equipment as mine, I would have shot the wedding myself and saved her all of the money." In our area, and with our clientele, our customers are neither intimidated nor impressed by 35mm camera equipment. Since most of our customers think that our good photo results come about due to the type of equipment we use anyway, we really can't afford to use 35mm equipment. Consequently, we use Hasselblad and Mamyia 2-1/4 cameras.

The View Camera

Although we have used a view camera for some of our figure studies, it's not a format that we favor or frequently use. Admittedly it has some definite advantages, such as larger film image (4x5-inches, 5x7-inches and so on) and the perspective and sharpness-controlling camera movements; however, its negative points keep it from being a format of choice for us for nude studies.

Film cost is considerably higher than with any other smaller format. In addition, a view camera is not an easy camera to work with, especially if there is a need to work quickly.

Further, it's bulky, heavy, and slow to maneuver. Once you start to load film, you lose eye contact with the subject and the composition; you can't see a subject through the camera's lens (since the lens is closed down) and hence you don't know if the subject has moved just prior to exposure of the film. View cameras also tend to intimidate, especially non-professional modeling-subjects.

Lenses

Being able to change lenses on a camera's body is very important in figure photography; it makes any camera more of a creative tool.

Owning a camera that allows you to change lenses is only a part of successful figure photography. Another, equally important part, is knowing which focal length of lens to select for your camera and when to select it.

These two things affect camera viewpoint, image size, perspective, creative distortion, and informational data for the composition.

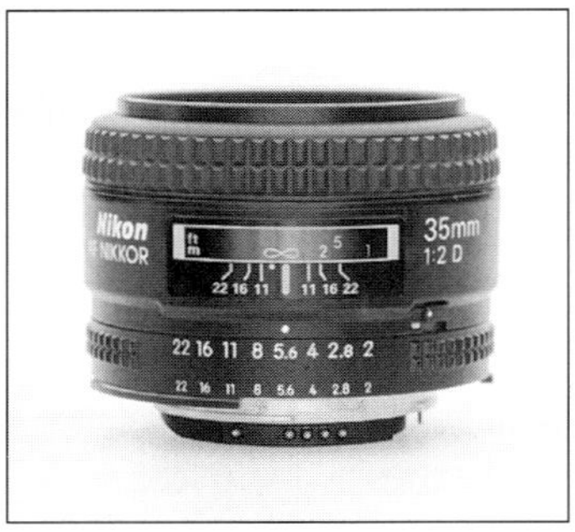

The Nikon AF Nikkor 35mm lens.

Focal-Length

When we shoot figure studies with a 35mm camera, we try to use three different focal-length lenses — a 35mm, a 50mm, and a 100mm Macro — during the course of the photo session.

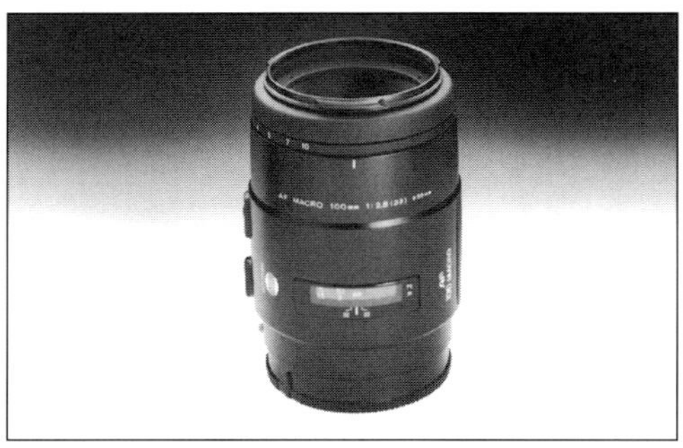

A 35mm, a 50mm, and a 100mm Macro are the three different focal-length lenses we like to use for figure studies. This is a Minolta AF Macro 100mm f/2.8 lens.

- **Four main aspects help to select the proper focal-length.**

Of the three lenses, the 100mm macro is the preferred focal length, because, compared with the other lenses, the 100mm Macro gives a better rendering to a subject's full-length figure. When using the 2-1/4-inch-square format, we favor using three other focal-lengths: a 60mm lens, a standard 80mm lens, and a 150mm lens. Of these three lenses, the 150mm is our lens of choice for the same reason as the 100mm Macro was in the 35mm format.

One of the reasons that we try to interchange lenses during the course of any given photo session is to increase pictorial variety; to give us and our subjects more and different picture choices and thus an opportunity to increase sales.

However, this is not the only criteria we use to decide which focal-length lens to use. We base our focal-length selection on four main questions:

1. How much space do we have to work in?
2. Do we want a normal or exaggerated perspective ?
3. How much of the scene do we actually want to record on film?
4. How much depth of field do we want?

Working space — The smaller the area that we have to work in—i.e., the shorter the distance from the camera to the subject—the more restriction there will be in choosing lenses. In tight quarters, we'll often be forced to select a fairly wide-angle lens in order to get all of the subject's figure recorded onto film. However, this may cause some image distortion; distortion that we would rather avoid, if we can, by moving farther from the subject and using a longer lens.

If we are forced to work at close quarters with a wide angle lens, we often try to minimize distortion by using an appropriate body pose that keeps the body parts all in the same plane. In other words we avoid placing parts of a subject's body closer to the camera's lens than other parts.

Normal or exaggerated perspective — A creative photographer does not arbitrarily choose a viewpoint and then select a lens that will give him or her a frame-filling image. There is more to selective lens choice.

For example, a camera viewpoint should be chosen to create the desired feel of perspective in the image. (Perspective is simply the relationship between things that are at different distances from the camera.) Camera viewpoint can affect the size relationship between your human subject and the background, or between different parts of a subject, such as her legs and her upper body. By moving a camera in, very close to a subject and using a wide-angle lens, the perspective can be very exaggerated. By moving the camera farther away and using a telephoto lens (such as a 100mm Macro for a 35mm camera or a 150mm lens for a 2-1/4 format camera), the perspective will be more geometrically "correct."

Angle of view — Whether you're deliberately trying to control perspective or not, the choice of lens focal-length enables you to control the image framing from the specific camera position you have adopted. Thus, the longer the focal-length of the lens, the narrower the angle of view will be and the less information, both horizontally and vertically, that will be included in the film frame. Conversely, the shorter the lens focal-length, the greater the angle of view there will be, and the more information that will be seen by the film.

Most of the nude studies that we photograph in our studio — whether head-and-shoulders, three-quarter length, full body or selected body parts — are taken with a 100mm Macro lens, when we're shooting 35mm. In the 2-1/4-inch-square format, we normally use a 150mm lens. Such lenses give us the angle of view (the amount of information; a fairly tight crop that eliminates distracting elements) that we look for in a composition. We also select such a focal-length because it allows us to work at a comfortable distance from our subjects, while at the same time making our subject appear prominent in the final image.

4. Depth of field. This is another factor to consider when deciding upon which focal-length lens to use. And the rule is simple. If you had three cameras (say 35mm cameras) set up next to each other, each with a lens of a different focal-length—such as 28mm, 50mm and 100mm—and each focused on a subject nine feet away and all set at the same f-stop, each camera would give you a different, apparent depth of field. It is because of this difference that one chooses one focal-length lens over another during any photo session.

The shorter the focal-length of the lens, the greater the apparent depth of field. The longer the focal-length of the lens, the shallower (or less) the apparent depth of field.

Thus, at a lens aperture setting of say f-11, the depth of field will be apparently greater with a 28mm lens than with a 100mm lens at the same f-stop setting, assuming both lenses were focused on the same given subject and were at the same distance from the subject.

If you wanted greater apparent depth of field than is possible with the smallest lens aperture you could use on a long lens, change to a shorter lens while shooting from the same distance.

If you want to limit depth of field to a very narrow zone, narrower than the widest lens aperture will provide, you should shoot from the same distance with a longer lens.

Of course, these changes will also affect your image framing and overall composition. Don't be tempted to change lens focal-length and then also change your shooting distance to maintain the same image framing. By maintaining basically the same image size in this manner, you would cancel out the effect the lens focal-length has on the depth of field.

As an aside, the reason that we keep saying apparent depth of field is because that's what it is. Depth of field is only apparent when you change focal-length of lenses.

Apparent depth of field — If you set up three similar cameras (say three 35mm cameras), positioned at the same distance from a given subject (e.g., 15 feet), each with a different focal-length lens (e.g., one with a 28mm, one with a 50mm and one with a 100mm lens), and set all to the same f-stop (for example, f-11), and then took a photo of the same subject with each camera, all of the print results would look different. The photo taken with the camera that had the wide-angle (28mm) lens on it would contain much more information and have much more apparent depth of field than the one taken with the 50mm or 100mm lens. By the same token, the photo taken with the camera that had the normal, 50mm lens on it would also show more picture information and have more apparent depth of field than the one taken with the 100mm lens (although less information than the one taken with the 28mm lens). This data is not too startling since it bears out the old photo axiom, the shorter the focal-length of the lens, the more the (apparent) depth of field.

However, what is startling is that if you went back into the darkroom and reprinted the negatives taken with the cameras that had the 28mm and 50mm lens on it and made new enlargements, ones that would yield prints that were exactly equal to the picture information shown by the print taken by the camera that had the 100mm lens on it, you would see an astonishing fact. You would see that the depth of field is identical in all three of the prints.

"Depth of field is only apparent when you change focal-length of lenses."

Therefore, the old rule that the shorter the focal-length of the lens, the greater the depth of field is not true. It only appears that way. In the typical shot, one taken with a short focal-length lens, a viewer is fooled into thinking that a lot of things are in focus and have great depth of field when in fact it isn't any sharper and has no more picture area in focus (no greater depth of field) than a similar shot taken with a long lens. A viewer is merely distracted into thinking it is because short -focal length lenses allow a viewer to see so much more information; it has a greater angle of view.

Film Selection

"Film represents a key ingredient in your photographic equipment."

Film represents a key ingredient in your photographic equipment. Although there are some basic guidelines that can be followed, choosing the right film for any photo session will often be a subjective decision rather than an objective one. In choosing any film for a photo shoot, you should take into account the film brand, type, color balance, and the film's speed.

Film Brand

There are a number of good films on the market today; however, we favor two: Kodak and Fuji. There may be a lot of technical reasons why one might choose one brand of film over another but with us, it's subjective. For our nude studies, we simply like the results we get with these two films. The Kodak films give excellent, warm skin tones, while the Fuji film yields a cooler look.

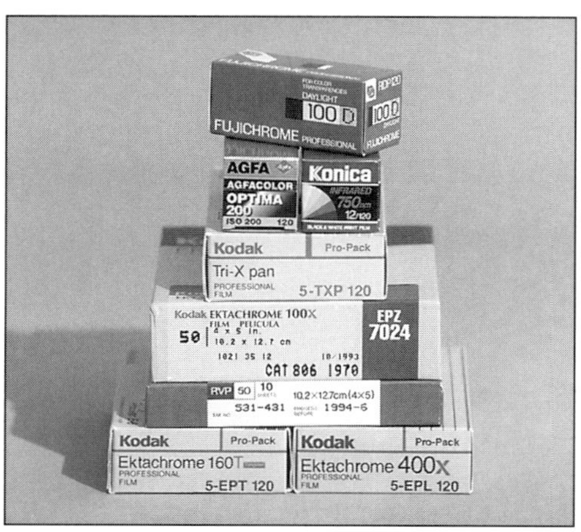

There are a number of good films on the market. We favor two: Kodak and Fuji. Try out different films to find the one or ones that suit you.

Film Type

If you want your final product to be prints of your images, then you should use a negative film (black and white or color) in the first instance.

If you want transparencies or slides, use a positive (color-reversal) film. Although you could shoot a subject on negative film and then copy prints onto slide film, you shouldn't. You'll lose something in the process: less color saturation, fidelity, and sharpness.

The same is true if you shoot with positive (color-reversal) film and then decide to make prints. It can be done, but something will suffer. Therefore, the best rule to follow is to shoot with the type of film needed in the first instance. Most of our nude studies are shot on color negative film (Kodak's VPS III), some with black and white film (Kodak's T-Max) and a few with positive film (Fuji's, Fujichrome).

Color Balance

Generally, film is made for use with one of two different color temperatures or lighting situations: daylight or tungsten. Therefore, you should always use the color balance of film that is compatible with the photo task at hand: daylight film for situations illuminated by daylight or flash; tungsten film for situations lit primarily by tungsten light (such as household lights).

Both natural daylight and flash (both of which are approximately 5500 degrees Kelvin in temperature) have a lot of blue color present in their light. If steps were not taken to correct this condition, photos taken with such film would all have a blue cast to them. As it is, daylight film has been designed to off-set this bluish color; it's been designed to give a viewer more natural looking color in the photo results. Thus, daylight film has been manufactured with an orange cast or bias to it so that when it is matched with the blue light of daylight or electronic flash, the color of the photo results will appear more correct, natural or normal to a viewer's eye.

On the other hand, tungsten lighting is a much warmer light source (about 2000 to 2400 degrees Kelvin) and has a lot of orange light present in it. To off-set this orange light and make any final photo graphic results shot with this type of film look more natural to a viewer, tungsten film has been designed with a blue basis or bias.

Although it is usual and typical to shoot the proper film for any given lighting situation — e.g., using daylight balanced film for situations lit by daylight or flash — this does not mean to say that you can not, or should not, deviate from this rule. When the situation calls for it, or when you wish to flex your creative muscles, you may well want to mix your film with different lightings.

For example, if you used tungsten film with daylight or flash to light your subjects, everything in your photo results would all be very bluish in color. If you use daylight film with tungsten lighting, your photo results will be very biased on the orange side. This, of course, is not normal, but who cares? If the shot you have pre-visualized calls for this sort of deviation, and otherwise meets with your creative intentions, then by all means, go for it.

Film Speed

If there is ample illumination, and you want optimum image resolution and quality, then the "rule" states that you should select the slowest film that is available. If you are going to be working in a low-light situation, and plan to handhold a camera, or if you want to deliberately create a grainy look in your final images, then the "rule" suggests that you use a fast film, with a high ISO rating: ISO 400, ISO 800 or even higher.

Notwithstanding the rules, when we do nude photography and work with color negative film, we prefer using Vericolor, ISO 160, VPS III film or Fujicolor Professional (ISO 100) color-negative film. With black and white film, we prefer the ISO 100 speed of Kodak's T-Max film. In the color-transparency films, we prefer Kodak's Professional Ektachrome 64 or Professional Fujichrome 50. Once in a while, when shooting outdoors in poor light conditions, we'll use a different Kodak color negative film: Vericolor, VPH 400 film. In poor lighting conditions, the final photo results have more snap to them when VPH 400 speed film is used.

Don't be Afraid to Experiment

Using different film brands, types, and speeds in a variety of situations will yield a great variety of photo results. By testing different films under widely varied conditions, you'll become proficient in reproducing those results consistently. However, before you experiment widely, we suggest that you start with one film brand, type, and speed and shoot only with that for awhile.

Learn all you can about that film and how it reacts to different lighting and filtration situations. Then, when you have established a base to work from, move on to another type. Continue testing until you have found the films you like to work with and know the reasons why you like working with them. You'll see that each film will give you a slightly different result. It's not that one will be better than the others; just different. By being aware of these differences, you can more wisely choose the correct film for each photographic task.

"Learn all you can about that film..."

Filters

The filters we most frequently use in our figure photography are soft-focus filters and color-warming filters. Once in a great while we'll also use a special effect filter, such as a four-pointed star filter, but this is rare. We restrict the use of such special effect filters to very appropriate situations; otherwise, their effect can detract from the aesthetics of an image, rather than add to it.

We also tend to avoid special-effect color filters such as deep blue, red, and green, as well as such devices as multi-image filters. We want our images to impress because of the poses, the settings, the lighting, and moods, rather than because of the effect of a filter.

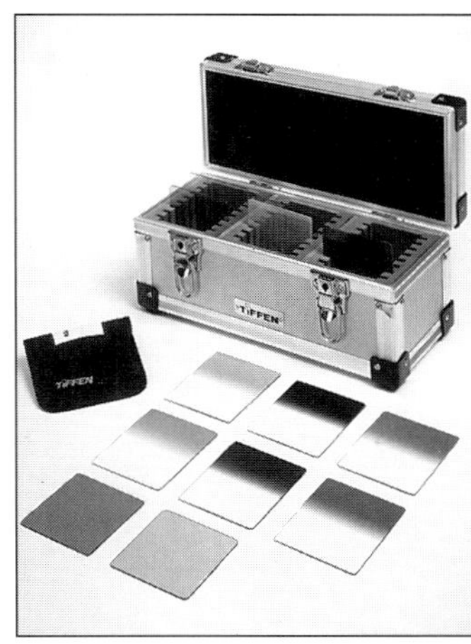

The professional line of Tiffen glass filters.

Soft-focus Filter

Most modern camera lenses produce images of incredibly high resolution, capable of recording a lot of sharp and minute details. When you shoot glamorous, romantic images of women, you usually don't want such totally unforgiving detail. The images would look too literal, too sharp, too harsh, and not very flattering to a female subject's face or figure. This is why we almost always use some sort of soft-focus or diffusion filtration when we photograph a female nude. Depending on the degree of soft-focus effect used, you can simply flatter and

- **We most frequently use soft-focus and color-warming filters for our figure photography.**

glamorize the female face and form, or go to the extent of giving an image a distinctly dreamlike, ethereal look. For full-length images, we frequently use a Softar #1 (made by Hasselblad) on our Hasselblad cameras, and a Softar #2 or #3 when doing tight head or head and shoulder shots.

Making your own filters — Rather than paying large sums of money for commercial filters (e.g., Softars are about $120 apiece), some photographers prefer to make their own. Some make soft-focus filters by smearing Vaseline on a clear-glass filter, a procedure which we neither favor nor follow. Smearing Vaseline has the advantage of giving you a wide range of possible effects; however, any one effect produced is not easily repeated (if at all) in exactly the same way on a later occasion.

Another trick which a number of photographers use is to take a blank filter ring and then attach a piece of netting obtained from a cloth store for a soft-focus filter effect. (The netting comes in various colors and weave-patterns.) Some pieces of material work well, some do not; some produce fair results, some great. In any case it requires a bit of experimentation until you hit on that just right combination that you might favor. This is too involved and time consuming for our taste. There is enough experimenting in photography without adding more problems.

No perfect filter — There are a few things that you should be aware of about soft-focus filters before you rush out and buy some. For example, there are numerous types and grades of commercial soft-focus filters on the market. As a result, there will be no one particular filter which will be the correct one to use for figure photography. There might be one filter you favor for one type of shot, another for another type of session and so on. But, no single soft-focus filter will handle every photographic job you plan to undertake (at least none that we have found). You must experiment until you find the type or grade you prefer, for the results you have in mind.

"...experiment until you find the type or grade you prefer..."

Halation problems — In addition, some soft-focus filters (especially glass ones) have a built-in problem called halation. This condition causes some filters to produce a distinct glow or halo-effect around the brightest parts of a photographic image. They might produce a glow around a white handkerchief or cloth that the subject might be draped with; or a glow around collars and cuffs of white shirts and blouses. This effect is most often inappropriate, if not undesirable, and should usually be avoided. This might mean going to a different brand or type of soft-focus filter, or eliminating the use of a soft-focus filter all together.

If you opt for a different type of filter in order to eliminate the halation problem, we might suggest that you entertain a filter or diffuser made of black netting or black dots. You can purchase black netting from a fabric store and make your own filters as we've previously noted, or you can buy ones commercially made. For example, Tiffen makes a fine set of black net filters; Harrison and Harrison also makes a set of soft-focus filters, but they are a little different. They're called Black Dot filters.

Grades of softness — Most soft-focus filters are rated or graded in degrees of softness. Thus a #1 grade of filter produces a slight degree of soft-focus effect; a #2 grade of filter produces more soft-focus effect than a #1 but less than a grade #3 filter. Unfortunately, this rule only applies to grades of filters with any one given manufacturer. Thus the rule would hold true for all Softar filters by Hasselblad, or all Tiffen SoftNet filters, but not when you compare one manufacturer's brand of filter with another. Thus, a Tiffen Soft Net #1 filter is not equal to the softening effect of a Hasselblad Softar #1.

Exposure compensation — Some soft-focus filters require some exposure compensation when you use them, others do not. What's worse, a grade #1 of one brand of filter may require a different

Opposite page: *This high-key image demonstrates a very simple concept. Once you have a scenario established (in this case, simple high-key), merely changing the pose can be enough to cause pictorial variety. When we shoot nude studies on high-key, we almost never use a soft focus filtration stronger than a Softar #1 by Hasselblad. Anything stronger than this tends to degrade the resulting images too much for our taste: colors become muted and less than saturated, and so on.*

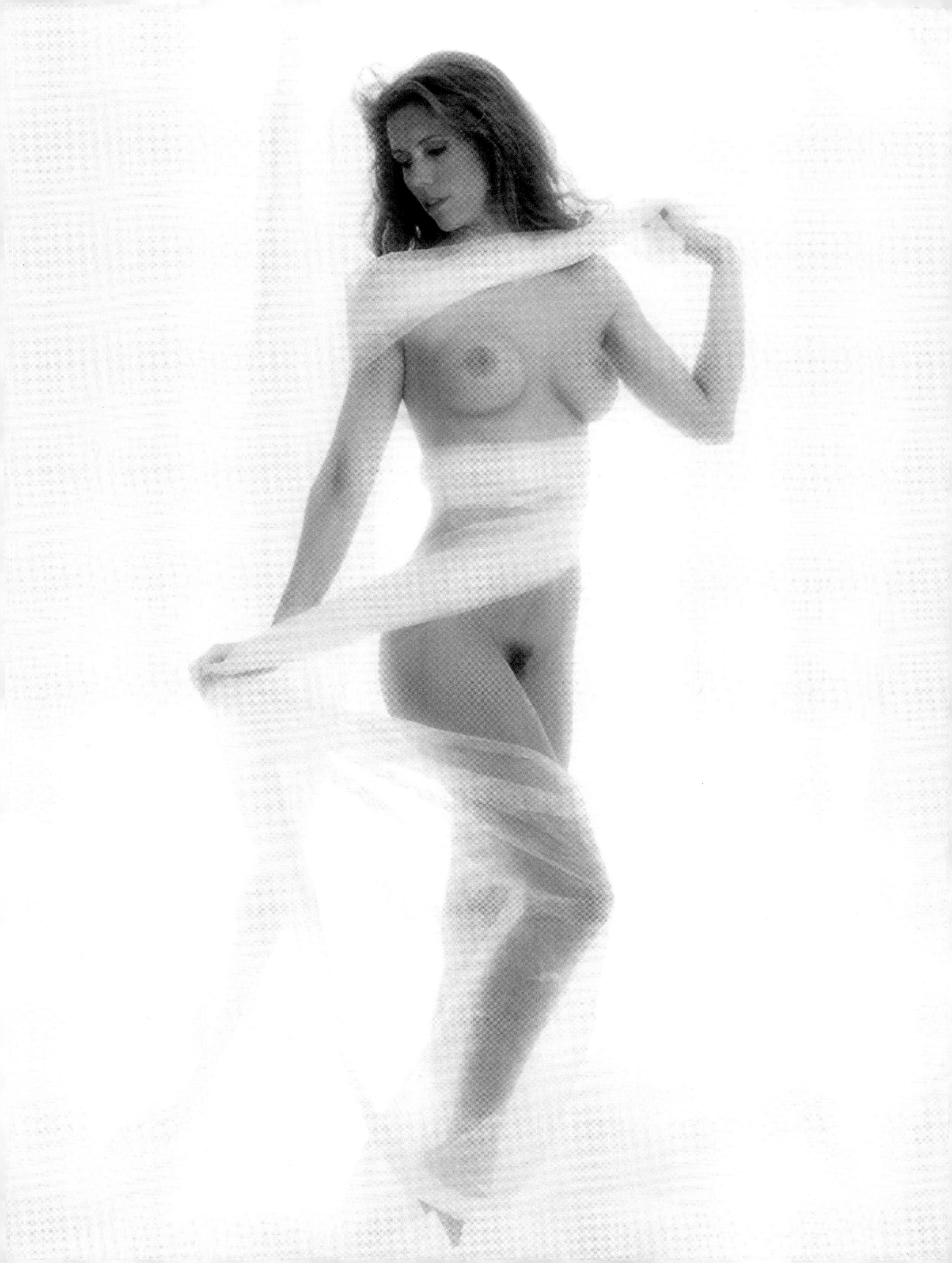

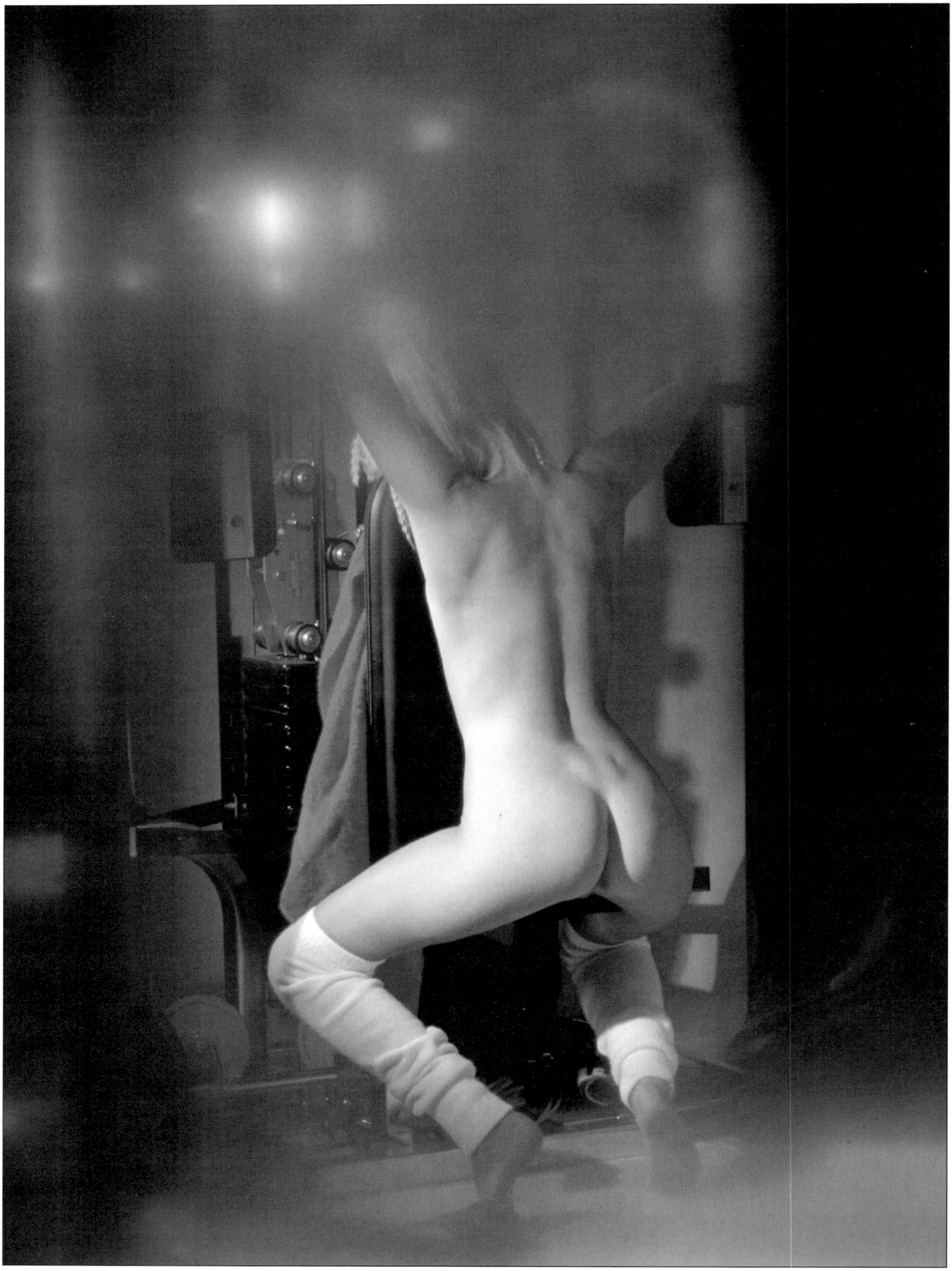

amount of exposure compensation than a #1 filter by another manufacturer. Other than the Softars by Hasselblad (which require no exposure compensation whatsoever when used individually), most all of the soft-focus filters we have ever worked with required some sort of an exposure adjustment from anywhere from 1/3rd of an f-stop to two full f-stops of over exposure.

From a very practical standpoint, what this all means is that if you're using a film with a very low ISO film speed, in a low light situation, you might find it impractical to use such filters; depth of field might become too limited.

Test the filter factor — Although commercially available filters usually come with full directions, including exposure-compensation information, we don't recommend that you blindly accept what a manufacturer says regarding exposure compensation information. Our experience has shown that they are usually wrong and off as much as 1/2 to 3/4ths of an f-stop. Therefore, to be on the safe side, test each filter yourself to find out exactly what the filter factor is.

Here's a simple way to establish the approximate light loss from any filter. Using a hand-held light meter, take an incident-light meter reading of any light source: flash or daylight. Let's assume the reading was f-16.

Now, pointing the meter in exactly the same direction and at the same distance from the previously metered light source, place the soft-focus filter over the meter's diffuser and take another reading. If the meter now reads a lower light value, such as f-11, you know that the light loss is due to the filter, and in our example, this would be one full f-stop or a filter factor of 2x.

Thereafter, every time you use that particular hypothetical filter on your camera, you would have to compensate by opening up your camera's f-stop by an additional one full f-stop.

Filters affect image quality — Soft-focus filters generally reduce image contrast and color saturation to some extent. This is not necessarily a bad thing. You can often use this to your advantage and create some very subtle, lovely figure studies, less harsh and blatant than those made without such filtration.

However, if the contrast level of your images appears too low, or the colors are too muted when you use a soft-focus filter, you might consider changing the light quality to illuminate your subject matter. Often you'll find that by using a harsher, more specular light source you'll achieve a better result. For example, you might have to change from a soft light source such as a soft box to a harder light source, such as a 24-inch bowl reflector, in order to achieve more contrast and saturation in your subject.

To use or not to use a filter — Whether soft-focus filtration is appropriate in the first instance for any given image depends very much on the type of image you're attempting to create.

For example, if we were shooting a strong graphic image, such as a silhouette, with bold, sharp lines, we would normally use a hard light source and no filtration at all. Absent such a situation, and due to the sharpness of modern lenses, we would never photograph a woman for a nude study without some sort of soft-focus filtration.

Warming Filters

Other than a soft-focus filter, there is another filter type we commonly use. It's called a warming filter and its purpose is to warm or give color to an overall bland photo scene. Since this type of filter is generally pink or salmon-colored, it's excellent for giving a healthy glow to skin tones. This is especially true if you are photographing outdoors where the light may be somewhat bluish due to open shade, or when subjects are under an overcast sky.

"...create some very subtle, lovely figure studies..."

Opposite page: *Although some soft-focus filtration devices can be homemade, we usually do not use such devices because it tends to lead to inconsistent if not non-repeatable results. However, we do keep our eyes open for new and different techniques and effects. Such is the case with this photo. We burned a small hole in the center of a small piece of a plastic drop-cloth and placed it over the camera lens. The effect produced images in which much of the subject was pin-sharp while the remainder went soft. The thin, plastic material we used in available from most paint-supply stores and is inexpensive. You can change the soft focus effect by simply adjusting the material over the camera's lens.*

Even when we photograph early in the morning or late in the day, when the sun is at its warmest color, the presence of blue light in the shadows sometimes bothers us.

To reduce or eliminate this blue condition, we'll use a warming filter. The ones we currently favor are the Cr.1.5 or 3.0 by Hasselblad, a Wratten 81A, a Tiffen No. 812, and a Singh-Ray warming filter.

Reflectors

Both outdoors and in the studio, we often use reflectors instead of electronic flash as secondary light sources. A well-placed reflector can raise the illumination on the shadow side of a subject by one or more f-stops, depending on the type and size of the reflector, the amount of light striking it, and its distance from the subject. Reflectors can also be used to back light or accent a part of a subject or scene. Reflectors are a wonderful compromise or alternative when flash is not available or practical.

"A regular mirror can make a very efficient reflector."

Reflectors are available commercially in many sizes and shapes — square, round, and rectangular — and come in a number of different materials and in varying colors. They can be matte, super matte, or highly reflective. They can be silvered, golden, white, or mirrored.

Even though all of these are readily available on the market, many of our reflectors are homemade, to suit our specific purposes.

Foamcore Boards

These boards come in white, and usually in one standard, 4x8-foot size. They are readily available from most art or hardware stores and make excellent reflectors. With an X-acto or carpet knife, they can be cut into any size or shape with ease, since they are only about 1/8-inch thick.

They can be used with their natural white surface or modified by covering all or part of the surface with pieces of material, such as silver or gold mylar, or even colored gels. The boards are inexpensive—about $10 per 4x8-foot board — very lightweight, and easily transportable and movable.

In addition to reflecting light and from a structural standpoint, a foamcore board makes a great gobo — an item used to hold back unwanted light. However, for this purpose, a board should be black. Since they come in white, your first inclination might be to paint it black. Don't do it. The boards are highly absorbent and paint will soak in, causing them to buckle. A better way is to cover the board with some black material.

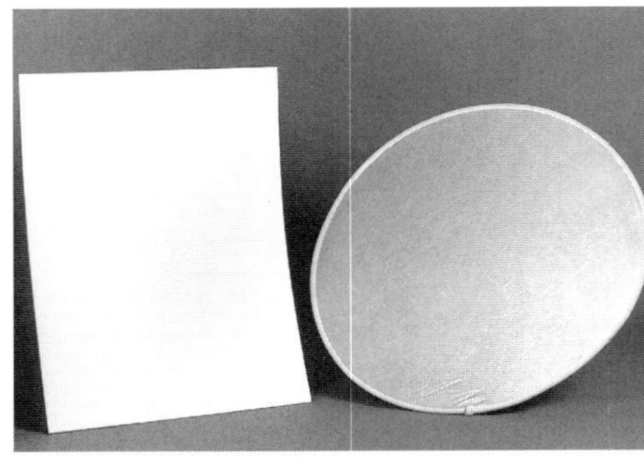

You can make your own reflectors with foamcore board. Foamcore is available at most art or hardware stores. With an X-acto or carpet knife, they can be cut into any size or shape.

Mirrored Reflectors

A regular mirror can make a very efficient reflector. Sometimes a mirror can be too efficient. A highly polished mirror will sometimes reflect almost as much light as is coming from the actual source. This is acceptable if the reflector is being used as an accent or back light, but is often inappropriate for a fill light.

Plastic mirrors are easier to use than. Plastic mirrors are lighter in weight and therefore easier to transport and maneuver. They can usually be purchased from companies that sell Formica. One of the standard size of 4x8 feet costs about $100. Although this size is often too large to work with, the plastic mirror can easily be cut by the supplier into any size or shape you want.

Although plastic mirror reflectors are heavier and cost considerably more than foamcore reflectors, their efficiency in reflecting light is far greater; although, slightly less light-efficient than top-quality glass mirrors.

Reflector Efficiency

The more dull or matte the surface of any reflector, the less light-efficient it will be; the less light will be reflected back onto a subject. The more specular the surface of any reflector, the more light-efficient a reflector will be.

A white reflector is less efficient than a mirrored one. However, a white reflector will produce a soft, reflected light; whereas, a mirrored reflector is much more light-efficient, but it will produce a harsh, bold, specular light source.

It's not that one is bad and one good; each type of reflector has its place and use for nude studies. A reflector should be chosen based on the type of results you seek, rather than simply because it's handy. For example, a gold reflector and a silver reflector are very close to being equal in reflective efficiency.

However, a gold reflector would usually be totally inappropriate for an Asian subject, and perfect for a Caucasian or African-American subject.

Making a Reflector

You can create reflectors of various kinds by using a wide variety of materials. For example, a white pillowcase, bed sheet, or even pieces of newspaper can make a great reflector.

For a more sturdy reflector, try aluminum foil adhered to a board with double stick tape or spray glue. It makes an excellent reflector. You can leave the foil in its original, flat form, or you can crumple it and then straighten it again sufficiently to enable you to adhere it to a board. The more flat the foil is on the board, the less specular the reflected light. The more crumpled the foil is on the board, the more specular the reflected light.

Each different treatment will give you a slightly different reflector effect. Some effects you make like, others not.

When to use reflectors — As is the case with a light source, a reflector should never be used just for the sake of using one. A reflector should be used only to accomplish a specific end result: back lighting a subject, accenting or highlighting a portion of a set, prop, or subject's body, or filling in shadows.

Although these same lighting goals can be accomplished with a regular light source (such as a flash), sometimes an additional light is not available or practical. In this case a reflector can be an ideal substitute.

Reflector size — As a general rule, a reflector should be at least the same size or slightly larger than the area to be illuminated. For example, if we wanted to rim light a standing subject with a strip of light from head to feet, of someone five feet tall, we would use a reflector that was at least five feet in height, but no more than six feet. For such rim lighting, the width of the reflector would not need to be very great — no more than six to nine inches.

If a reflector is too big in height or width, it may put light in areas other than the place intended. If it is too small, it usually will not adequately illuminate the desired area. In either case it would be poor light control not to have the right size reflector. This is one of the reasons why we prefer to tailor-make our own reflectors.

"...we prefer to tailor-make our own reflectors."

Selecting And Using Exposure Meters

Accurate and consistent exposures are essential for top-quality photography. It doesn't matter what lighting situation you might be faced with (tungsten light, daylight or electronic flash), or what key of lighting you might be in (high-key, low-key or medium key), your film should always be receiving an adequate amount of light (or exposure) to get the information (your subject matter) properly recorded onto the film.

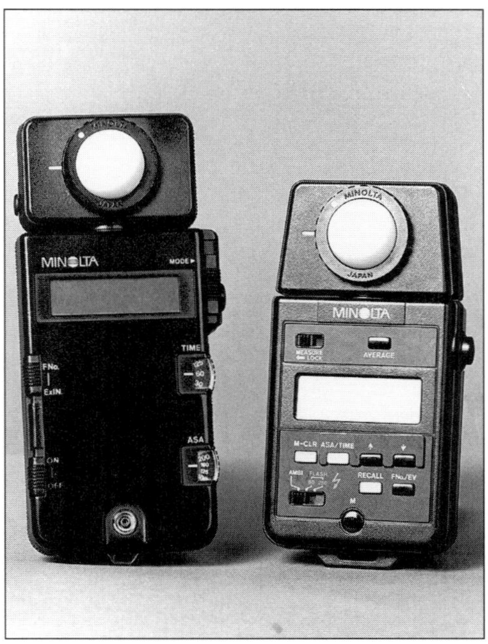

Meters, like these from Minolta, can help you to achieve accurate and consistent exposures needed for top-quality photography. Your film should always be receiving an adequate amount of light for good results.

"...you should use a good exposure meter."

To help accomplish these results, you should use a good exposure meter. For most of our figure photography, we use a hand held light meter in the incident-light mode.

The hand held meters we use at the present time are the Minolta Auto Meter III-F, the Minolta Flash Meter III and IV, and the Ultra-Pro by Gossen.

Obtaining Exposure Data and Bracketing

Once a meter reading is taken of a given lighting condition, it usually is a simple matter to transfer the obtained information (the f-stop and shutter speed data) over to your camera, and then take the photo.

However, many photographers go further; they bracket their exposures. They take a meter reading, set their camera according to the information supplied by the meter, and then take a photo. But, they then will back this photo up by taking the same shot at several other exposure settings, such as 1/2 and 1 f-stop over and under the first metered exposure to ensure the best possible exposure results.

Although we have used this bracketing-exposure method on some rare occasions, we generally find it wasteful and time-consuming.

Even though we don't favor bracketing, we recognize that it is a matter of personal taste and style, and each photographer must work in the manner he or she feels most comfortable.

Many years ago, Sheila and I studied with a well-known fashion photographer. We were with him when he shot an ad campaign for a national company. His assignment was simple. He had to take five different shots, involving five different settings of one model wearing five different outfits.

The cost of the shoot, including the professional model, the location setting, the props, stylist and the photographer, was high; about $50,000 for the day. Consequently, it was important to avoid the need for a re-shoot. The photographer's technical safety net was to use exposure bracketing.

To get his five images, he expended 10 hours of his time and exposed a total of 2700 frames of film. Ever since that experience, we have resolved to rely on exposure accuracy rather than on bracketing exposures. This, of course, requires that one be very knowledgeable and comfortable with the concept of lighting and exposure.

Take Multiple Meter Readings

Even though you may not bracket your exposures, don't just meter the subject and setting at the beginning of a photo session and leave it at that. You should meter a lot during the course of your photo session too.

Every time there is a major move of your subject in relationship to the lighting setup or vice versa, a new meter reading should be taken for accuracy and consistency.

How and Why We Measure or Meter Light

We start all our shots by metering only the main light source at the subject's position, with the incident-light dome of the meter directed toward the main source of illumination.

During this procedure, all other lights are turned off. Once we have obtained information about the main light source, all other lights we intend to use (back lights, background lights, accent lights, and fill lights), whether from direct electronic flash, reflectors, or ambient light, are then metered separately.

Each light source has its power adjusted to emit slightly more or less light than the main light, depending on the effect or mood we are trying to create. The main-light meter reading is used as the standard.

All other lights are adjusted around this standard value. If the main-light value on the subject shifts up or down — as it often does during a studio sitting when a subject's distance from the main light changes — it's a simple matter to re-meter the main-light source and then move it closer to, or farther from, the subject, or adjust its power, so that we can remain with the initial f-stop and shutter speed setting that had been previously selected.

Whether indoors or outdoors, using ambient light, electronic flash, or reflected light, this constant monitoring by metering helps us maintain consistently good exposures for each frame of film shot during an entire photo session. This procedure also eliminates the necessity for bracketing.

Camera Support

In our studio, we follow a simple rule when it comes to tripods: we almost always use one, even if we're working with a 35mm camera. We consider a tripod an essential item of basic equipment since it helps ensure stability and the sharpness of a final image.

Tripods

The camera support we use in our studio is by Arkay. It's a relatively expensive one, on a 7-foot stand mounted atop a very sturdy, three-wheeled dolly-base. For our location photography, we use a much more portable tripod, without wheels; ones by Tiltall and Bogen. Since stability is the main purpose for using a tripod, when we have a choice, we always go for a heavier, sturdier tripod than what we might need.

For example, if we are using a 35mm camera, we will use a tripod that is primarily designed for, and which can support, more weight, such as a 2-1/4-square-inch camera. For our medium-format cameras, we use tripods that are designed for and can support the weight of a 4 x 5 view camera. Following this guideline helps us get the stability we need.

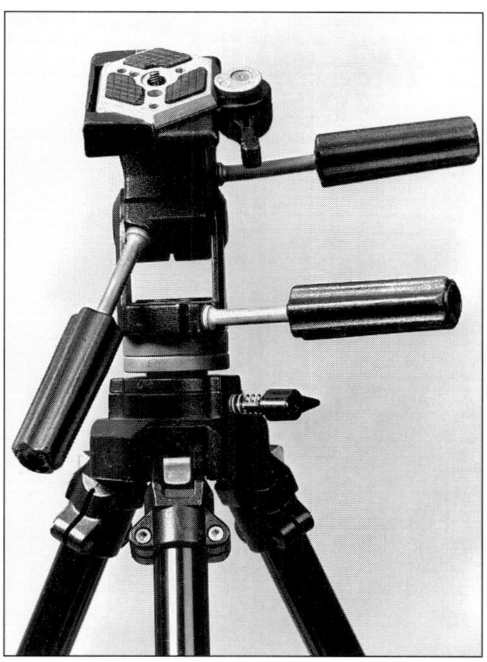

A good sturdy tripod is an essential item of basic equipment. It helps to ensure stability and the sharpness of a final image.

Modifying a tripod — Sturdiness is not the only consideration; smoothness of motion is also an important factor. Unfortunately, most of the more elaborate tripods that we have seen come with separate, individual controls (three separate handles) for controlling the motion. Typically, one control is designed for camera height, one for horizontal swing, and one for vertical tilt.

Unfortunately, these handles don't promote ease of camera handling. As a result, we don't like these types of separate controls and therefore modify all of our tripods with a Leitz ball-and-socket head. This head has only one knob, allowing us the ability to control camera height, swing, and tilt all at the same time. We find this much easier and faster than using a tripod that is not so equipped. However, the Leitz head is not cheap, costing about $150. If this is too much for your budget, you might consider a very viable alternative. Bogen is now making a very good similar adapter for a lot less money.

Buy a versatile tripod — As if the above were not enough, size (specifically height) is another consideration. Most of the better and sturdier camera tripods stand about 30 to 36 inches tall when their legs are not fully extended. Since most of these have telescopic legs, when they are fully extended their height extends to about six feet or more.

We have found times when having a camera only 30 or 36 inches above the ground is just too high. What if you wanted to shoot from a lower camera angle (such as 12 to 16 inches) and use a tripod? Therefore, it becomes important to have a tripod that is versatile and which will accommodate. One that we know of that allows its legs to be opened more fully, holding a camera lower to the ground, is the Bogen model 3068.

- **A good sturdy tripod is an essential item of basic equipment.**

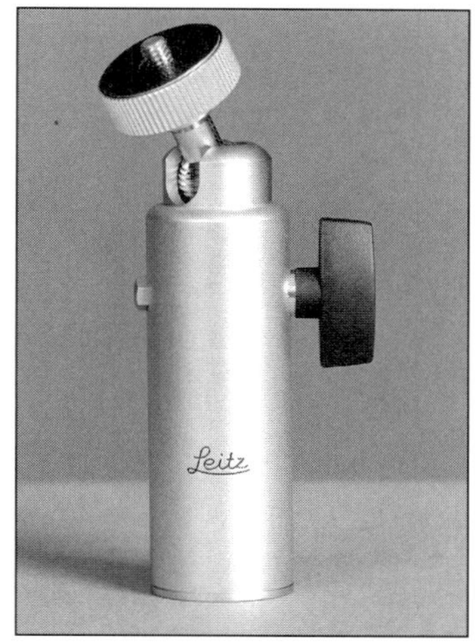

A Leitz ball-and-socket head.

CHAPTER SEVEN

Lights and Lighting Techniques

"dozens of lighting options to choose from..."

There are a number of different sources or types of illumination that could be used for nude photography. For example, one type of light source that could be used is daylight. Other types of light sources include electronic flash and tungsten light.

The number of different light sources can also be increased if you consider that different types of light sources can often be mixed to create even more varied sources of illumination. For example, daylight can be mixed with flash, flash mixed with tungsten lights, and tungsten mixed with daylight.

Lighting options could be increased even further if you also consider another variable and factor: the quality of light (i.e., hard light versus soft light) produced by any given type of light source.

In other words, one could use soft tungsten light with hard tungsten light, or soft electronic flash with hard tungsten light. This condition gives dozens of lighting options to choose from for almost any photo situation.

As a result, and before any film is ever exposed, lighting (in terms of quantity of lights, type of lights and quality of lights) should be well thought out with subjects and settings illuminated by design and not by chance. At first blush, this whole process sounds rather formidable.

However, its not as difficult as it might sound, especially if you think of lights as falling into one of three primary categories: main light; fill light; and other lights. It also helps if you think in terms of building your lighting around a subject and setting, one light at a time.

Main Light

How many lights must be used for nude photography? If we were in a totally dark environment, we wouldn't be able to photograph anything without the benefit of at least one light. This one light is usually referred to as the main, key, or primary light. The reason it's called by these names is because it has the sole obligation of sufficiently illuminating the subject matter of a given photo scene (which, in nude photography, will usually be the subject), so that it can be adequately recorded onto film.

This one light has another key role. It's also responsible for setting the standard for which all other lights should follow. Once a main light has been chosen, brought onto the set, positioned, and its strength of light metered, all other lights which are going to be used (including a fill, back light, background light, or accent light), should then be set and adjusted in relationship to the power output of the main light.

Thus, all the other lights to be used should be set to a power setting either equal to, just lower than, or just stronger than, the given main light.

How much lower or stronger should these other lights have their respective powers adjusted? This will depend on the lighting effect desired as well as the type of film being used (the latitude of the

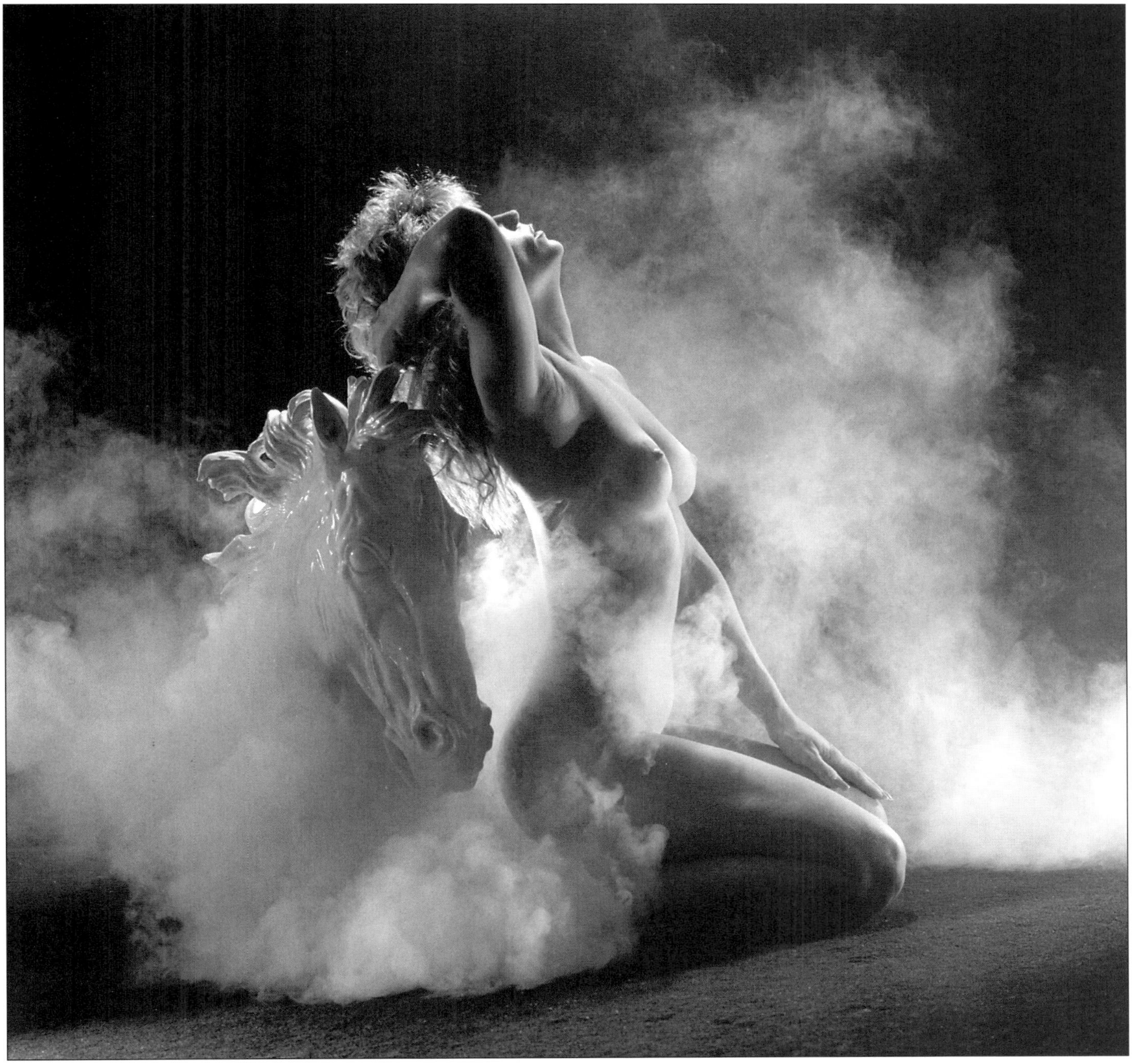

Above: *If you are going to use fog in a photo scene, then you should usually light it separately. If you don't, it will tend to look dark and even a little "dirty." Notwithstanding this general rule, we chose to only light a portion of the fog in this scene; the part that was striking the subject. By doing so, it helps direct a viewer's attention directly to those portions of the subject we wanted seen. As a general rule, and depending upon you taste, fog should be illuminated by an accent light whose power had been set to no less than one full f-stop less than its companion main light, of equal value to the main light, or to an output that is no more than one full stop more than the main light.*

film). For example, you will have more options if you're using black and white film and different options if you are using color negative film.

In other words, when using black and white film, you might like the dramatic effect of an accent light that has its power adjusted to two or three f-stops under the power of your main light. If you were to switch to color transparency film and wanted to get the same effect, you'll usually find that adjusting the accent light's power to about one full f-stop of power less than the main light will give you the same result.

This is because color transparency film has far less latitude than black and white film and thus does not see light as efficiently. As we have already noted, there can be a problem choosing any main light (or any light for photography for that matter) because there are a lot of variables and choices.

A main light can vary in power output, size, shape, light quality and it can come from a number of different sources: natural daylight, electronic flash, tungsten bulbs, and so on. Notwithstanding all of these variables, there are some things that one can look to and use as guides. In this chapter, we shall be developing some of these points.

Fill Light

In any photo scene, the existence of a main light (any main light) means at least a few things to most photographers. First, it means that there will usually be some sort of shadows created by the key light and, secondly, that such shadows will usually fall on or about the setting, subject or both.

In addition, a subject and setting lit only by a main light will usually mean that the photo scene will have a lot of contrast. Whatever the main light strikes will be bright. Whatever it doesn't will usually be dark; a contrast will thus exist between the light and dark areas.

The difference between these light and dark areas (i.e., the ratio of lighting difference between the light and dark areas, which is often expressed in ratio-terms such as 2 to 1, 4 to 1, 6 to 1) is commonly referred to as a contrast range. A fill light serves to lighten the shadow areas created by a main light as well as to control (or reduce) the overall contrast range of a photo scene.

"A fill light serves to lighten the shadow areas..."

More succinctly stated, the stronger the fill light (i.e., the more closely a fill light source equals that of a main light source in power output), the less contrast there will be. The darker the shadows, the more serious or somber the mood, the lighter the shadows the more light and airy the mood.

Because of this, it would seem that one should never photograph without the benefit of some sort of fill light source. From a very practical standpoint, this is not necessarily the case.

Sometimes, depending on the quality (the hardness or softness) of the main light, and the overall pictorial effect desired by the photographer, a fill light might not be used at all.

In such a case, the contrast range will usually be great (such as 6 to 1 or more), the mood austere, and the images created by only the illumination of a main light, very dramatic.

Like the main light, the fill light can come from one of several different direct lighting sources. It could also come from indirect sources; from light reflected from a portable reflector, off a nearby wall, a sheet, or a sandy beach on which the subject is posed. In addition, a fill light can be most any size or shape, although typically, it is usually the same size or larger than the subject matter to be photographed and the same size or larger than a fill light's counterpart, the main light.

Although it might seem that the guidelines of a fill light are rather loose, there are a couple of things that are very definite. For example, a fill light should never have its power output equal to or stronger than its companion main light. If it does, it'll cease being a fill light source; it'll totally overpower the shadows created by the main light and, in effect, become a main light itself.

In addition, a fill light should not create its own shadows, at least none which could be perceived by the camera. If it does, the shadows would conflict with the main-light's shadows and this would look very unnatural in the photo.

To help guard against such conditions, follow some simple rules: use only a soft

Opposite page: *This image was captured on Kodak's T-Max 100 black and white film, using a four light set up. A top light, mounted on a boom stand just above the subjects, was housed in a 6-inch bowl reflector and acted as the main light. Three accent lights, each housed in a 4-inch snoot-type reflector, rounded out our lighting. One accent light was set at 90 degrees to the right of camera axis and was directed onto the female subject's hair. Its power was adjusted to equal that of the main light. A second accent light was placed about 110 degrees to the right of camera axis and was directed onto the female subject's buttocks. Its power was set to be one full f-stop less than the main light. The last accent light was set about 70 degrees to the right of camera axis and was directed onto the male subject's face. Its power was adjusted to be three full f-stops less than that of the main light.*

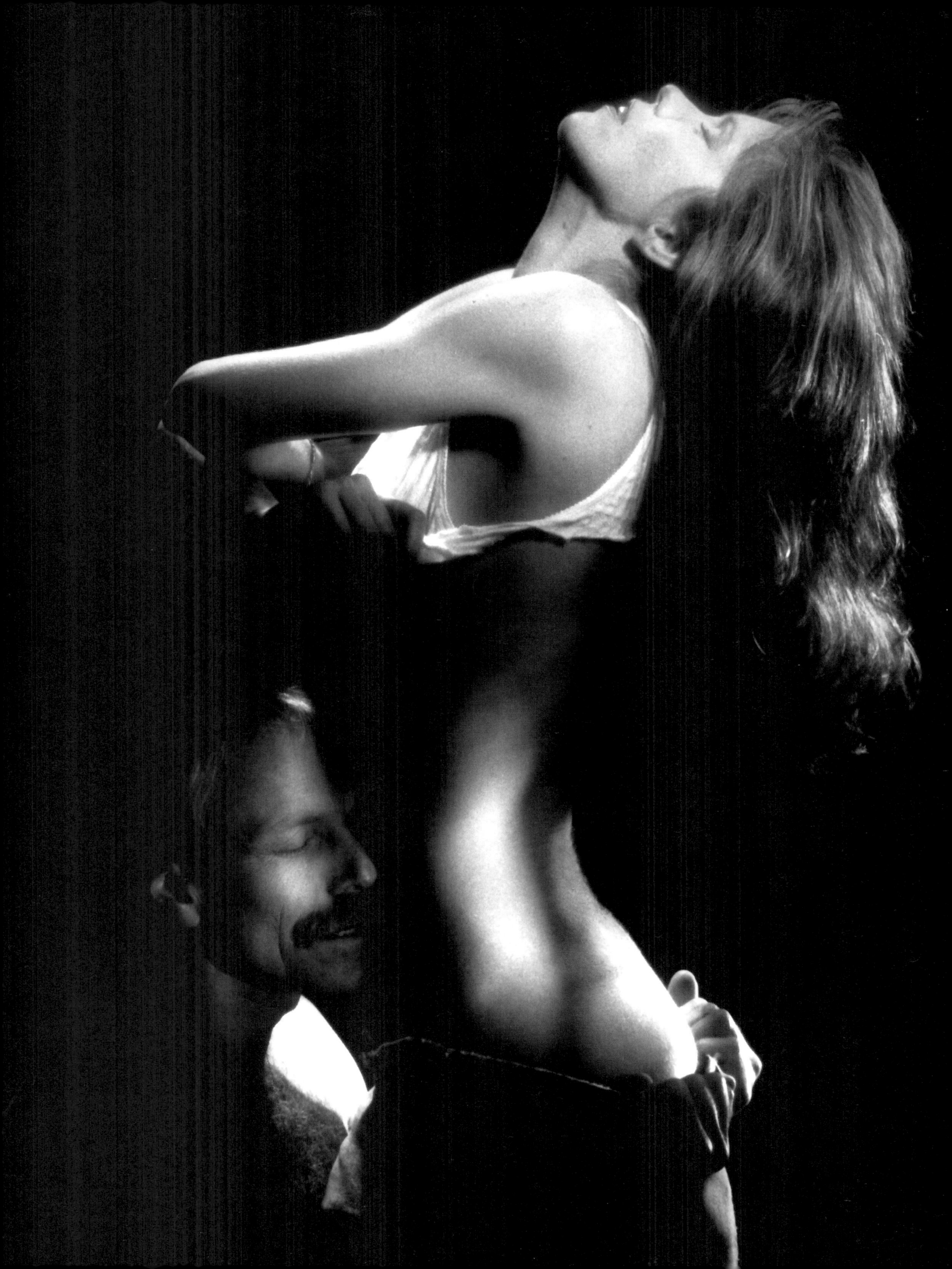

"...there are many other lights which can be used in nude photography."

light fill light source, making certain that it is larger than the main light it's paired with and that the fill is always set to a lower power output than its companion main light.

Other Lights

In addition to the main and fill lights, there are many other lights which can be used in nude photography. These other lights have the specific function of illuminating parts of a subject, setting, background, or props. These lights include back lights, hair lights, background lights, and accent or kicker lights. During any given photo session, one or more of these lights may be used in combination with any other of these lights, depending on the photographer's wishes, as well as the results and effects sought. But, this explanation might seem to be too vague to be of much value. Therefore, to keep things simple, keep a few general rules in mind:

1. Never use any light just to use a light.
2. Use a light only if it is going to accomplish a specific purpose.
3. If you want to see something, light it. If you don't, don't.
4. Lighting should be based upon a subject's nose axis.

Of these four rules, only the last one needs some explanation.

Look at Diagram 7-1 (See page 124). Notice how the subject's nose is pointed toward, and in line with, the camera's position and an imaginary line which we have labeled the 0 degree line. As a general guide, and referring to a light's placement, a top, back, accent or kicker light usually gets placed anywhere along the arcs of, or within, the quadrants of C or D, directed, of course, toward the subject.

Now look at Diagram 7-2 (See page 124). Notice that neither the camera nor the subject's body have been moved. Only the subject's head has been turned away from the camera (to the right of camera; to the subject's left; counterclockwise from the subject's initial position). Note also that because the subject's head has been moved, all of the arcs have moved too; they have moved proportionately in the same, counterclockwise direction: to the subject's left. The area of the other lights (back lights, kicker/accent lights) still lie within and on arcs and quadrants C and D. All the lights have merely followed the subject's nose axis. By following this rule, some of the mystery of light placement is removed. It makes it easier to know where to place a light in relationship to a subject.

No lighting placement should ever be so rigid that you force your subject or subject matter to conform to its placement rather than the other way around. Lighting — with a few exceptions — should be flexible so that it accomplishes the lighting goal.

Accent or kicker light — The function of an accent or kicker light is to highlight or accent one or more portions of a setting, prop, the subject's face or body that are to appear in a photo scene. These lights are usually easy to discern since they're usually of the spotlight type and most often are housed in rather long and slender, four or five-inch snooted reflectors. Housings such as these make lighting very directional and easily controllable, producing a hard, precisely limited light. Even though such light housings are typical for accent lights, an accent or kicker light does not even have to be a true light source. An accent or kicker light can be in the form of an appropriately sized, shaped, and placed reflector.

The exact placement of a kicker or accent light and its power output will often not be decided until the subject is actually posed on the set or at the location. It's generally at this time that a decision will be made as to which portions of the subject's body, set or props should be accented, to what extent (i.e., how much power) and where such lights should precisely be placed. One word of caution when it comes to using accent lights. Don't. If you don't know where to put an accent light or if you are not sure if you should have one, then don't use one. Keep your lighting as simple as possible and use accent lights with restraint, especially until you are really confident of your basic lighting techniques.

Back light — This light can be similar to an accent light in type, but its placement generally differs. It's often positioned directly and squarely behind a subject, pointed toward the subject. Its height can be set as low as the floor, up to and level with the back of a subject's head, or anywhere between these extremes, depending on which part of the subject's body you wish delineated with light. Its purpose is usually to provide graphic separation between a subject and a background, to outline the subject's body, to highlight the subject's hair, or some combination of all three.

Top light — This light, which can be of any size or shape, and in any form of housing, is most conveniently used on a boom stand, suspended above, and slightly behind, a subject. It's sometimes called a hair light and its purpose is to visually separate a subject from the background as well as to provide ideal illumination for the back and top of a subject's head, and sometimes, shoulders.

When we want a rather hard edge to a top light, we'll use a small light, one housed in about a six-inch silvered bowl reflector. For a softer look, a light housed in a small soft box is ideal.

Background light — A background light serves two major purposes: to illuminate a background so that it can be seen and recorded on film, and to graphically separate a subject from it. Depending on the size, reflective quality and the emphasis you wish to place on a background, you might use one or several lights to accomplish your purpose.

Regarding power, and as a general proposition (assuming you're using color negative film), a background light could have its power set anywhere from two stops under that of the main light power setting to three stops over the main light setting, depending upon the effect you are trying to create. Regarding its size, and depending on the area that needs to be covered, you can use lights in small, six inch bowl reflectors, in umbrellas or in large light-banks.

To obtain uniform illumination on a large background, and at a minimum, you should use one light on either side of the background, directed toward the background's approximate center. While lighting a background is usually not complicated, there is one word of caution.

When you're using large, powerful background lights, watch out for a condition called halation; it's unwanted flare. Halation causes a subject's outline to glow, appear ethereal, ghost-like and less than sharply defined in the final photo results. This condition is usually caused by placing a subject too close to a background, and by having the background lights too powerful so that excess light spills off and reflects from the background back onto a subject's person. Although flare, like most other conditions, can sometimes be used creatively for a special effect, most often it'll be a condition which you will want to avoid.

The Basics

With so many different types of lights and lighting techniques which can be used for nude photography, it becomes important to keep a few basics in mind.

1. You only need one light.
2. Sometimes you might use two or more lights.
3. Build lights one at a time
4. Sometimes you might use two main lights.
5. Typically a main and fill light are used.
6. The quality of the light sources must be considered. This, by necessity, must take into account:
   a) Size of a light source
   b) Proximity of a light source
   c) Diffusing materials for a light source
   d) Housings for a light source

• **There are a few basics of lighting you should keep in mind.**

One Main Light

We sometimes forget a very rudimentary principal. Whether it be from electronic flash, tungsten, daylight, or other form of illumination, some very beautiful nude studies can be made by just using one light; a main light. This is because a main light does more than simply provide the illumination needed to record an image on film. It is responsible for providing the modeling and texture in a subject, and setting the mood for a photo scene.

Thus, and using only a single (main light) light source placed at about 45 degrees to the right or left of the camera-subject axis, an appreciable portion of a subject's body (opposite from the main light source) will go into deep shadow.

This portion of a subject's body which has received the main light illumination, will, because of the angle of the light, be perceived by the film as having a fair amount of depth and texture.

This single-light concept can be very effective for certain types of shots; it can create an air of drama, somberness, or mystery. However, the moment you add a fill light source (even one which has its power setting adjusted low, to emit an f-

"This single-light concept can be very effective..."

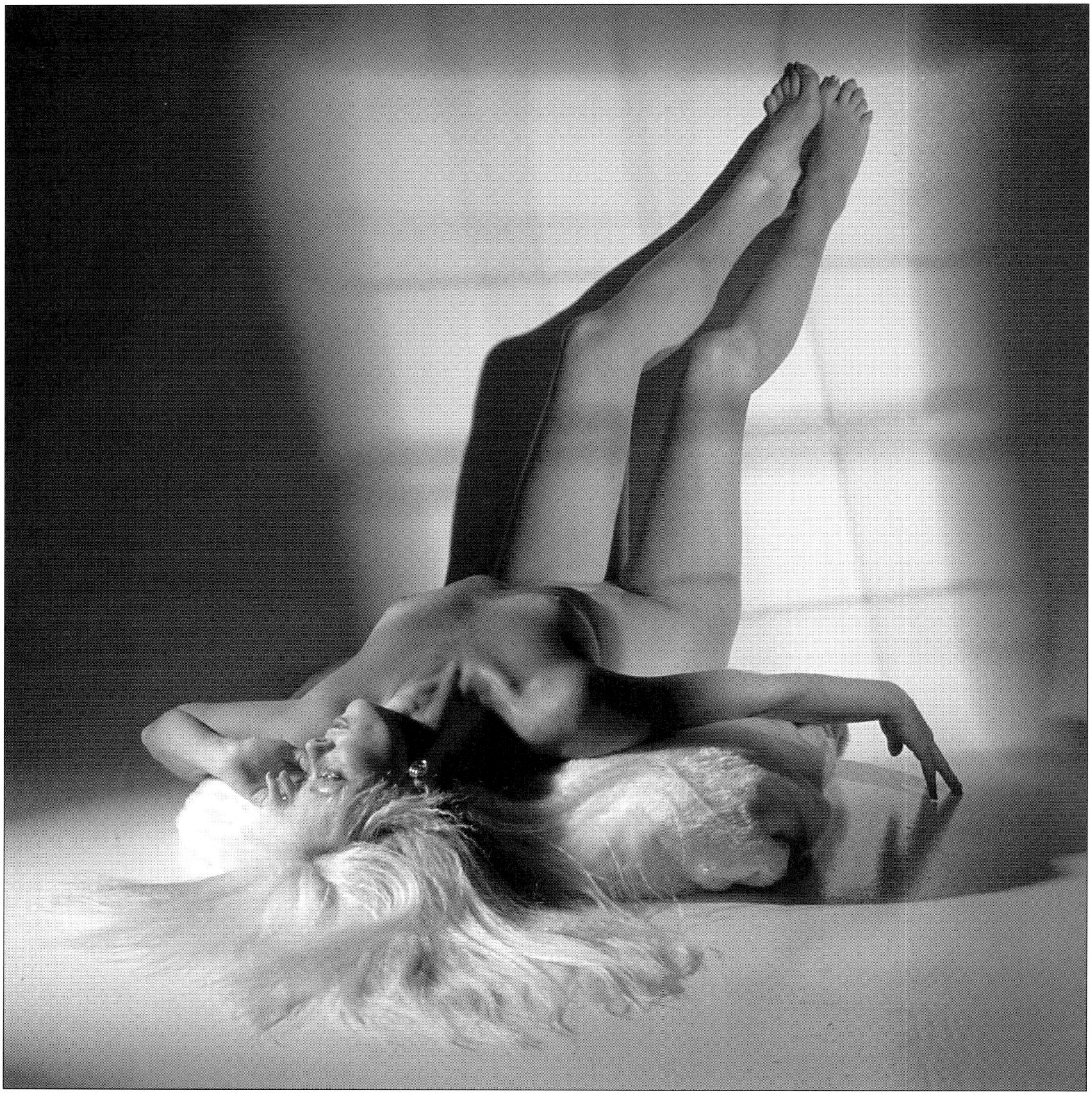

***Above:** In this image, we wanted the subject's entire being to reflect a total lack of strain and tension, much as though she were lying in a room , in the early morning sunlight, contemplating the day that was just beginning. The lighting was kept simple. We used a Bowens Monospot flash, to the right of the camera position, as the main light. We put a "window-pane" grid over the light to create the window effect and placed a yellow gel over the light. This light was directed at the lower portion of the subject's torso, her legs, and a portion of the white background sweep. The light was intentionally not focused critically, so that the window-pane pattern on the background would go soft, so as not to be too prominent and distracting. A second light, on the floor and about 90 degrees to the left of the camera-subject axis, was in a bowl reflector with a 4-inch snoot and a yellow gel. It was directed onto the subject's hair, face, and shoulders. Its power was set equal to that of the main light.*

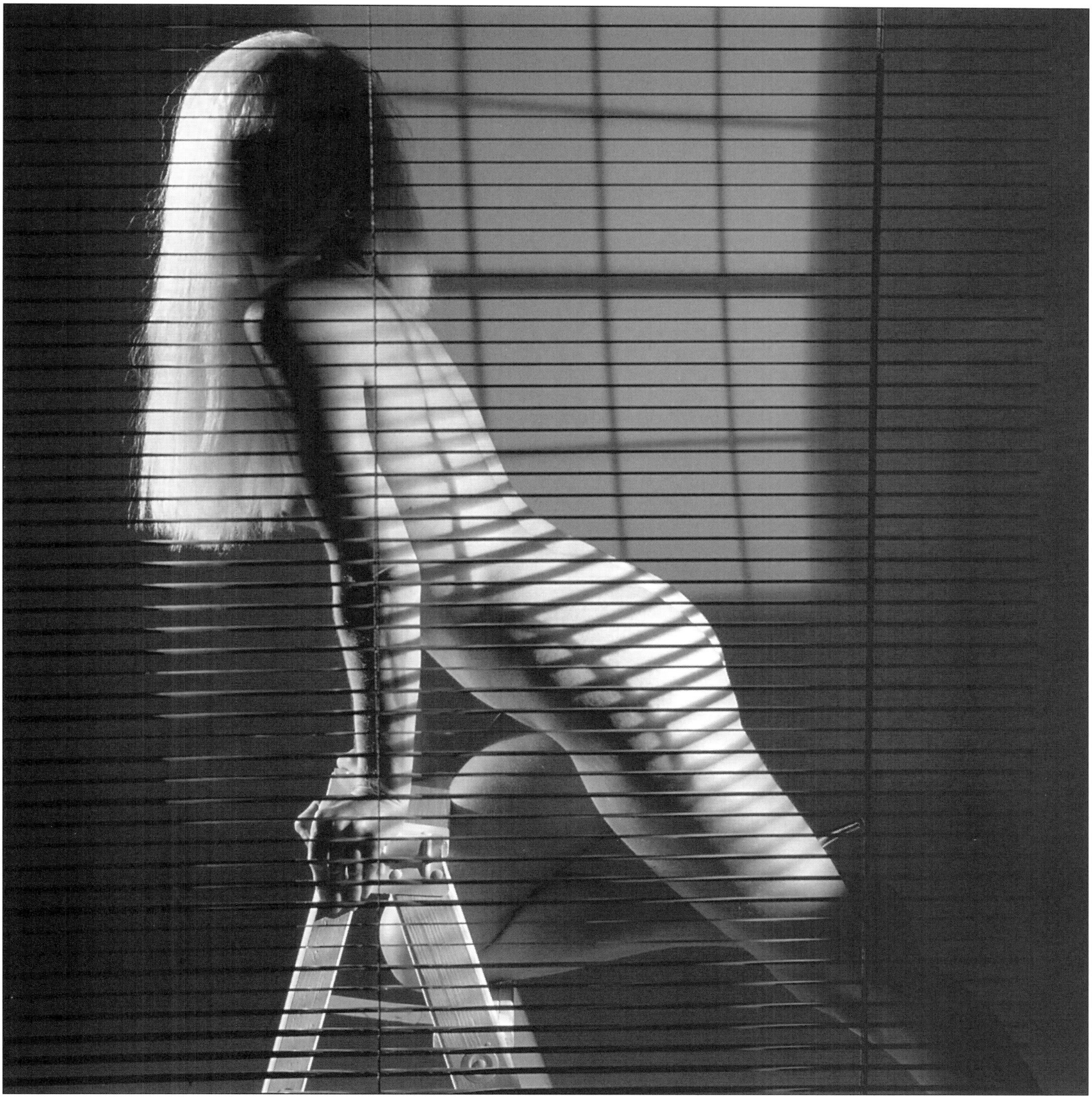

Above: *We enjoy working with both horizontal and vertical blinds because they give us the ability to create some very stunning, different-looking figure studies. Once a blind is in place, there are two ways in which we can light the scene so that it appears that the subject has shadows falling onto her from the blind. One way is to light the blind with hard, frontal lighting, to create sharp shadows on the subject's body. However, we don't favor this approach because it forces us to work with the subject in very close proximity to the blind, restricting the posing options. In addition, when a blind is illuminated directly from the front, it becomes prominent in the photo. A second, more preferred way, gives us more control and better results. We put no frontal light on the blind at all but place a Bowens Monospot flash, with a "blinds" grid pattern over it, behind the blind. This light creates the shadows for the subject's body but gives a viewer the impression that light falling through the blinds is causing the illumination to appear on her. This is the technique we used for this image. We placed the Monospot main light behind the blind, almost 90 degrees to the right of the camera-subject axis. We shielded the side of the light with barn doors, to keep any of its illumination from striking the real blind. To highlight the hair, we introduced a light with a 4-inch snoot and a yellow gel, placing it about 90 degrees to the left of the camera-subject axis. Its power was set to equal the power of the main light.*

• **Take care not to over-light you subject. When in doubt, start with just one light.**

"Don't try to work with all the lights you intend to use, all at one time..."

stop of two or three f-stops under that of its main light counterpart), the air of drama, somberness and mystery lessen, or are eliminated. As a result of this, there is some caution that should be exercised.

A number of photographers — especially ones just starting often commit a cardinal lighting sin: over-lighting their subject, setting or both. They'll use too many lights. Most often you will use more than one light for your nude studies. However, when in doubt, start with just one light; a main light. You might find that this one light will serve your needs.

Two or More Lights

Even though using one light can produce some dynamite photos and can give even a novice photographer a number of lighting options from a lighting placement point of view, multiple lights can do more. If you consider lighting a subject with two lights — for example, one main light and one fill light, one main light and one kicker light, or even two main lights — lighting options increase dramatically. For even more pictorial variety, consider lighting the subject with more than two lights: a main, a fill, and one or more accent lights; a main and two kicker lights; or a main light, fill light, and top and back light. We could expand this concept a lot further. It's not that one type of lighting will be better than another, just different, with each type of lighting setup having its definite place in nude photography. Some of these lighting setups you will like, and some you won't.

Build Lights One at a Time

If you intend to use two or more lights to light a subject, setting, and props, then make it easy on yourself. Place and meter each light separately, working only with one light at a time. Don't try to work with all the lights you intend to use, all at one time. It can be too confusing.

If you intend to use four lights (such as a main, fill, background and accent light) for a given shot, put each light into the place you think each should go, but don't turn them all on; not just yet. Start with the main light.

After it's in place and you evaluate its lighting on the subject and are satisfied with its placement, take a meter reading at the subject's position. When you're satisfied with the lighting value, temporarily turn the main light off and start all over but this time with the fill light. Follow the same procedure. Once you are satisfied with this light's placement, its affect on the subject , setting and props, and with its power output, turn it off and go on to the next light.

Once you have placed and measured the light output of all of the lights intended to be used, and are otherwise satisfied with the lighting, then and only then should you turn on all of the lights. Finally, before you expose any film, take one final light measurement of the main and fill light sources.

Make certain that their total, combined power output is still in keeping with the light value you wanted. If it is, your lighting is ready and you're ready to expose film. If not, start again.

Two Main Lights

There is a general lighting rule which states that a main light should be at least the same size or larger than the subject matter you are trying to photograph. If you wanted to photograph a can of soda, a 12 by 12 inch soft box, , would do the job of lighting it quite nicely. Anything much larger would usually be overkill.

However, if we had the job of photographing a person's entire figure, a 12 by 12 inch light source would usually be too small; the entire body would not receive the same quantity (or quality) of illumination. To avoid this lighting inequity, for lighting a person's entire body, we would often use a six foot or larger soft box.

Not everyone has large light sources at their immediate disposal. Fortunately, there is another way to approach and solve the problem of lighting a person's entire figure, without resorting to a large light source, use two smaller main lights. By using two lights as main light sources — e.g. a 12 or 24 inch soft box for a subject's face and a three or four foot soft box, set to the same power output as the first for lighting the remainder of a subject's body, a subject's entire body can receive adequate and even illumination.

Keep in mind that while your two main lights might differ in size, shape and type, their power outputs — the quantity of light falling onto the subject from each source — must be equal. If not, if one of the lights is more or less powerful than the other, you might be lighting with one main and one fill light, or one main and one accent light or some other combination, but you will definitely not be lighting with two main lights. Also, when you double-light a subject in this fashion, you should still think of the subject as being illuminated by only one primary source. This means that the shadows must not provide conflicting, confusing information. If the body light casts shadows toward the right side, the face light should do the same. If they do not, then you must make certain that such conflicting shadows are not perceived in the final photo result.

Main And Fill Illumination

Most nude studies are probably lit by using two lights (a main and a fill light) rather than just one (only a main light). Accordingly, when you use two lights (even if your two lights are the same or different in size, shape and type), their power outputs — i.e., the quantity of light falling onto the subject from each source — must not be equal. A fill light must always be less in power output or f-stops than its companion main light, even if it is only one half of an f-stop less than the main light.

Remember that the function and effect of a fill light is greatly dependent on the character of the main light. Depending on its power setting or distance from the subject, compared to the main light and its power setting and size, the fill light will play a greater or lesser part in determining the ultimate atmosphere and drama in an image.

The less powerful a fill light is, compared with its main light counterpart and in terms of f-stops, the more dramatic the subject will be lit and photographed. Accordingly, being able to control the power of a fill light source further increases any photographer's lighting potential.

We like to keep our lighting as simple as possible, consistent, of course, with our preconceived concept of what the final photographic image should look like. If you wanted to record something with detail, it should be adequately lit. If you wanted to record no detail in a specific area, then don't light it. If you want subdued detail, use an appropriate amount of light. To do all this well, you need to be very familiar with the exposure-latitude characteristics of your film, and well-versed in your lighting and exposure techniques.

When looking at the photos throughout this book, you will see many lighting variations illustrated and described. They should be helpful in giving you some understanding of the basics of practical lighting, as well as provide you with some ideas for your own shooting. By no means are they exhaustive of all the lighting setups you could employ.

Light Quality

When a subject is lit by only one (main) light, there will be portions of her face and/or body which will be illuminated by the light and other portions which will be in shadow. Depending upon the light's placement, these portions of light and dark may or may not be equal in area. If you examine this lighting closely on the subject, you'll see a line of demarcation; a line which separates the lit area from the dark, shadow area.

When this line of demarcation is very prominent, pencil thin, and sharply defined, the light quality produced from such a source is called hard light. When this line is very subtle, broad, and it's not easily discernible where the light ends and shadow area starts, the light quality is called soft light.

How do we know if we want a subject to be illuminated by hard or soft light? Initially, one doesn't. Its only through practice, experimentation, and looking at a lot of images taken by other photographers that one becomes proficient in being able to select the right quality (hard or soft) of light.

In other words, for some jobs you may want a four foot soft box as a main light, placed three feet from the subject (very soft light). For other jobs you may want a light housed in a 6-inch bowl reflector (hard light), or something in between. It'll all depend upon what result you like and seek. Each type of light (hard and soft light) has its place in nude photography.

However, whether it be hard or soft light, some beginning photographers confuse a point that is important to note: a light's quality (hard or soft light) has nothing to do with its quantity, power or total output of illumination. A light source could emit a lot of strong light (e.g., f-32 light) and be either hard or soft light or it

"...a light's quality has nothing to do with its quantity..."

could emit a very small amount of light (such as f-2.0 light) and still be hard or soft light too. This point is so important that it bears repeating.

The power output of a light source has an affect on one's photography (such as on the potential depth of field that is possible), but has no bearing on a light's quality. If you had two identical lights, connected to identical power packs, each placed at the same distance from a subject and at the same angle, with the power of one set at 200 watt-seconds and that of the other set at a higher watt-second output (e.g., set at 800 watt-seconds), the quality of light falling onto the subject from each light source would be identical.

Using the higher (800) watt-second light would merely give you the luxury of working at a higher f-stop setting (i.e., two f-stop smaller lens aperture), thereby giving you considerably greater depth of field than if you had used the 200 watt-second power source.

At this point you might well ask the question that since power has nothing to do with a light's quality, what does affect it? A number of factors can affect the quality of any light source: its size, its proximity or distance from the intended subject, the type of material the light must pass through, the type of housing a light source is contained in, and even a housing's color and texture.

Size of a light source — As a general rule, the smaller the light source, the harder the light produced. Conversely, the larger the light source, the softer the light produced.

For example, a light which is housed in a four-inch bowl reflector will produce harder light than the same light housed in a 24-inch bowl reflector. However, size is relative. A 24-inch bowl reflector will yield soft light compared with a light in a four-inch bowl reflector but hard light if it is compared with a light housed in a 30-inch bowl reflector.

Proximity — The size rule just noted is not quite as hard-and-fast as it may initially appear. That's because what really matters is not the absolute size of the light source, but its size in relationship to the size of the subject — and that varies with the light-to-subject distance.

A three foot soft box, placed three feet from a subject will emit soft light. However, if you placed that same light six feet from the subject, in effect it no longer would be a three foot light source; it's only about one foot. Its effective size is inversely proportionate to the square of the distance which it has been moved. This is a very fancy way of saying that the closer any light is placed to a subject, the larger it will appear from the subject's viewpoint.

As a result, the softer the quality of the light falling on the subject will be. Conversely, the farther that same light is from a subject, the smaller its apparent size will be and the harder the resulting light quality.

Diffusing materials — Before a light strikes a subject, if you allow it to pass through some translucent material (such as plastic, nylon, or linen), it will cause the resulting illumination to be softened. This softening effect is largely due to two major factors. First, because of the diffusing material, the source is usually made effectively larger; therefore, the light is softer.

For example, if you placed a 20x20-inch diffusion screen in front of a bare bulb, the effective size of the light source would no longer be just the size of the bare bulb. It will have been increased to about the size of the diffusing material: 20x20 inches.

Second, and to some extent, the light is also softened because the diffusing material renders the light less directional; light passes through and out of the material in a number of different directions. All of this sounds well and good, and relatively straight forward; however, there are compromises.

When you place any diffusing material in front of any given light source, you will always reduce (to some extent) the effective brightness of the illumination. (Power will be reduced.) The denser the material used, the more power that will be needed to pass any given amount of light through it, just to maintain a given f-stop. For example, take any light (one without any diffusing material on it) and place it in front of a subject. Measure the light output by taking an f-stop reading at the subject. Say that the reading indicated an f-stop of f-11.

Now, put one thickness of nylon or white linen in front of this light source and take another meter reading. You will

- **To reduce the effective brightness of a light, place a diffusing material in front of the light source.**

"...the larger the light source, the softer the light produced."

note that the f-stop has been reduced; it might indicate f-8 or even lower.

To get the same f-stop (power) measurement that you had before (before the diffusing material was put into place) you would need to increase the power output of your light source. How much you'll have to compensate will all depend upon the thickness and type of diffusing material being used. It could be as little as 10 or 20 percent or as much as 200 or 300 percent or more power.

If you don't have the ability to increase the power dramatically, you could opt for an alternative measure. You could open up your camera's f-stops to compensate. (In this example, if you had f-11 before diffusion material was used and f-8 afterwards, you would compensate by opening your camera's lens by at least one whole f-stop.) If you did not want to do this, you might entertain another solution: move the light source closer to the subject. This, of course, would help to compensate for a loss of power output.

However, by doing so, you will change the quality of the light source. Moving the light closer to the subject will give you an added softness because you have now effectively made the light source larger from the subject's viewpoint. If you were seeking hard light, this would not be a very acceptable solution; if you were after soft light, it would be.

You will need to experiment. It will only be through experimentation that you will discover the most effective and expedient ways and materials for softening illumination to a degree that suits your specific purposes. We might prefer ripstop nylon for a diffusing material; you might prefer plastic.

Light housings — A housing is something a light (or lights) fits into and which serves to direct and reflect the light's illumination out onto a photographic subject matter. Examples of typical light housings are bowl reflectors, umbrellas, and soft boxes.

By definition, a bare bulb does not get put into a housing; therefore, the light emitted is not direct nor reflective. Since light from a bare bulb scatters in all directions (360 degrees), it's non-directional, and is often considered a soft light. Since a light housing — any housing — makes a light directional (more or less), it's therefore usually harder light than light

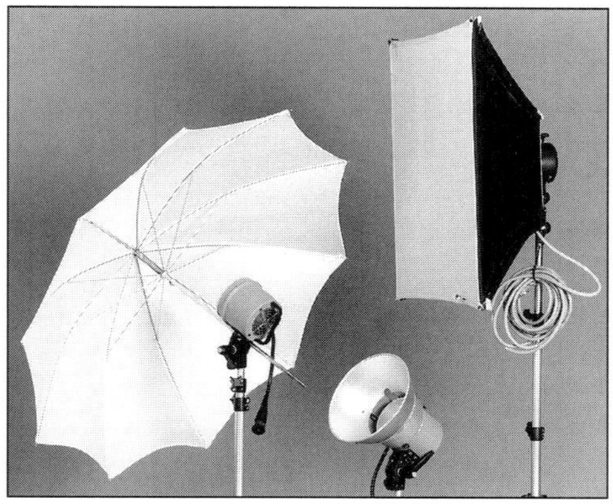

Here are three light modifiers: an umbrella (left), a bowl reflector (center), and a soft box (right). Each of these housings will produce a different quality of light from the same, given flash source.

from a bare bulb light source. Hard light is relative. Accordingly, the rule still applies: the larger the light housing, the softer the light emitted therefrom compared to the same light contained in a small-sized light housing.

As a result, most bowl reflectors produce harder light than umbrellas because they are usually smaller. By the same token, umbrellas usually produce harder light than soft boxes, if the umbrellas are smaller. A small-sized soft box will usually produce harder light than a much larger light panel or soft box.

If you want body contours or the texture of a subject's skin to be sharply defined, a light housed in a relatively small bowl reflector, yielding hard light, might be the answer.

However, if you want the contours or skin texture of a subject displayed more subtly, an umbrella light or soft box may be an appropriate choice. As a further point of reference, and if we were dealing with a subject who had pock-marked skin, hard light would not be our lighting choice. Hard light would not glamorize the subject's skin; it would accentuate all of its flaws. We would opt for a large light panel or soft box; we would want very soft light.

This is just one of the reasons why no one light source could possibly suit our needs. Because of all of the variations, we long ago learned that no single light source can handle all of the lighting situations we usually encounter. We would suggest that you be prepared to have some lighting choices available. No single

"...most bowl reflectors produce harder light than umbrellas..."

"A golden reflector is useful outdoors under a blue sky..."

housing will be the only right choice for all of your photographic situations too; it will all depend on the results you're after. After experimenting with a number of different light housings, you will eventually find certain housings and combinations that you favor.

Housing color and texture — The color and texture of a housing's interior surface will also have an effect on a light's quality. For example, a housing with a matte, white interior will yield a slightly softer, more "gentle" light than one with a shiny, highly polished silvered or golden interior surface. A light in a 24-inch bowl reflector that has a matte, white interior will produce a somewhat softer light than the same light housed in a 24-inch silvered bowl reflector.

A golden reflector is useful outdoors under a blue sky or in open shade. In such conditions, it makes a very suitable fill reflector, enabling you to warm up shadows that might otherwise be unacceptably blue.

Lighting Techniques

Now that we have had some discussion about lighting basics, we'll briefly discuss how basic lighting setups are obtained and how you can use them to create various lighting effects for your figure photography.

Lighting the Nose Axis

Earlier in this chapter, when we discussed other lights, we reported that lighting of a subject's face should be constructed based on the subject's nose axis. Look at Diagram 7-1 and note how the subject's nose is pointed toward and in line with the camera's position. We have called and labeled this imaginary line the 0-degree line. As a general guide, and referring to a light's placement, a main and fill light are most often placed anywhere along the arcs of or within the quadrants of A and B, directed toward the subject.

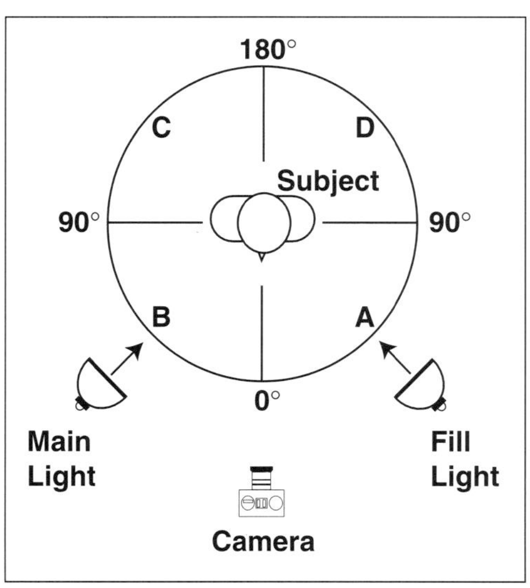

Diagram 7-1: Lighting the nose-axis

Now, look at Diagram 7-1A. Note that neither the camera nor the subject's body have been moved. Only the subject's head has been turned away from the camera. Note also that because the subject's head has been moved, all the arcs have moved too; they have moved proportionately in the same, counterclockwise direction: the the subject's left.

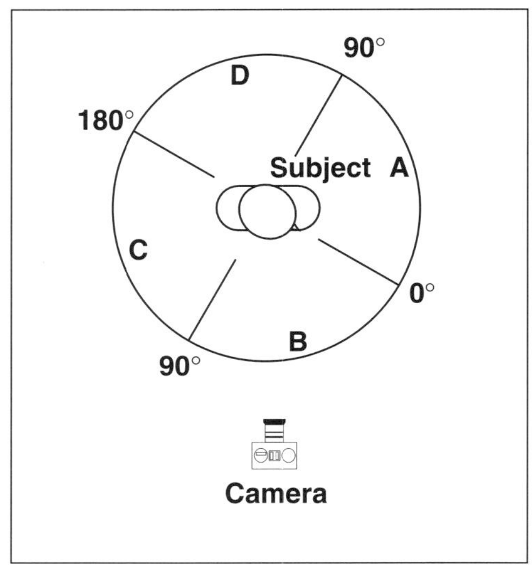

Diagram 7-1A: Change in the nose-axis.

Notwithstanding, the placement of the main and fill lights still lie within the relocated arcs of A and B, as it originally did in Diagram 7-1. All the lights have merely followed the subject's nose axis. In like manner, if the subject had moved his or her head to the right, all of the arcs would have moved proportionately and to the right.

By following this nose-axis rule, it makes it easier to know where to place a main and fill light in relationship to a subject. Perhaps another example will make this proposition easier to understand.

If we were to light a subject's face by placing a main light at the 0-degree position, square to the nose and face, the front of the face would be illuminated evenly. This even type of lighting is often

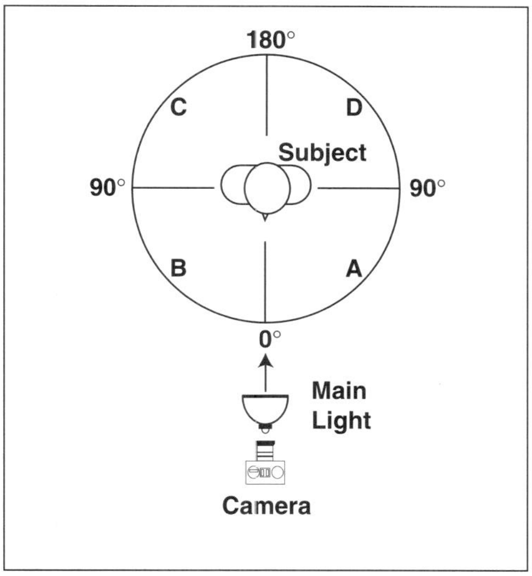

Diagram 7-2: Glamour lighting — subject's face and body are facing camera and light.

referred to as glamour or flat lighting; virtually no shadows are seen at the camera position. (See diagram 7-2.)

If we keep the camera and the subject's body in this same position, but have the subject turn her head 90 degrees to the right or left of camera-body axis and put a light at this position, the nose axis has once again created a 0 degree position and the face is once again evenly and glamour lit. (See diagram 7-2A.)

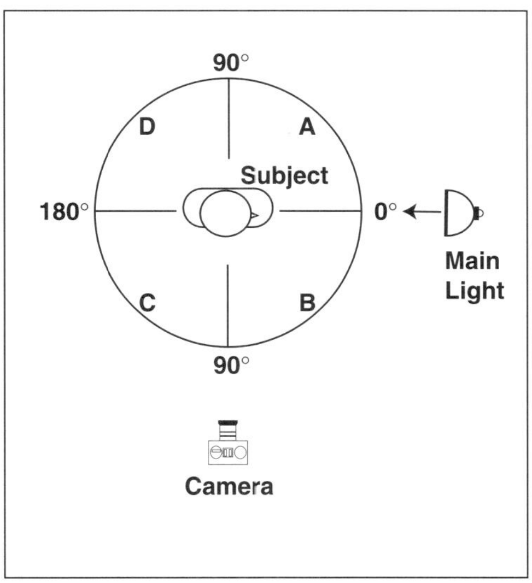

Diagram 7-2A: Glamour lighting — subject's face turned 90 degrees.

Now, look at Diagram 7-3. If we don't move the subject's face but move the main light to the 90-degree position, to the right or left, the subject's face would now be in a lighting pattern called split lighting; one-half of the face would be in light and the other in deep shadow. Between these two extremes — between the 0-degree (glamour) and the 90-degree (split) positions — along arcs A or B, lie the positions for creating other standard main-lighting patterns. Each pattern used will give a subject's face a different look. Not all patterns will be flattering to all subjects, nor appropriate for all pictorial moods or themes.

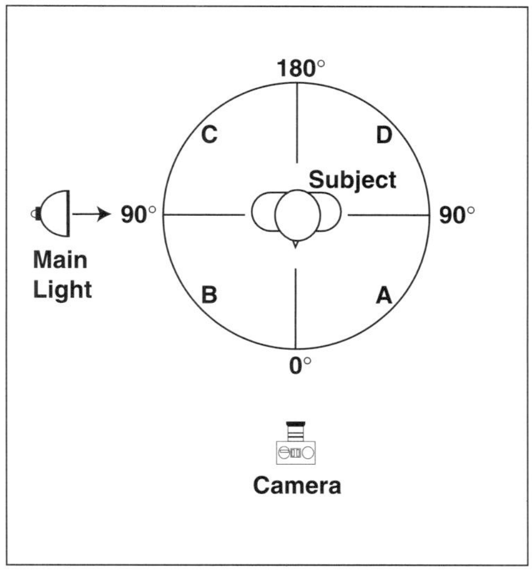

Diagram 7-3: Split lighting

For example, frontal glamour lighting reduces contrast, minimizes lines and wrinkles, flattens the facial modeling, and minimizes skin texture. However, this is not appropriate illumination if your aim is to produce a dramatic mood.

Glamour lighting usually creates no appreciable shadows, generating no drama or mystery. Little is left to a viewer's imagination. On the other hand, split lighting dramatically increases contrast, significantly accentuates lines and wrinkles, and helps to accentuate contours and texture. It is a great lighting pattern to use for creating a mood of drama and mystery, since a portion of the face is left in deep shadow.

Although sharp side lighting is frequently flattering to a subject's figure, it is often not as flattering to the female face as is glamour lighting. As a result, a compromise is often made, such as placing a main light somewhere between the 0 and 90 degrees point; somewhere around the 30 to 70 degree point, to the right or left of the 0-degree axis. Although this type of lighting compromise does solve a lighting problem, there is a better way: double lighting.

When you double light a subject, you use two main lights. One main light would be designated to light only the subject's face and the other main light would be for the subject's body. Since two lights are used, each light should follow the nose-axis rule. With this lighting approach, and to ensure that you are lighting the subject correctly, it'll be easier if you think of a subject as having two noses. One nose would obviously be on the subject's face while the other is a hypothetical one and located in the middle of a subject's chest.

For example, look at diagram 7-4 where the subject's face and body are both facing the 0-degree position. A main face light could be placed at the 0-degree position while a second main light illuminates only the body. This second, body light could be positioned obliquely — on the side, to the right or left of the 0-degree axis — for a flattering rendition of the body contours.

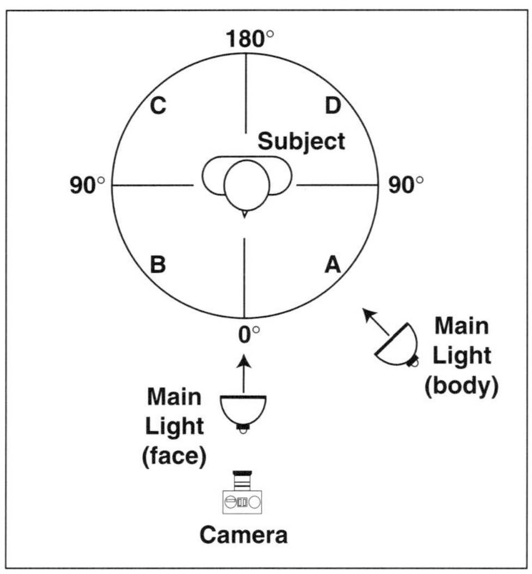

Diagram 7-4: Double lighting — subject's head and body facing the camera.

There are two warnings when you work with two or more main lights: shadows and power. First, be careful not to generate distinct, sharp shadows that contradict each other, at least none that can be seen by the camera. It will look unnatural. Second, make certain that both main lights are set to emit the exact same amount of power (f-stop). If one is stronger than the other, in effect it will become a main light and the weaker light will become a fill light source.

"There are many lights to choose from..."

Our lighting placement is most always based upon a subject's nose axis (hypothetical or real), not on the location of the camera. For example, if we had a situation where we had a subject turn her head to her left, 90-degrees from the camera-subject axis (see diagram 7-2A), we frequently place a main light in line with her new nose-axis position.

Even though this position would place her face 90 degrees to the camera axis, it would be 0-degrees to the light axis. This would be extremely flattering light for her face; it would be glamour lit; there would be frontal, shadowless light falling on her face. The subject's body, however, would be another matter.

Since the main light would be 90-degrees to the right of the body's nose axis (the hypothetical nose which we put in the center of the subject's chest), the body would not be glamour lit, but side-lit. This type of lighting can be very flattering for most figures. With one main light, we have been able to accomplish two goals: glamour light the subject's face and add texture and dimension to a subject's figure. Let's take another example.

Refer back to diagram 7-2. Assume that we place a main light on the 0-degree subject-camera axis. Since both the body and face are shown square to the main light, both are receiving flat, glamour lighting. As we have already noted, such lighting can be flattering to the female face, but less flattering and dull for the body, primarily the bust and waistline. Flat lighting of this type tends to make a subject's bust appear flatter while emphasizing or exaggerating the width of the waistline and hips.

Look at diagram 7-5, the nose axis of the subject's face and the camera are at

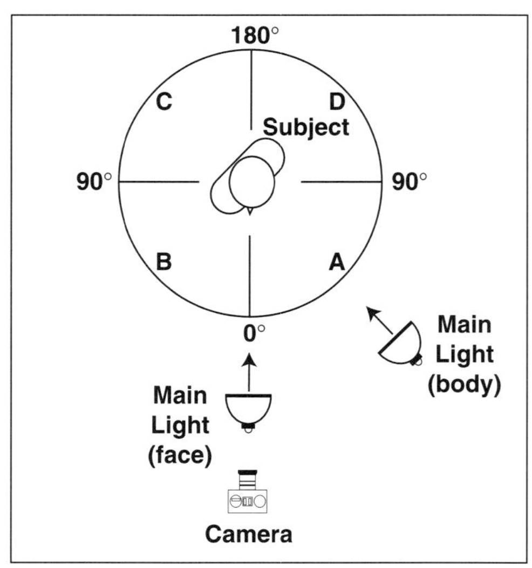

Diagram 7-5: Double lighting — subject's head facing camera with body at a 45 degree angle

the 0-degree position; the body is turned at 45 degrees to the camera position. You will note, however, that both the subject's head and body are in the 0-degree position for lighting purposes. (We gave a hypothetical nose to the subject's body.) In this situation, you have the option of lighting the face and body separately with two lights, one at each 0-degree position as indicated in diagram 7-3, or using just one light source placed on either 0-degree line. You'll have to practice and experiment to see which lighting procedure you like.

Lighting in the Studio

There are many lights to choose from on the photographic market and almost every professional has his or her favorite lighting setups. However, until you gain proficiency and confidence, it's best to work with just a few lights and relatively simple setups. This will lead you to consistent results and keep you from becoming overwhelmed by too many equipment choices.

Main lights — Even though we tailor-make our lighting setup for each photo situation, more often than not we usually favor using one of the following five light sources as a main light: a light housed in a four-inch snooted housing or 6-inch bowl reflector, an 18-inch bowl light with a grid spot and plastic diffuser cap, a four or six-foot white umbrella with a plastic diffuser cap, or, our own Shero light (developed by ourselves), which is a large, 40 x 88-inch silver or white-lined light panel unit.

Fill lights — For a fill light source, we frequently use our own, white-lined Shero light, a 3x4-foot, white-lined soft box, or a white or silver-lined three-foot or six-foot umbrella. Occasionally we'll use a smaller fill source, such as one or two four-inch snooted lights or even a white matte reflector. Again, it all depends on the effect we are after.

Power packs — We have approximately 20 different power packs in our studio, ranging in power output from 100-watt-seconds to 2400 watt-seconds. At present we use and favor power packs by Norman, Dyna-lite, Balcar, and Broncolor.

The reason we have used many different brands is because of versatility. No one brand can satisfy all of our lighting needs. We're not suggesting that you need 20 power packs but you should have at least two; each pack should be in the 1000-watt-second range. Unlike packs in the lower wattage range, a 1000 watt-second power pack will allow you to use more than one light at a time. In addition, and because of its relatively high power output, you'll be able to shoot at a smaller lens aperture (higher f-stop setting) for greater depth of field.

Basic studio equipment — To keep your lighting setup relatively simple in the beginning of your figure photography, we suggest starting with a four-foot or six-foot white-lined umbrella as a main light. Buy one that gives you the option of allowing its opening to be covered with diffusion material or a screen. This option, of diffused or undiffused light, makes a single umbrella source more versatile. For a fill source, a white-lined three or four-foot soft box are a good choice. To your basic lighting setup, add two accent or kicker lights, preferably with four or five-inch snooted housings, one top light in a six-inch silver-lined bowl reflector, two background lights, one 4x6-foot white foamcore reflector, and one 3x6-foot mirrored reflector.

A good flash exposure meter and a good, sturdy boom stand, as well as regular light stands, should round out your equipment needs.

For the background lights, we suggest two flash units, each housed in a six-inch silver-lined bowl reflector, paired with two, three-foot silver-lined umbrellas. These two lights will afford ample versatility for your background illumination. In addition, and should the need arise, the bowl reflector lights could be taken from the background, the umbrellas removed, and then used as additional accent lights.

- **Be careful of halation when working with a high-key setting.**

High-Key Lighting

Our definition of a high-key image is simple: everything in the photographic image (background, foreground, props, and so on) is white with or without detail except the subject; the subject should be the darkest entity in the image. If you're going to use some material to adorn part of the subject's body, it's best if the material is white or, a light or pale color.

When we construct our high-key lighting, we make certain that our white background receives much more light than

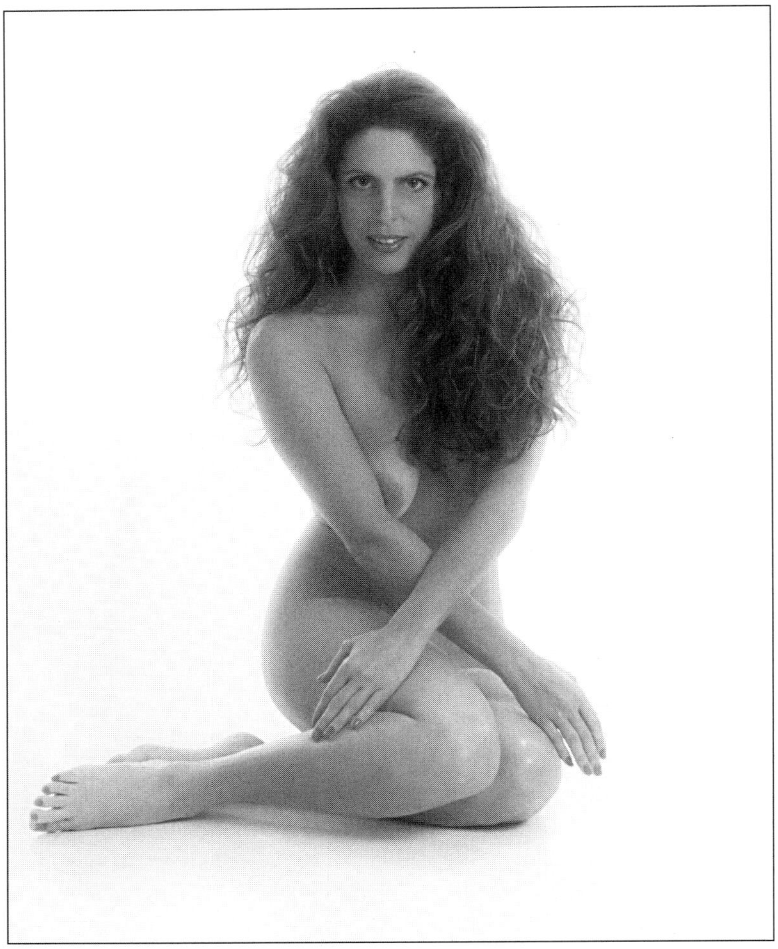

These images, and the ones on the next page, were shot in a high-key setting and by high-key lighting to deliberately create an atmosphere of lightness. Although I prefer nude studies in low or medium key settings because they tend to be more dramatic, high-key is a favorite among most of our clientele.

All of these images were shot with a seven-light setup. Two silver-lined, three foot umbrellas were used for the background. The power of these lights was adjusted to emit two full f-stops more light than the main light on the subject. A third light, housed in a 5-inch bowl reflector, was mounted on a boom stand and placed above and slightly behind the subject, to illuminate the top and back of her hair. The main light (a Balcar) was a 6-foot, white-lined, umbrella with a plastic diffuser cap over the light source. It was placed about 30 degrees to the right of the camera-subject axis. A fill light in the form of a 3x4-foot soft box was placed about 20 degrees to the left of the camera-subject axis. Its power was adjusted to give two full f-stops less light

(continued on next page)

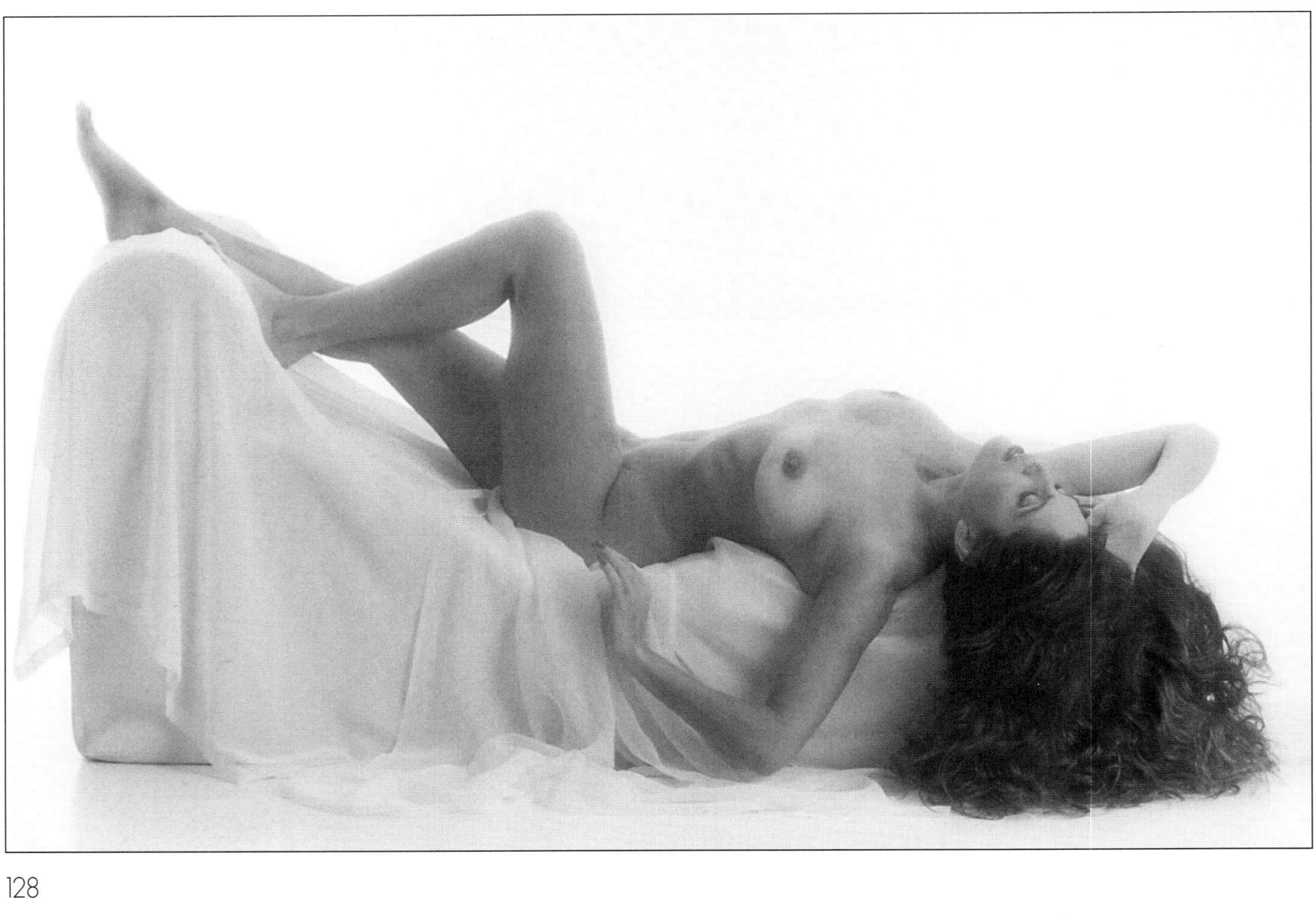

than the main light. The final two lights — two snooted kicker lights — floated; they were usually placed approximately 90 degrees to the left or right of camera-subject axis or behind her but they were always directed onto the subject's back and the back of her head. The power of these accent lights, as well as that of the top light, was set to equal the main light's output.

The only exception to the placement of the snooted lights is the photo to the right. In this image, we placed an amber gel over the snoots and allowed some of their light to directly illuminate the subject's body. As you can readily see, and compared with the other images, the result was to add a warm glow to the subject's overall person.

These images were shot at f-16 with a Softar, soft focus filter over the 150mm Hasselblad lens.

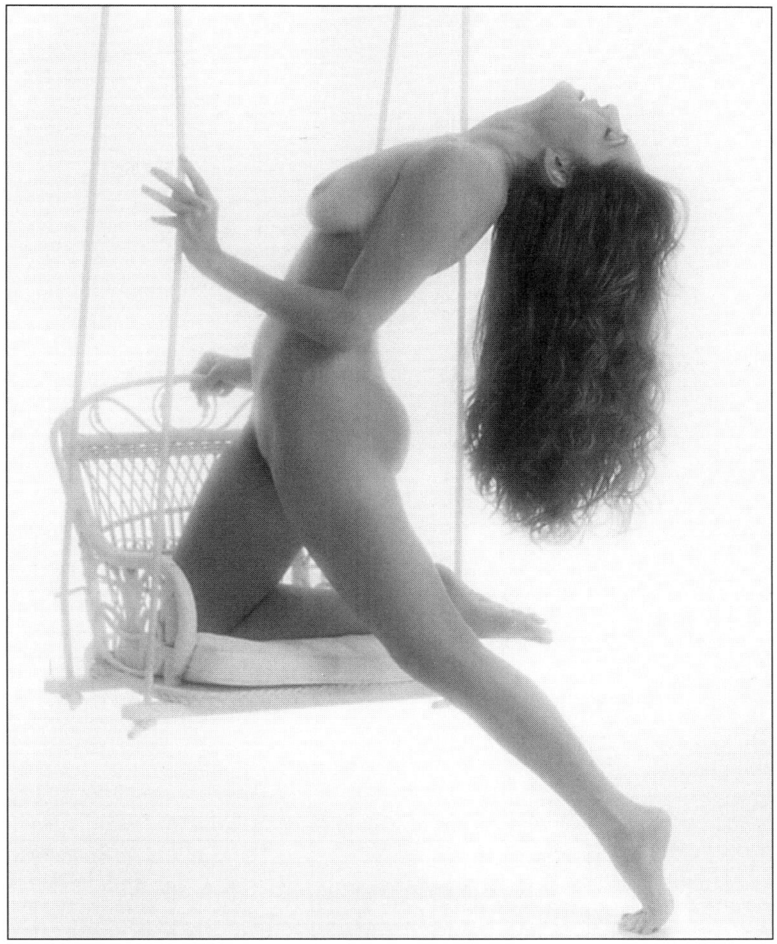

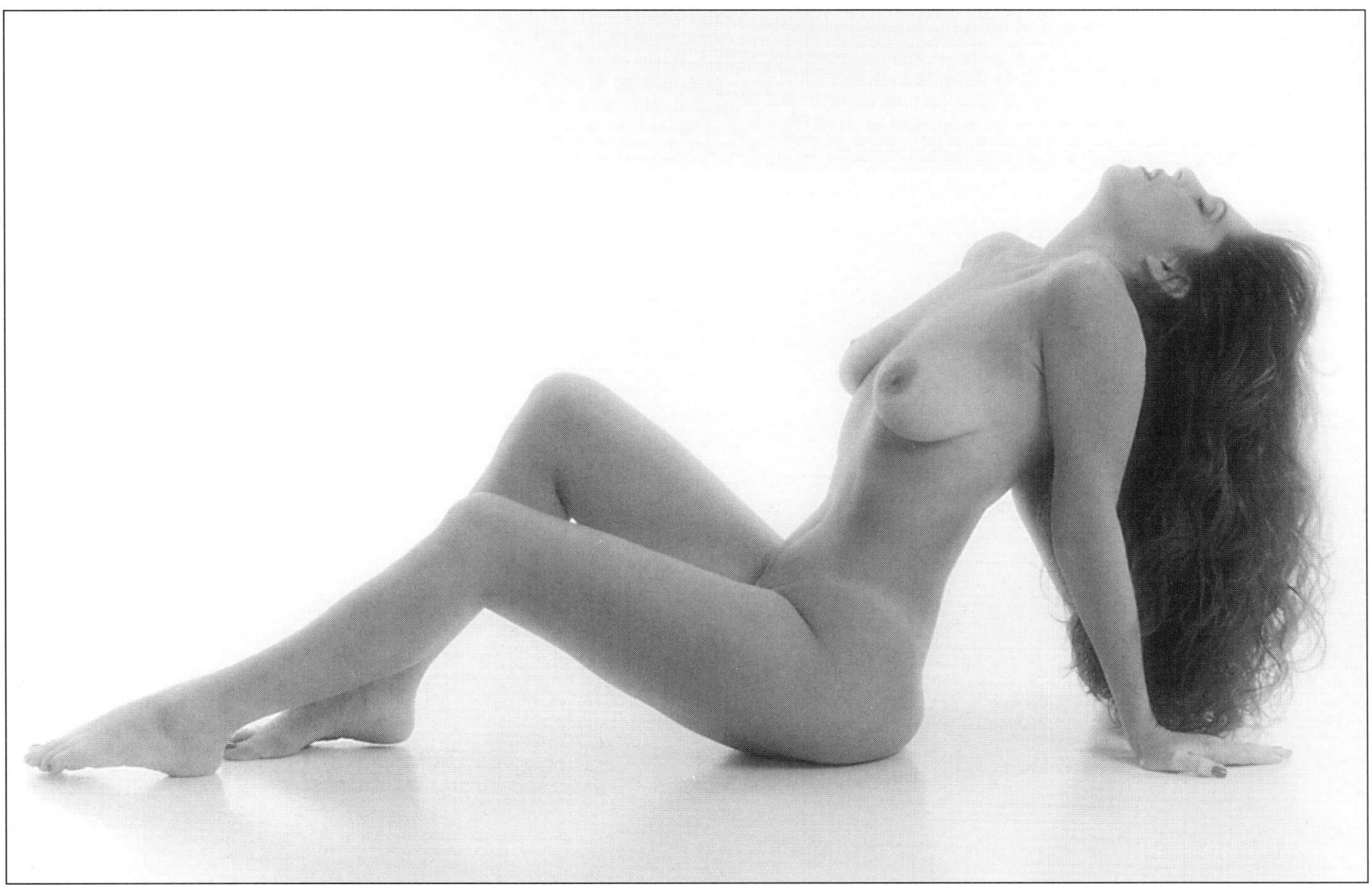

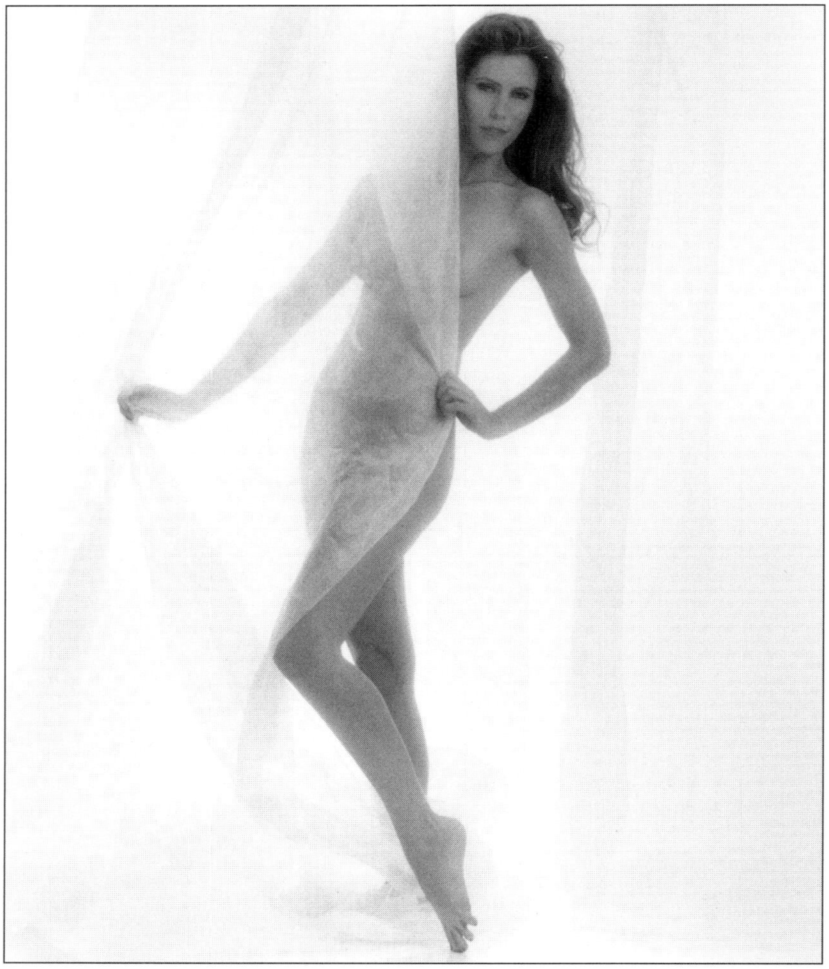

Above, Right and Opposite page: *Here are a three more images shot in the the high-key setting. This setting is quite unusual for figure photography but the results can be very dramatic and stunning. These images also demonstrate two different figure photography categories: personal (above and opposite page) and impersonal (right).*

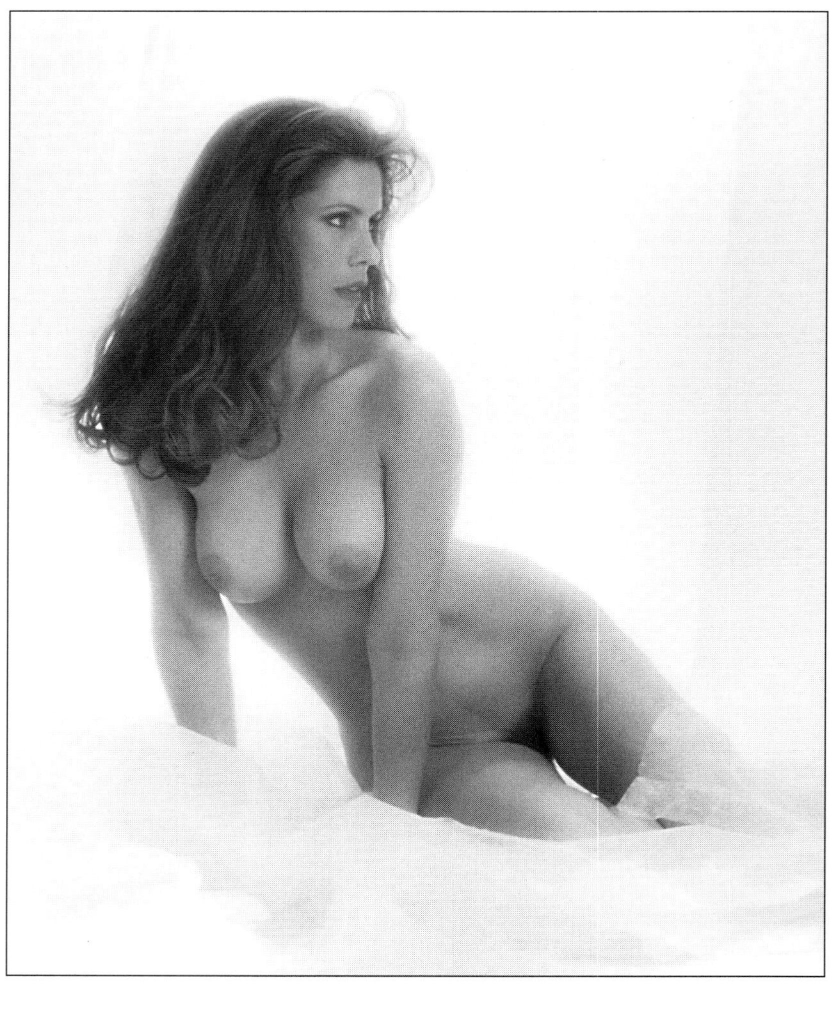

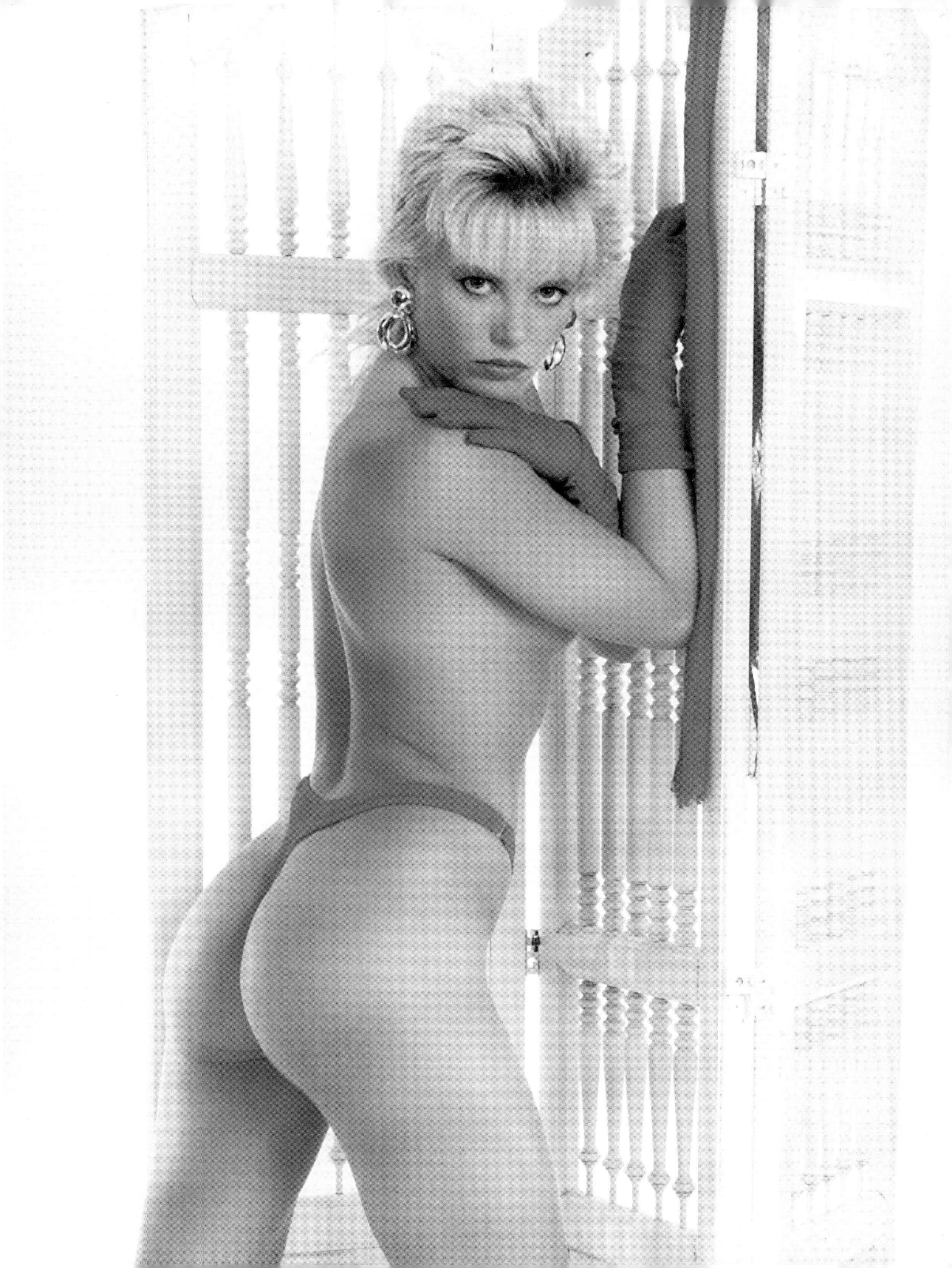

our subject, the props, and the remainder of the set. The goal is to have the background record on film as pure white, without any detail in it, while the foreground, setting and props record as white with or without detail, depending upon the results sought. Depending on the type of white background material used, this means that the background must usually receive two f-stops or more incident light than the light falling onto the subject from the main light.

This assures us that the subject's face and figure will be the darkest reference points in the image, while everything else records as a clean white. Even though this sounds rather simple, there is a word of caution. Be very careful of radiation (halation). If you set up a high-key setting, adjusting your background lights to emit a lot of power, and then have your subject stand too close to the white background, radiation will occur. The light will bounce off the background and surround the body, washing (flaring) most of it out.

For example, in our studio, we have our high-key main light set to emit just under f-22 light. Our background lights are set to f-45.5 light (based upon an incident meter reading; f-64.5 reflective). This is a lot of light coming from and off our background. If we were to stand our subjects any closer than 10 feet from it, their bodies would glow. Parts of their bodies would be obliterated by the bouncing light and not recorded onto film, all due to halation.

The setup — For creating a high-key lighting setup, four lights are usually adequate. Begin by setting up a background sweep of white, seamless background paper (or some other white reflective material) supported by two stands. For a full-figure shot, a nine-foot wide material is adequate, although we would prefer to use at least 12-foot wide material. Have the subject stand at least six to eight feet from the background. This distance will help guard against possible unwanted flare around the subject, provided your lights are not set to emit too much power.

"This simple four-light setup represents a good starting point..."

Next, set up two background lights of equal power. We use two three-foot silver-lined umbrellas. Place one to the left and one to the right of the background, at about a 45-degree angle in relationship to the background. Aim each just beyond the background's center, as shown in diagram 7-6, so that the entire background is evenly lit. With both of these lights turned on, take a meter reading at the center of the background, noting the indicated f-stop reading. Turn these lights off, position your main light and turn it on. (We usually use a 6-foot, white lined umbrella with a plastic diffuser cap for a main light.) Adjust the power of the main light to emit two and one-half f-stops less light than your background lights.

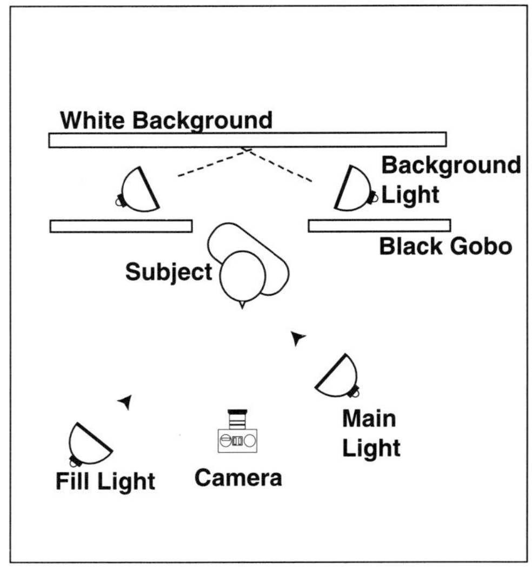

Diagram 7-6: High-Key lighting setup.

Let's assume an incident meter reading at the background was f-16.5. The main light should then be adjusted to emit light at the subject's position at a value of f-8. The camera's f-stop setting must then be based on the main light's output on the subject. In this example, we would set our camera to f-5.6.

Next, position your fill light (we usually use a four foot soft box) and adjust its power, based on the lighting ratio that you prefer for the results. Using the above example, we would, typically, adjust our fill-light's power to emit no more than f-5.6 of light; sometimes even f-4 or slightly less. It would depend on how dramatic we wanted the final high-key result to appear.

This simple four-light setup represents a good starting point from which you can derive some beautiful high-key results. We sometimes use setups that are a bit more elaborate, including kicker lights for the subject, for the floor area, etc.

Low-key Lighting

As with high-key, we must have a common understanding of what low-key is before we can talk about lighting for low-key. Our definition of a low-key image is simple: everything in the image is black with or without detail (background, foreground, props, and so on) except the subject; the subject should be the lightest entity in the image. If you're going to use some material to adorn part of the subject's body, it's best if the material is black or a dark color.

When we construct our low-key lighting, we use a set that has black carpeting on the floor and black material on the background. The goal is to have the background record on film as pure black, without any detail in it, while the foreground, setting, and props record as black with or without detail, depending upon the results sought. Since the floor and background are not being directly lit, we're assured that they will reflect no appreciable light from the main or fill lights we use. We're also assured that the subject's face and figure will be the lightest reference points in the image, while the background records as jet black.

Although black background paper could be used, we have found it to be unacceptable. It will not record as the deep black we generally desire. Spill light, from the main and fill lights, even when protective gobos are used, strikes the background and usually illuminates it to some extent.

This condition keeps it from recording totally black. This is one of the main reasons why we favor using velvet or some other black, absorbing material.

The setup — For low-key photography, there are many lighting choices. For example, for a main light, and depending on whether you're going to light the subject's face and body with one or more separate lights, you could use anything from snooted spots, white-lined diffused umbrellas, a large soft box, a large light panel unit, or some combination of these lights.

No matter which main-light setup we start with, we are likely to change it one or more times during the course of any given session. As a photo scene is changed, so should the lighting, otherwise all scenes and resulting photos start to look alike.

If we decide to use a fill light, then it's most often a four foot soft box. Sometimes we'll use a white foamcore reflector, just

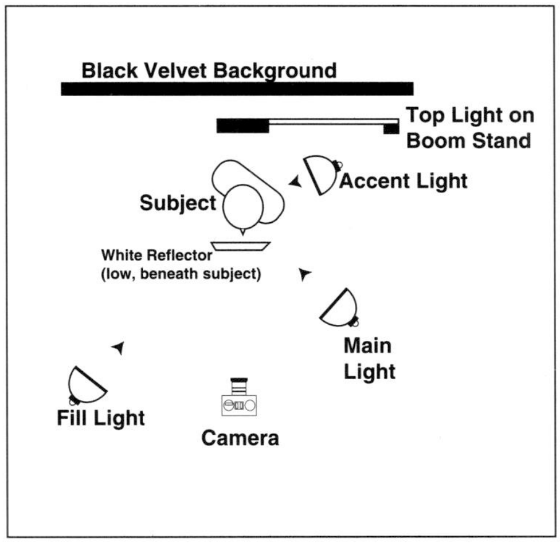

Diagram 7-7: Low-Key lighting setup.

out of the camera's view, as a fill, kicker, or rim light source. Depending on how we want a subject to be represented in the final image, we might add a top light and an accent light or two (the four-inch snooted type) behind or to one side of the subject. These snooted lights are great for highlighting one or more portions of the subject's body.

Finally, it's common for us to add a back light. A back light helps to separate the subject more clearly from a black background, to further outline the subject's body, and increase the overall feeling of depth in the image.

Outdoor Lighting

When you're shooting outdoors, especially when working with non-professional models, you should be prepared to work fast. This means being mobile and as unburdened by lighting and other equipment as possible. This is the time to keep your lighting simple.

- **Be prepared to work fast when shooting outdoors.**

Typical lighting setup — A number of photographers we know prefer to engage in outdoor nude photography using solely natural daylight as a main and fill light source.

Although such photographers may espouse a number of different reasons why they prefer using only natural light, we're convinced that one reason in particular has to head the list: it's easier. We favor using electronic flash as a main light and the natural daylight as the fill source, or the natural light as main light and electronic flash as a fill source; it allows us to have more control.

We'll often supplement the lighting by using a gold or white reflector for accent

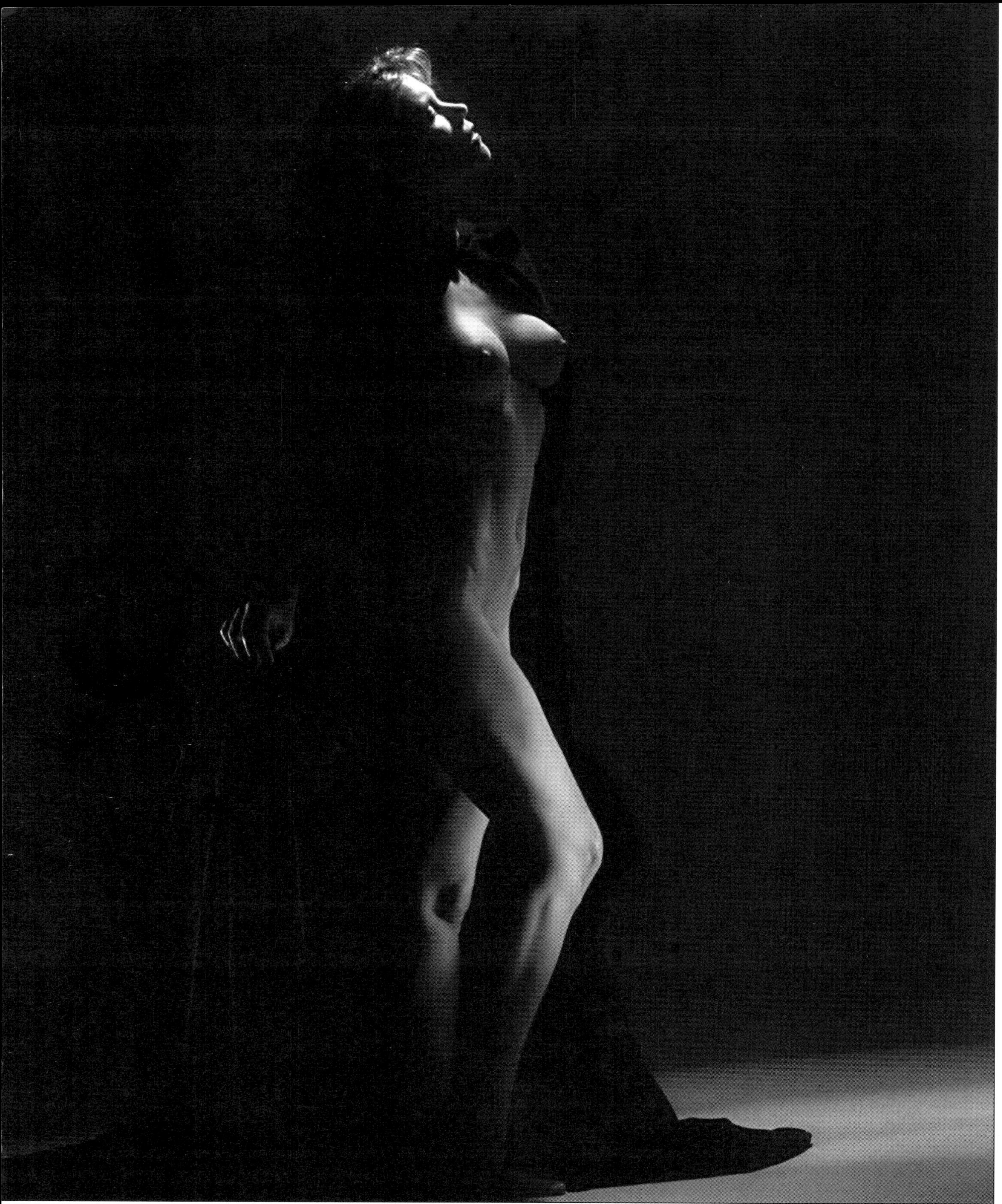

Above and Opposite page: *These two images (above and opposite page) demonstrate how easy it is to achieve pictorial variety. Once the lighting had been set and the image captured for the image above, it was a simple matter to achieve a different "look" for the subject. For the photo on the opposite page, we simply modified the pose and moved the camera closer, the lighting remained the same. We used a three light setup for both images. A Norman light, in a 6-inch bowl reflector, was placed directly above the subject on a boom stand. This was our main light. Two other Norman lights, each in a 4-inch snoot housing and covered with an amber gel, acted as accent lights.* *(Continued on next page)*

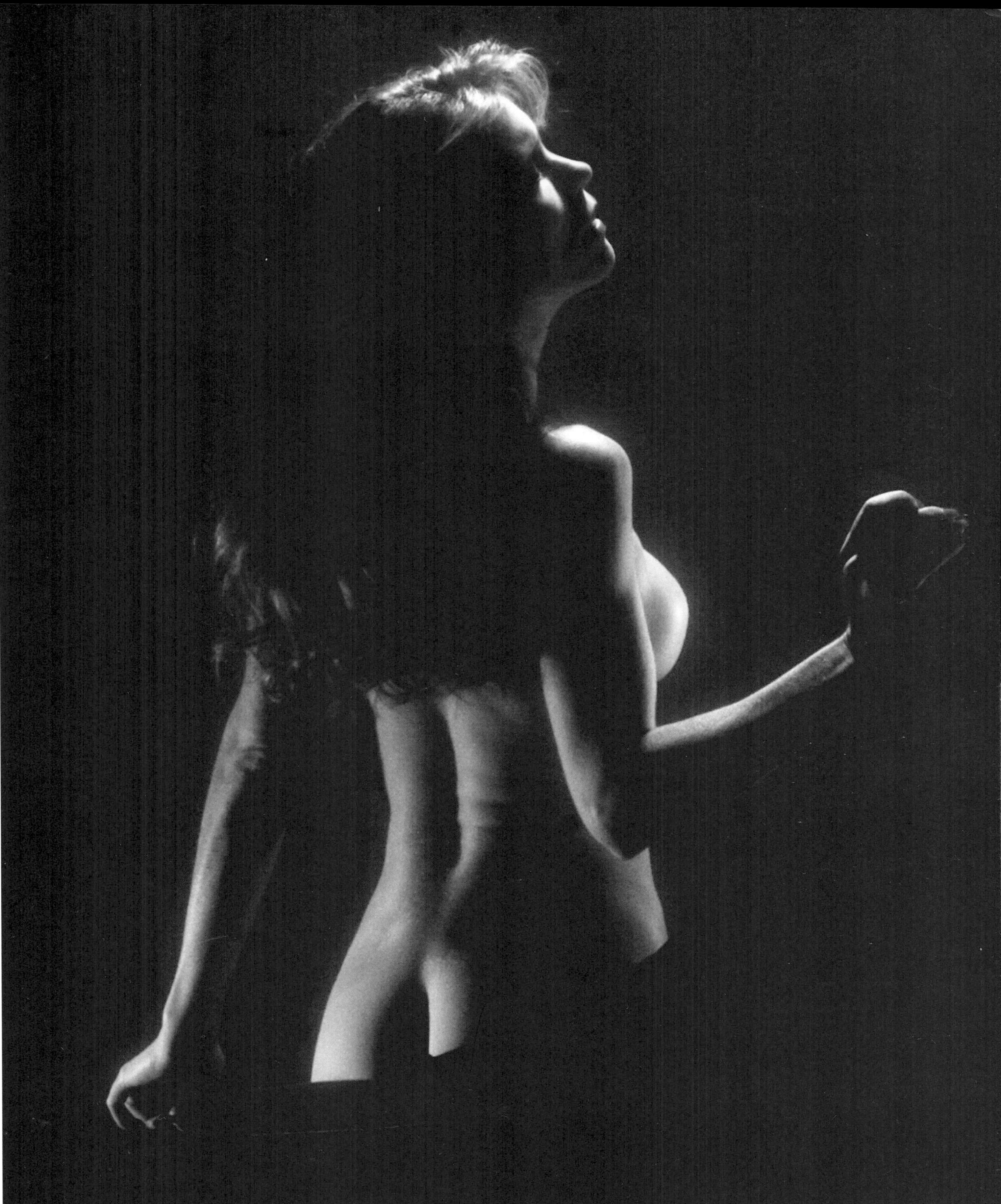

Each accent light was placed approximately 110 degrees to camera-subject axis; one to the right and one to the left. The subject was wearing a heavy velvet robe, which absorbed light like a sponge and she was photographed on a white background sweep. The background photographed dark (which was the effect we wanted) because we keep all the existing light from striking or spilling onto it.

illumination. Because outdoor illumination tends to be variable and unpredictable, (and we don't always get to work at the optimum time of day or even in ideal weather conditions), we usually disfavor working with natural light alone.

By augmenting the natural light with flash, we have more control and the photo results are more predictable and consistent. Flash also gives us the ability to put some sparkle into our final images, regardless of what the natural light conditions happen to be.

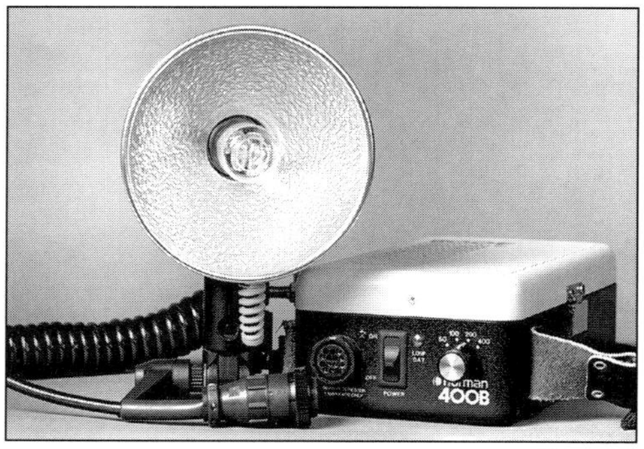

The Norman 400B flash unit.

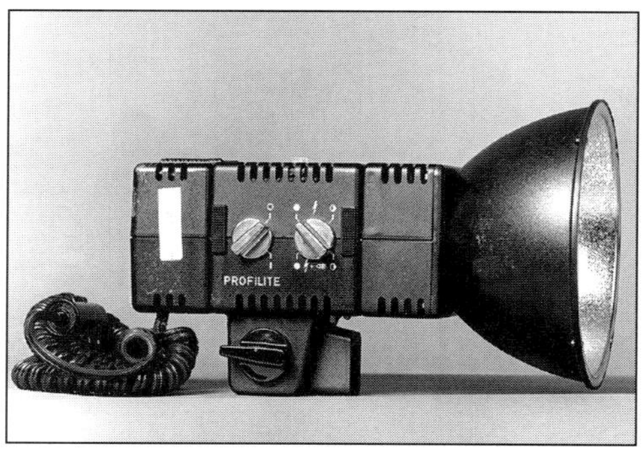

The Multiblitz flash unit.

Ideally, we prefer working with studio flash heads, housed in one of our own Shero light-panel units, with studio power packs. However, in the field, this is usually not practical. Household current is often not available and time constraints prevent us from bringing a bulky generator for using studio-type lighting. This is especially true if we are planning to change locations frequently during the session. As a result, we usually use portable flash units.

Although there are a number of very good portable, battery-operated units on the market, we have found the Multiblitz and the Norman 400B portable flash units particularly good. The Multiblitz is configured so that it can be used either with an external portable battery (which is quite heavy) or with household current; it's very dependable and is easy to set up and dismantle.

On the other hand, the Norman 400B uses smaller, lighter portable batteries as its power source but has two times more power output than the Multiblitz. The Multiblitz is a 200 watt-second unit but can easily be adjusted to emit 100 watts with just a turn of a switch. On the other hand, the Norman 400B is a 400 watt-second unit but can be quickly adjusted to emit 200, 100 or even 50 watts of power by just turning a dial.

The last time we checked, both units were selling for about the same price. As between the two units, we use our Norman units more often: they're lighter, more powerful and offer more versatility regarding power. When used behind a 3x6-foot light panel, covered with a bed sheet, or with our Shero light housing, either the Multiblitz or Norman flash lamp heads will produce extremely soft lighting. They'll produce somewhat harder lighting if used with a white or silver-lined umbrella, and still harder light when used with only their standard six-inch silvered bowl reflectors.

From an efficiency standpoint, each is more power-efficient in their own respective bowl reflector rather than housed in a light panel.If time or rough terrain is a factor, and we have at least some good daylight, we will compromise. We'll use only natural light and no electronic flash.

However, to get some brilliance into a scene, we'll frequently use one or two portable reflectors. Typically, one will be a 3x6-foot plastic mirror, often covered with amber gels. It will act as main-light source, reflecting the natural light (altered by the amber gels) back onto the subject's face and figure. A second plastic mirror would be used behind or to the side of the subject, to act as a back or accent light. The unaltered, direct natural light would be used as the fill source.

If you had no reflectors and wanted, or had to use, only natural daylight, you could. Use natural light as the main light source and take advantage of what might be around the subject to serve as a fill reflector. For example, you could use the natural light bouncing off of a white or bright wall, a sandy beach, or even large rocks as a fill light source.

Backgrounds outdoors — Keep backgrounds simple, uncluttered and to pay attention to the background lighting values. You must avoid spoiling otherwise good figure studies by having a background drastically under or overexposed, or messy and cluttered.

Once you have selected a photo site, take at least two meter readings. First measure the light value striking the subject and then meter the background area. Compare the meter reading from the background with the lighting on the subject. If the background measures too bright or too dark in relationship to the subject lighting, the simple solution is to increase or decrease the main and fill lights for the subject, to bring them more in line with the background illumination. If the lighting on the background is bright (say f-32 light) and the lighting on the subject a lot darker (say f-5.6), the background would be entirely too hot, unless you were intentionally trying to create a high-key effect.

If you weren't, then you could introduce flash onto the subject to raise the foreground light value; from f-5.6 to a much higher value (say f-16 or f-22). If this is not practical, you'll have little choice but to relocate to another area or wait for a different time of day, when the lighting on the background and subject are more in keeping with the lighting ratios you want.

If you had the problem where the background was a lot darker than the light falling onto the subject, the solution would be the same: relocate or wait. Adding lights to a dark background or gobos for a hot one will usually not be a practical solution to the problem. This is because it's usually time-consuming and takes a fair amount of additional equipment. There is another way to solve the problem when you're dealing with either a dark or bright background, provided you're using a leaf-shutter camera.

For example, say that we wanted to photograph a subject positioned in the shade of a tree and that a light meter reading at the subject's position indicated f-4.0 at 1/30th second. Assume further that the light falling on the background was much hotter than you wanted; a meter reading indicated f-11 at 1/30th second. Also assume that you don't want to relocate or wait until a different time of

"Keep backgrounds simple..."

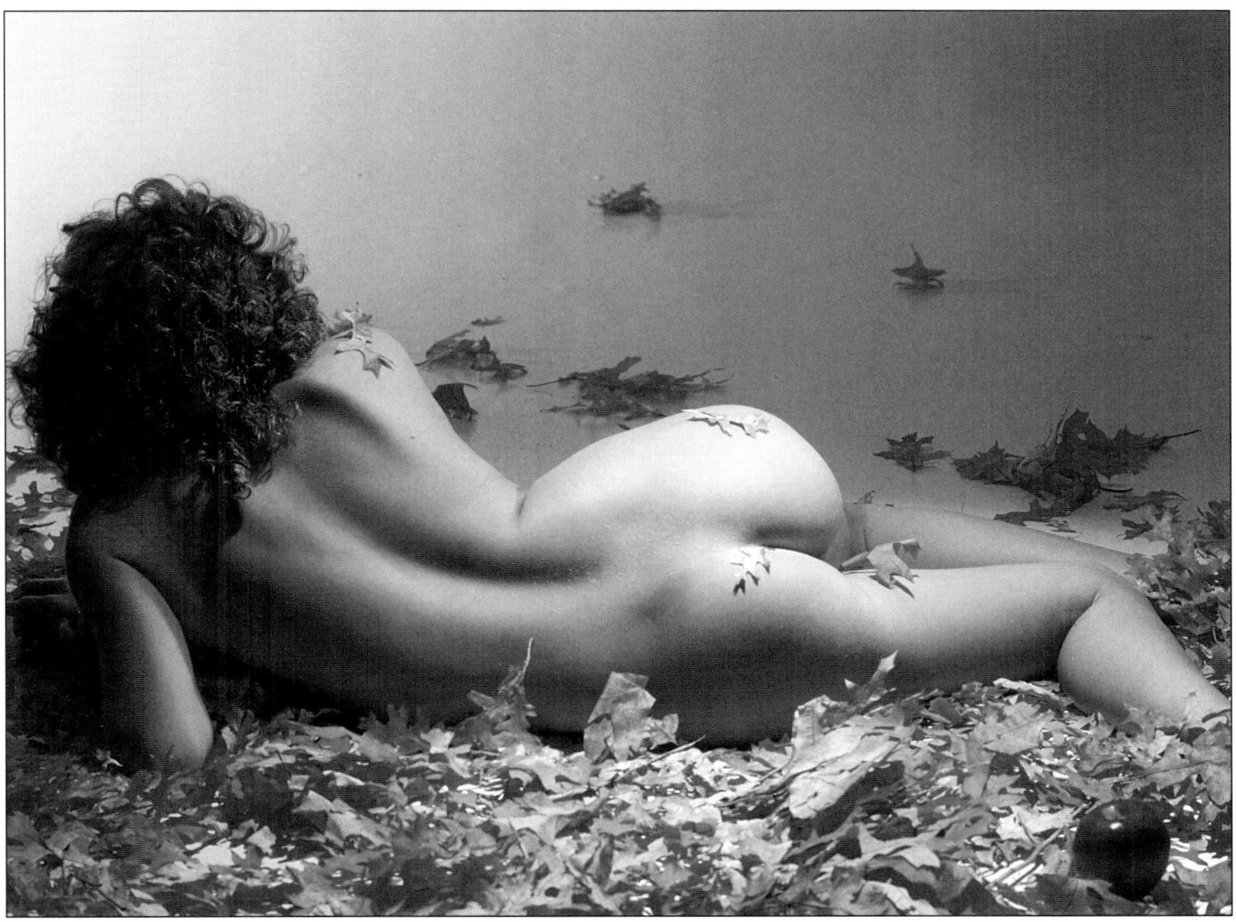

"It's an easy way to add pictorial variety to outdoor shots."

day. Could you still take good photos under these lighting conditions? Yes. Introduce flash and control the background with your shutter speed control.

If you use electronic flash, at least as a main light, exposure of your subject can be based on the flash. The camera's f-stop should be set according to the output of the main light. The more distant background can then be exposed and made to appear as dark or light as you would like, based on the natural light. This background exposure is controlled by setting the camera's shutter-speed dial.

Based on our above example where the light on the subject was f-4.0 at 1/30th second and f-11 at 1/30th second on the background, we would introduce flash on the subject to the extent of f-11. However, since flash is controlled by f-stops, we would set our camera to f-8, not to f-11. Why? Because an f-8 f-stop setting will give us one full f-stop of density or overexposure on our film, a good film exposure. And, for this particular shot, once this f-8 f-stop was set on our camera, it would be cast in stone. As long as we had f-11 flash falling onto the subject, we would not change our f-8 f-stop setting.

The next thing we would do is bring the background light value in line with this f-8 value. If we didn't change anything but took the photo with our camera set at f-8 at 1/30th second, the subject would be properly lit (having received one full f-stop of overexposure from the flash-main light), the background will be properly lit (having received one full f-stop of overexposure from the ambient light), but the background would not be the tonal value we wanted: it would be a light, not the dark value we wanted.

If we set the shutter speed dial to 1/60th second, the background would appear a little dark in the resulting photos, and a lot darker if we set it to 1/125th second. Although either setting would be acceptable, we would most likely opt for the 1/125th setting; f-8 at 1/125th second.

By putting our camera to this setting, the subject would be perfectly exposed by the f-11 flash, while the background was underexposed, receiving two full f-stops of less light than the metered value. This would give us a very rich, deep color on the background. This variable-exposure method for the background will yield images that differ greatly, even in one identical location with similar subject poses. It's an easy way to add pictorial variety to outdoor shots. In some shots you can make the background very light, even to the point of being high-key, or at least pale in tone, while in other shots, you can make the background very dark.

Conclusion

We have reached the end of our book. We trust that you have enjoyed reading it and have gained some insight into this wonderful photographic field. Should you have any questions, comments or even suggestions which we might incorporate into our future books, please feel free to contact us in care of Amherst Media.

Good luck!

Index

A

B

C

D

E

F

G

Other Books from Amherst Media, Inc.

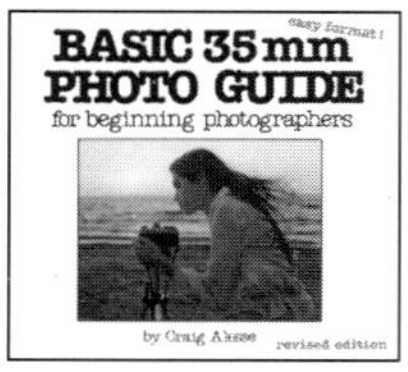

Basic 35mm Photo Guide

Craig Alesse

Great for beginning photographers! Designed to teach 35mm basics step-by-step — completely illustrated. Features the latest cameras. Includes: 35mm automatic and semi-automatic cameras, camera handling, f-stops, shutter speeds, and more! $12.95 list, 9 x 8, 112 p, 178 photos, order no. 1051.

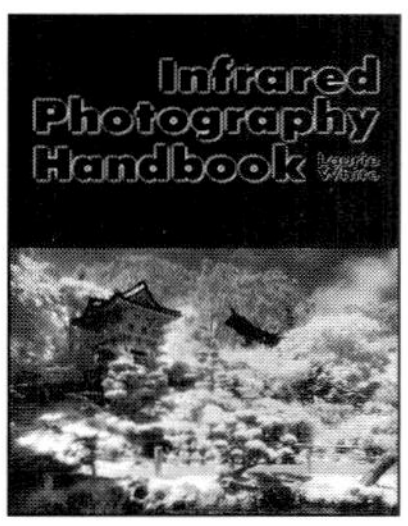

Infrared Photography Handbook

Laurie White

Totally covers black and white infrared photography: focus, lenses, film loading, film speed rating, heat sensitivity, batch testing, paper stocks, and filters. Black & white photos illustrate how IR film reacts in portrait, landscape, and architectural photography. $24.95 list, 8 1/2 x 11, 104 p, 50 B&W photos, charts & diagrams, order no. 1383.

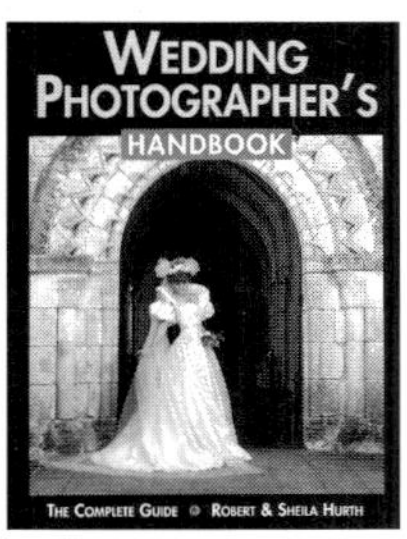

Wedding Photographer's Handbook

Robert and Sheila Hurth

The complete step-by-step guide to photographing weddings – everything you need to start and succeed in the exciting and profitable world of wedding photography. Packed with shooting tips, equipment lists, must-get photo lists, business strategies, and much more! $24.95 list, 8 1/2 x 11, 176 p, index, b&w and color photos, diagrams, order no. 1485.

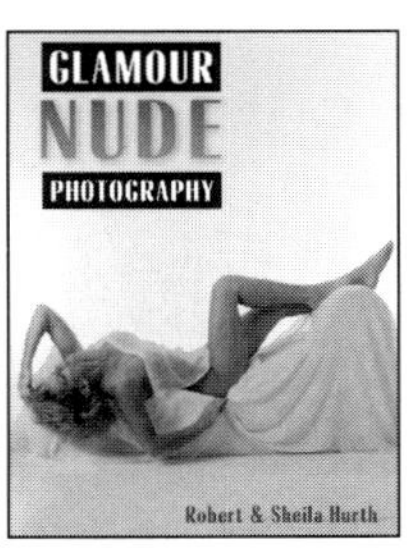

Glamour Nude Photography

Robert and Sheila Hurth

Create stunning nude images! Robert and Sheila Hurth guide you through selecting a subject, choosing locations, lighting, and shooting techniques. Includes information on posing, equipment, makeup and hair styles, and much more! $24.95 list, 8 1/2 x 11, 144 p, over 100 b&w and color photos, index, order no. 1499.

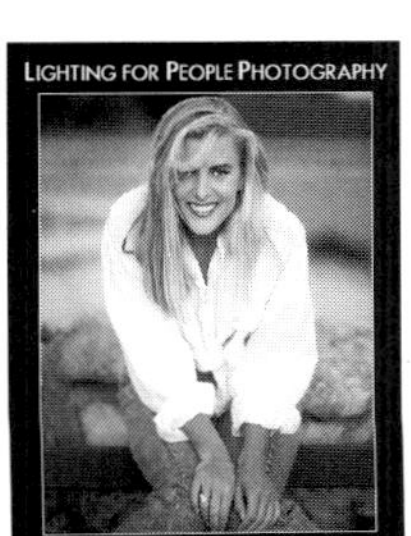

Lighting for People Photography

Stephen Crain

The complete guide to lighting and its different qualities. Includes: set-ups, equipment information, how to control strobe and natural lighting, and much more! Features diagrams, illustrations, and exercises for practicing the lighting techniques discussed in each chapter. $24.95 list, 8 1/2 x 11, 112 p, b&w and color photos, glossary, index, order no. 1296.

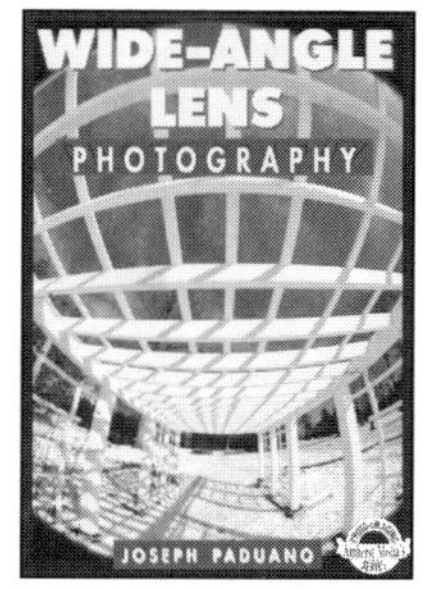

Wide-Angle Lens Photography

Joseph Paduano

For everyone with a wide-angle lens or people who want one! Includes taking exciting travel photos, creating wild special effects, using distortion for powerful images, and much more! Part of the Amherst Media's Photo-Imaging Series. $15.95 list, 7 x 10, 112 p, glossary, index, appendices, b&w and color photos, order no. 1480.

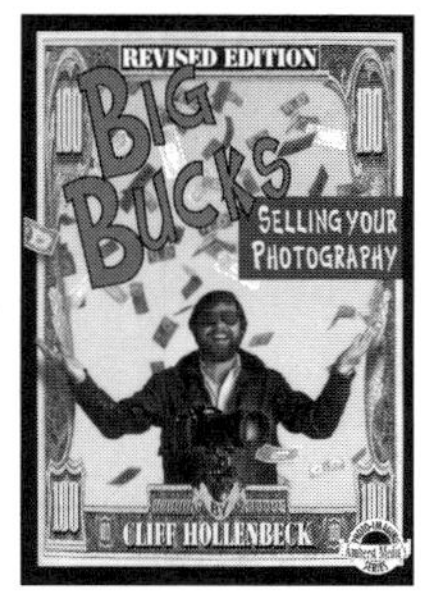

Big Bucks Selling Your Photography

Cliff Hollenbeck

A complete photo business package for all photographers. Includes secrets to making big bucks, starting up, getting paid the right price, and creating successful portfolios! Features setting financial, marketing and creative goals. This book will help to organize business planning, bookkeeping, and taxes. $15.95 list, 6x9, 336 p, Hollenbeck, order no. 1177.

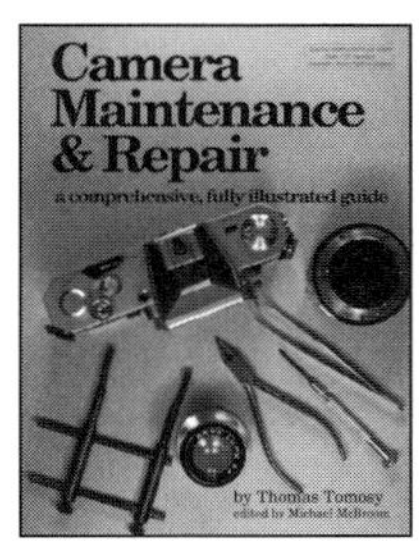

Camera Maintenance & Repair

Thomas Tomosy

A step-by-step, fully illustrated guide by a master camera repair technician. Sections include: testing camera functions, general maintenance, basic tools needed and where to get them, basic repairs for accessories, camera electronics, plus "quick tips" for maintenance and more! $24.95 list, 8 1/2 x 11, 176 p, order no. 1158.

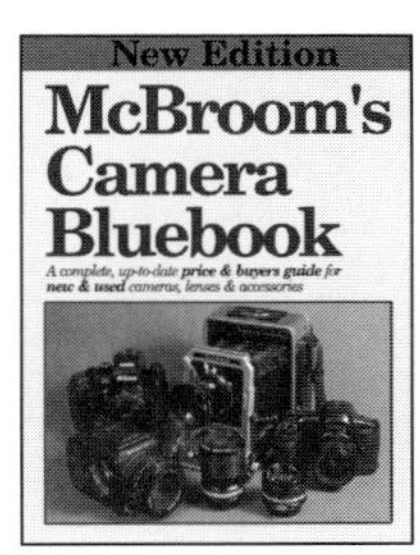

McBroom's Camera Bluebook

Mike McBroom

Comprehensive, fully illustrated, with price information on: 35mm cameras, medium & large format cameras, exposure meters, strobes and accessories. Pricing info based on equipment condition. A must for any camera buyer, dealer, or collector! $24.95 list, 8x11, 224 p, 75+ photos, order no. 1263.

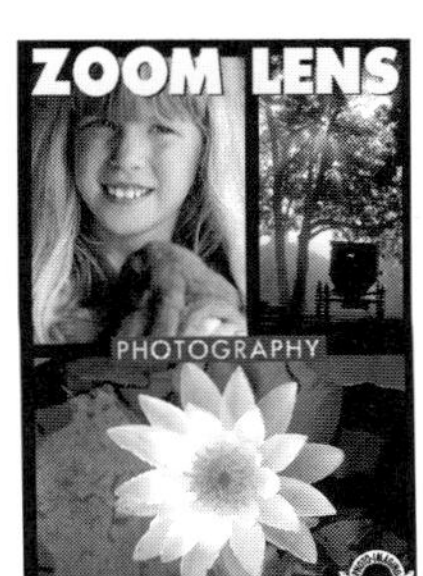

Zoom Lens Photography

Raymond Bial

Get to know the most versatile lens in the world! Includes how to take vacation, landscape, still life, sports and other photos. Features product information, accessories, shooting tips, and more! Part of the Amherst Media's Photo-Imaging Series. $15.95 list, 7 x 10, 112 p, b&w and color photos, index, glossary, appendices, order no. 1493.

Other Books from Amherst Media, Inc.

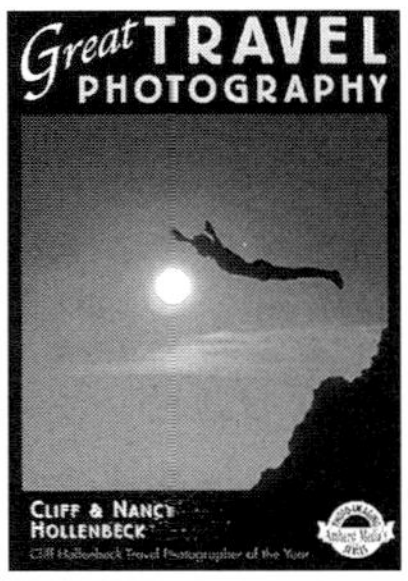

Great Travel Photography

Cliff and Nancy Hollenbeck

Learn how to capture great travel photos from the Travel Photographer of the Year! Includes helpful travel and safety tips, packing and equipment checklists, and much more! Packed full of photo examples for all over the world! Part of the Amherst Media's Photo-Imaging Series. $15.95 list, 7 x 10, 112 p, b&w and color photos, index, glossary, appendices, order no. 1494.

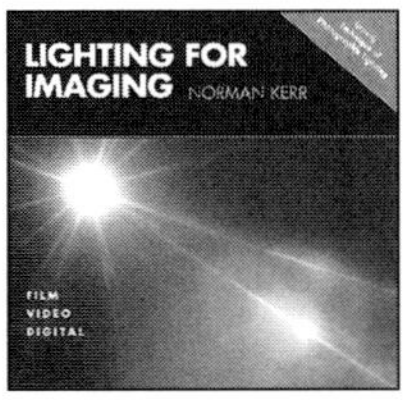

Lighting for Imaging

Norman Kerr

This book explains light: what it is, how to use it, and how to control it. It shows how to use any light source for any form of photographic imaging — including film, digital, or video. Learn to use light like an expert: from taking videos of your family trips to polishing your professional work. $26.95 list, 8 1/2 x 11, 144 p, color and b&w illustrations, order no. 1490.

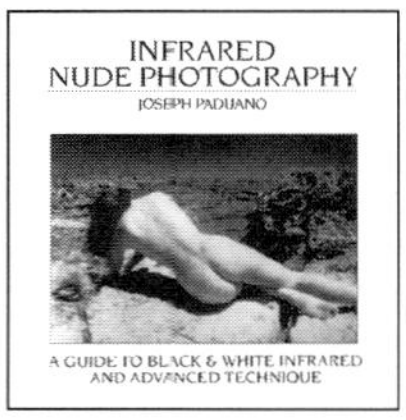

Infrared Nude Photography

Joseph Paduano

A stunning collection of natural images with wonderful how-to text. Over 50 infrared photos. Shot on location in the natural settings of the Grand Canyon, Bryce Canyon and the New Jersey Shore. $19.95 list, 9 x 9, 80 p, over 50 photos, order no. 1080.

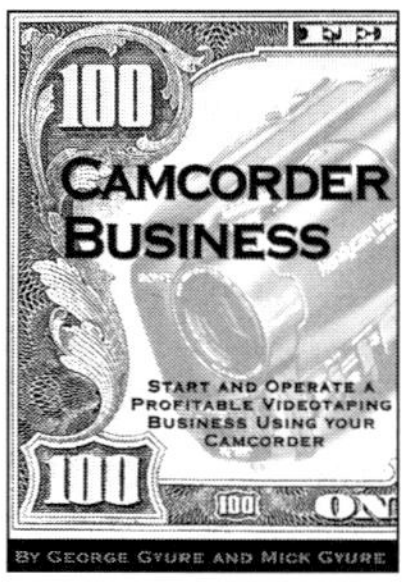

Camcorder Business

Mick and George A. Gyure

Make money with your camcorder! This book covers everything you need to start a successful business using your camcorder. Includes: editing, mixing sound, dubbing, technical and business tips, and much more! Also features information on covering a wedding or other special events for a client, legal and industrial videos, and more. $17.95 list, 7 x 10, 192 p, order no. 1496.

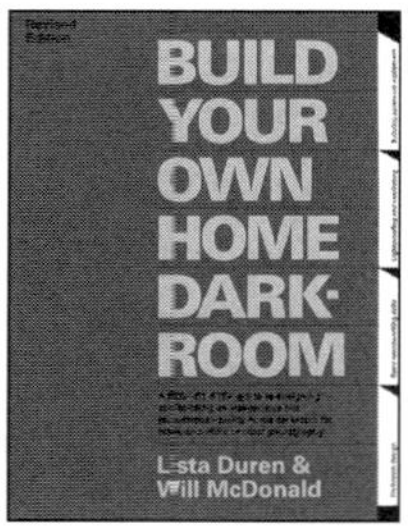

Build Your Own Home Darkroom

Lista Duren & Will McDonald

This classic book shows how to build a high quality, inexpensive darkroom in your basement, spare room, or almost anywhere. Information on: darkroom design, woodworking, tools, and more! $17.95 list, 8 1/2 x 11, 160 p, order no. 1092.

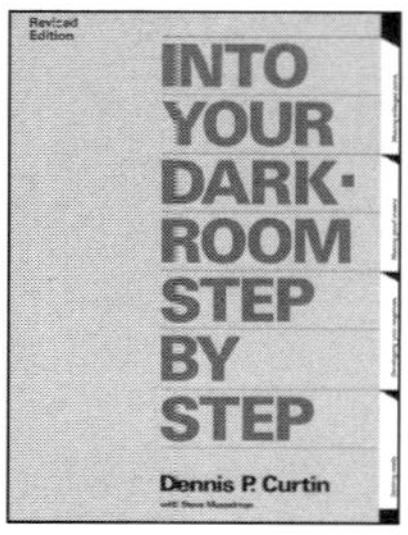

Into Your Darkroom Step-by-Step

Dennis P. Curtin

The ideal beginning darkroom guide. Easy to follow and fully illustrated each step of the way. Information on: equipment you'll need, set-up, making proof sheets and much more! $17.95 list, 8 1/2 x 11, 90 p, hundreds of photos, order no. 1093.

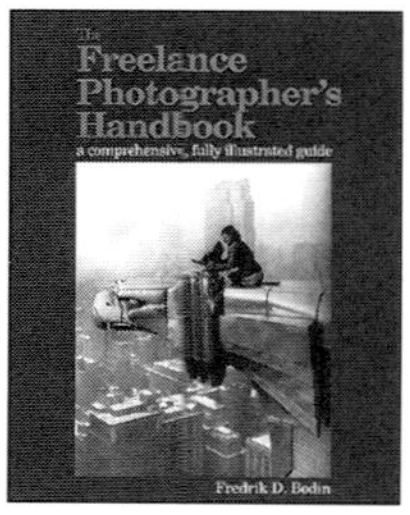

The Freelance Photographer's Handbook

Fredrik D. Bodin

A complete handbook for the working freelancer. Full of how-to info & examples. Includes: marketing, customer relations, inventory systems, portfolios, and much more! $19.95 list, 8 x 11, 160 p, order no. 1075.

More Photo Books Are Available!

Write or fax for a *FREE* catalog:

AMHERST MEDIA, INC.
PO Box 586
Buffalo, NY 14226 USA

Fax: 716-874-4508

Ordering & Sales Information:

Individuals: If possible, purchase books from an Amherst Media retailer. Write to us for the dealer nearest you. To order direct, send a check or money order with a note listing the books you want and your shipping address. U.S. & overseas freight charges are $3.50 first book and $1.00 for each additional book. Visa and Master Card accepted. New York state residents add 8% sales tax.

Dealers, distributors & colleges: Write, call or fax to place orders. For price information, contact Amherst Media or an Amherst Media sales representative. Net 30 days.

All prices, publication dates, and specifications are subject to change without notice.
Prices are in U.S. dollars. Payment in U.S. funds only.

CUT ALONG DOTTED LINE

Amherst Media's Customer Registration Form

Please fill out this sheet and send or fax to receive free information about future publications from Amherst Media.

CUSTOMER INFORMATION

DATE

NAME

STREET OR BOX #

CITY STATE

ZIP CODE

PHONE ( )

OPTIONAL INFORMATION

I BOUGHT *GLAMOUR NUDE PHOTOGRAPHY* BECAUSE

I FOUND THESE CHAPTERS TO BE MOST USEFUL

I PURCHASED THE BOOK FROM

CITY STATE

I WOULD LIKE TO SEE MORE BOOKS ABOUT

I PURCHASE BOOKS PER YEAR

ADDITIONAL COMMENTS

FAX to: 1-800-622-3298

IF MAILING, FOLD IN NUMBER ORDER ALONG DASHED LINES.

①

②

Name________________________________
Address______________________________
City_______________________State_____
Zip__________________ — __________

Place
Postage
Here

Amherst Media, Inc.
PO Box 586
Buffalo, NY 14226

③

IF MAILING, PASTE UNDERSIDE OF FLAP, OR TAPE HERE.